The Social Work of Museums

D0143944

At first glance, museums may not seem to be engaged in social work. Here, however, Lois H. Silverman brings together relevant visitor studies, trends in international practice, and compelling examples that demonstrate how museums everywhere are using their unique resources to benefit human relationships.

In this groundbreaking book, Silverman forges a framework of key social work perspectives to show how museums are evolving a needs-based approach to provide what promises to be universal social service. In partnership with social workers, social agencies, and clients, museums are helping people cope and even thrive in circumstances ranging from personal challenges to social injustices. *The Social Work of Museums* provides the first integrative survey of this emerging interdisciplinary practice and an essential foundation on which to build for the future.

The Social Work of Museums is not only a vital and visionary resource for museum training and practice in the twenty-first century, but also an invaluable tool for social workers, creative arts therapists, and students seeking to broaden their horizons. It will inspire and empower policymakers, directors, clinicians, and evaluators alike to work together toward museums for the next age.

Lois H. Silverman is a scholar, project innovator, frequent speaker, and consultant to social agencies and to museums around the world. A three-time recipient of Indiana University's Teaching Excellence Award, her publications include *The Therapeutic Potential of Museums* (1998) and *Transforming Practice* (2000). She holds a PhD from the Annenberg School for Communication, University of Pennsylvania, and an MSW from Indiana University School of Social Work.

The Social Work
of Museums

Lois H. Silverman

LONDON AND NEW YORK

First published 2010
by Routledge
2 Park Square, Milton Park, Abingdon, Oxon OX14 4RN

Simultaneously published in the USA and Canada
by Routledge
711 Third Avenue, New York, NY 10017

Routledge is an imprint of the Taylor & Francis Group, an informa business

© 2010 Lois H. Silverman

Typeset in Garamond by
HWA Text and Data Management, London

British Library Cataloguing in Publication Data
A catalogue record for this book is available from the British Library

Library of Congress Cataloging-in-Publication Data
A catalog record for this book has been requested

ISBN10: 0-415-77520-5 (hbk)
ISBN10: 0-415-77521-3 (pbk)
ISBN10: 0-203-86296-1 (ebk)

ISBN13: 978-0-415-77520-5(hbk)
ISBN13: 978-0-415-77521-2 (pbk)
ISBN13: 978-0-203-86296-4 (ebk)

For my mother, Marlene, my father, Harvey, and my sister, Lisa, with love and gratitude beyond words

and

To my muse, Freddie

Contents

Illustrations

Preface

All my life I have been seeking to understand the remarkable magic of museums. As people engage with objects and each other, museums become containers and catalysts for personal growth, relationship building, social change, and healing. Museums have long been institutions that care for the world's treasures. It is my passionate belief that the most important and essential work museums do is to use their unique resources to benefit human relationships and, ultimately, repair the world. I hope *The Social Work of Museums* will inspire and empower others toward these goals.

The seeds for this book have been sown over twenty-five years as a museum educator, scholar, professor, and museum consultant – years that have blessed me with some of the most inspiring teachers, colleagues, and friends one could hope to meet. At Pennsbury Manor historic site outside of Philadelphia in the mid-1980s, I became a museum professional with the caring mentorship of the late Alice Hemenway. In 1990, I completed my doctoral studies at the Annenberg School for Communication, University of Pennsylvania, under the brilliant intellectual direction of Larry Gross. My dissertation on visitor pairs in museums was also guided by D. D. Hilke, a pioneer in the study of museum visitors, and the support of a Smithsonian Institution Fellowship. I will always be grateful to Alice, Larry, and D.D. for nurturing the foundations of my career.

This book took root in my encounters with social service agencies, social workers, and social work clients for whom I have felt not only an instant bond but a profound respect. Their deep intuitive understanding of human frailty, strength, and resilience is just the knowledge that museums need. During my tenure at Indiana University, with generous support from the Institute of Museum and Library Services, I fulfilled a fledgling dream to bring museum staff, social workers, clients, and students together to explore *The Therapeutic Potential of Museums*. That three-year project, begun in 1997 with thanks to the open-minded support and insightful input of Suzanne Koesel, MSW, LCSW, senior vice president of Centerstone; Judith Kirk, assistant director of the Mathers Museum of World Cultures at Indiana University; and other wonderful colleagues in Bloomington, affirmed my faith in the great value of dancing between disciplines. It also inspired my own return to school to earn an MSW at the Indiana University School of Social Work.

In my social work classes and practica, especially during my internship at the amazing Fountain House in New York City, the worldwide model clubhouse program for people with mental illness, a vision for this book began to grow. I am particularly grateful to professor Eldon Marshall, whose enthusiasm and support throughout the entire research and book proposal process provided generous sunshine for blooming. I am also indebted to Carol Stapp, director of the Museum Education Program at The George Washington University, who, along with her students, has nurtured and influenced the development of this work in countless ways over many years. Like many museum professionals, I am still a student of social work. However, I've learned enough to recognize that social workers are the perfect partners to help museums fulfill their social service potential and that museums have much to offer in return.

When I began this project, I had planned to identify best practices and provide definite guidelines for museums' engagement in social work. Instead, my research soon revealed that a "how-to" approach would be both premature as well as limiting. It is also my professional judgment that innovation, like people, thrives best in an atmosphere of possibility and strength rather than confinement and criticism. Therefore, I have focused on what I believe we most need at this point in time: a theoretical framework to organize, integrate, and inspire expanding practice and provide a foundation on which to build. Museum staff and social workers are among the most creative and resourceful people in the world. I am confident in readers' abilities to move this exciting work forward in important ways.

One of the hardest tasks of this survey has been choosing from among equally important projects. For every example in this book, I have only for reasons of space reluctantly left out many impressive others. I have tried to reflect a balance of countries, museum types, museum sizes, and audiences to illustrate significant trends as well as to capture the range and diversity of the social work of museums. I apologize to the many pioneers and institutions whose work is not described in these pages. It is exciting to know that there is more relevant work than a single volume can hold.

The process of creating a book about relationships has overwhelmed me with gratitude for the precious relationships in my life. This book owes its existence to many people who have given their time and talents with stunning generosity and grace. I apologize to anyone I inadvertently forget to mention by name. Although I wrote alone at a desk with only my beloved dog Honey and cats Trouble and Casper nearby, this work is in fact the collective product of a remarkable community.

I am grateful to Matthew Gibbons, editor; Lalle Pursglove, assistant editor; James Benefield, John Hodgson, and Routledge Press for believing in this project. Their patience and unflagging support of this first-time book author is deeply appreciated. Thanks are also due to friends and authors Jeffrey Ankrom, James Capshew, Robert Fischman, Elaine Heumann Gurian, Carol Polsgrove, Richard Sandell, Lee Sandweiss, Bob Vernon, Lisa Williams, Matt Williamson, and Barbie Zelizer, who provided valuable guidance early on about the publishing process. I am especially grateful to Jay Rounds and Sheila Watson for their helpful comments.

This book has benefited tremendously from the care and insight of many professional colleagues who are also dear friends. I am grateful for the thoughtful suggestions and advice of Melody Childs, Marcia Doran, John Encandela, Daryl Fischer, Ben Garcia, Bjorn Involdstad, Loreta Involdstad, Judith Kirk, Randi Korn, Lotte Lent, Paul Marsh, Eldon Marshall, Kris Morrissey, Mark O'Neill, Deborah Perry, Lisa Roberts, Carol Stapp, Darrell Stone, Nina Warnke, Cathleen Weber, Shari Werb, Ray Williams, Douglas Worts, and Bob Vernon. Their support and encouragement have been priceless.

As soon as I began this project, I started looking for a compelling cover image. From a half a world away in Australia, artist Wayne Roberts's stunning painting leapt forth from the Internet as the perfect visual representation of the social work of museums. What synchronicity it was to find such a gifted artist who, as I learned later, often donated his work to support important social service organizations and causes. I am honored that Wayne's beautiful art graces the book's cover and that its use will benefit Médecins Sans Frontières, courtesy of Wayne and Routledge Press.

I am also grateful to those who have made possible the photographs that enliven these pages. I'm thrilled to include original work from Kevin Atkins, Fiona Barnett, Tamara Bournival, Wendy Bush, Edward B. Flowers, David Hassell, Emily Radecki, and Lynette Yeo Balota. Many thanks to models Nivee Amin, the Bournival family, Irwin Glasberg and family, Sol Goodman, Freddie Shaw, Darrell Stone, Jeff Stone, and Jamie Waldon. For assistance with securing images and permissions I thank Pat Bakunas, Marla Berns, Robin Bisha, Priscilla Borges, Vicky Cahan, Danielle Curry, Fiona Davison, Anne Decker, Alla Dvorkin, John Encandela, Betsy Escandor, Peggy Glowacki, Bruce Grenville, Kathy Hackett, Valerie Harris, Karen Jepson-Innes, Euripedes Junior, Lara Kelland, Lynda Kelly, Henry Law, Elena Letona, Katie Marchetti, Jeannine Mjoseth, Mark O'Neill, Pamela Parlapiano, Shabana Pathan, Diane Pelrine, Patricia Pitaluga, Carol Ann Scott, Lisa Silverman, Lisa Snow, Eva Stanley, Olinka Vistica, Mark Vivian, and Cynthia Wroclawski. Figure 3.1 by David Hassell was taken in The Raymond and Laura Wielgus Gallery of the Arts of Africa, the South Pacific, and the Americas at the Indiana University Art Museum, Bloomington.

For assistance in securing permissions to use quotes as chapter epigraphs, I thank Elizabeth Clementson, Kristine Frost, Christa Heschke, Pamela Quick, and Michael Schwartz. Chapter 1 epigraph, from George Eliot (and B. Hornback, editor), *Middlemarch: An Authoritative Text, Backgrounds, Review and Criticism,* is reprinted by permission of W.W. Norton & Company, Inc. Chapter 4 epigraph, from Jung, C.G.; *Collected Works*, Vol. 16, reprinted by permission of Princeton University Press. Chapter 5 epigraph, from George Santayana, *The Life of Reason, or the Phases of Human Progress,* reprint permission granted courtesy of The MIT Press. Chapter 6 epigraph, from Madeleine L'Engle, *Walking on Water: Reflections on Faith and Art* is copyright © 1980 by Crosswicks, Ltd. and reprinted with permission of McIntosh & Otis, Inc.

For additional information and assistance I also wish to thank Marcus Appelbaum, Tansy Barton, Leslie Bedford, Leslie Bushara, Natalie Collins, Fiona

Davison, Stephen Demanchick, Lon Dubinsky, Brandi Lee Emerick, John Falk, Craig Fees, Susan Ferentinos, Paul Johnson, Carlo Lamagna, Christine McLean, Claire Mehalick, John Powles, Trish Regan, Ellen Sieber, Caroline Skehill, Courtney Spousta, Catherine Wakeling, and Cynthia Wroclawski.

There are seven individuals who have been utterly essential to the completion of this project. I will be forever grateful to each member of this "dream team" for their remarkable generosity, endless patience, and incredible talents. It is impossible to prioritize them. Thank goodness for alphabetical order.

Kevin Atkins, close friend, photographer, and technical expert extraordinaire, contributed to this project in countless ways. From shooting and preparing photos to solving every conceivable computer problem to providing constant support and encouragement, Kevin's assistance was heroic. It was my luckiest day when Marlene Chambers, former head of publications at the Denver Art Museum, agreed to serve as consulting editor. Her scrupulous precision, tireless analysis, and wise counsel have improved this product greatly. It has been an honor to work with Marlene and benefit from her vast experience. Since day one, Melissa Jane Hight has been my right hand, conducting hours of library research, locating obscure resources, and managing the entire bibliography, all with a constant smile. Melissa's awesome research skills and calm, loyal support have kept me grounded along the way. When the photo and permissions work took on a life of its own, my dear friend Bette Lucas stepped in graciously and saved the day. With impressive skill, infinite patience, and infectious optimism, Bette shepherded the communications and paperwork to a perfectly organized conclusion. Over many years, Jessica Mott, founder of Whole Person Health, has nurtured my dreams and helped me to speak my truth. From friendship to intellectual engagement, Jessica, a gifted healer and practicing midwife, has helped me give birth to this book. Early in this process I met Anne Roecklein, a visionary artist and photo permissions expert. On all matters visual and artistic, Anne provided invaluable opinions and advice, generously answering my endless questions with insight and sensitivity. Last but most surely not least, Darrell Stone, MSW, has exemplified the spirit of social work as well as friendship in walking this path with me. Drawing upon our shared experiences in social work school as well as her vast professional expertise, Darrell critiqued chapters, offered opinions, helped select photos, and kept me on-track and energized. Thank you, Darrell, Anne, Jessica, Bette, Melissa, Marlene, and Kevin.

When all is said and done, it is those closest to me whose love and support, as always, has sustained me in every way possible over these past few years and made this journey worthwhile. I am grateful to my chosen brothers John Encandela and Gary Covey for their abiding friendship and deep understanding. My better-than-brother brother-in-law David Siegler is a truly special friend whose encouragement, kindness, and good humor always lighten the load. Words can hardly convey my gratitude and love for my partner, Frederick Shaw Anderson, whose unconditional love and support has transformed my life since the day we met. From photo production to cooking, calming late-night panic to cheering me on, Freddie's love and generosity is the pure white space on which the lines were written. This book exists because of him.

Finally, it is my mother, Marlene; my father, Harvey; and my sister, Lisa, to whom I owe everything. All my life, they have supported me, encouraged me, and believed I could do anything I set out to do. It is because of their love and guidance that I can. For nearly five decades, they have taught me about museums, about relationships, and about caring. For this and so much more, I dedicate this book to them with all my love.

Lois H. Silverman
June 2009

Figure 1.1 Musée d'Orsay, Paris. Photo by MacTabbie.

Chapter 1

In the service of society

What do we live for, if it is not to make life less difficult to each other?

George Eliot

In an old art museum with a well-worn floor, a tour group gathers around an enthusiastic guide and a famous painting of flowers. People are soon sharing moments: where and when they have seen flowers like this, who they know that loves bright colors, and what they think of the work. A petite woman with long, grey hair offers her opinion of the artist's technique. A tall, slender man nods in agreement, and the two exchange quick smiles. Like countless other groups enjoying the world's art in museums, this man and woman, along with their companions, are exercising their minds, expressing their identities, and recognizing potential friends as they interact with one another. For this group, the moments are particularly powerful. Just two hours ago, the woman could not remember her name or what day it was, and the man had been sullen and withdrawn. Like many of their companions, who are all residents of a local nursing home, the woman and man are experiencing the progressive impairment of cognitive and social functioning caused by dementia. Unfortunately, they are far from unique. By the year 2040, the prevalence of dementia will more than triple worldwide, reaching epidemic proportions in India, China, and elsewhere (Ferri et al. 2005). Yet, in this museum, viewing art, they find their thoughts and voices and connect with the social world. Which museum is this? It might be any one of a growing number, like the Metropolitan Museum of Art in New York and the Ateneum Art Museum in Helsinki, that now offer tours to foster positive mood and social interaction for people with Alzheimer's disease and their caregivers. Who is the woman with the long, grey hair and the slender man? As statistics would suggest, they are our neighbors, our parents, ourselves.

Far away in a children's museum, a ten-year-old boy and his father are working on a challenge. In a hands-on exhibit about making music, the boy reads aloud instructions that tell how to string the oddly shaped instrument before them. The father, who cannot read, listens carefully, trying hard to do it right. Sensing his father's frustration, the boy repeats the directions, more slowly this time. The father hooks the string, turns the peg, and plucks the taut nylon: the sound of success! The boy moves in closer to his father, whom he is seeing today for just the third time in his life. The father embraces his son. Like many other families in children's museums, this pair is sharing some quality time and building their relationship. Their need is particularly intense: after this two-hour visit, supervised by a social worker, the father will return to prison and the boy to his grandmother's house. Both will eagerly await their next meeting. Millions of parents and children in the European Union and United States alone, particularly those of low income, endure significant separation as a result of adult criminal behavior and subsequent incarceration (Mumola 2000; Correctional Association of New York 2007; European Committee for Children of Imprisoned Parents 2007). Yet, while making music in the children's museum, these two take critical steps toward a stronger father–son bond. Which museum is this? It could well be the Please Touch Museum in Philadelphia, Pennsylvania, or the Providence Children's Museum in Rhode Island, where cohesion is fostered for many families, sometimes through innovative collaborations with local courts and family service agencies. Who are this father and son? They are a family with needs like all families.

Across the ocean, in a drafty basement, a dozen dedicated activists, artists, and neighbors are holding a weekly meeting. Tonight, they will move forward with their dream of starting a museum to teach future generations about tolerance. In a long-awaited moment, one person unveils a table full of photographs and historical objects recently collected from area residents. Many people weep as they recognize the faces of loved ones and their cherished belongings. Like others who work together to found a museum, these neighbors have forged a close new group capable of dramatic accomplishments. In this case, the group provides more than a bit of support to its members, who are all survivors of brutal persecution that literally destroyed their community. Together they face the tangible reminders of a shared history that inspires them further toward their goal. Horrifically, millions of people around the globe live amidst repeated outbreaks of violence (World Health Organization 2002), and "millions ... have died as a result of their membership in a specific ... group" (Toft 2003: 3). United in their mission to build a museum, this group has become stronger. Many museums that empower some people and enlighten others have begun in a similar way, for example the District Six Museum in Cape Town, South Africa, and the Vilna Gaon Jewish State Museum in Vilnius, Lithuania. Who are these neighbors who came together? They are people who wanted change.

Scenes of change

As these scenes suggest, change is plentiful in museums today – for the people using them and for the entire profession. On display is a growing belief among practitioners, policymakers, and the public alike in the power of museums to inspire hope and healing, improve lives, and better the world. Museums have long been considered institutions that benefit society, most familiarly through the activities of collecting, preserving, and educating about valuable artifacts and art. Today, the world's museums are embracing starkly bolder roles as agents of well-being and as vehicles for social change. Many museum scholars and writers have noted this "transformation" of the museum field, fueled by external as well as internal economic, political, and social forces and characterized by "the desire by museum professionals to position the museum to be relevant and to provide the most good in society" (Anderson 2004: 1). According to even a small sampling of their observations, museums have become "socially responsible" (Gurian 1988; Sandell 2002; Janes and Conaty 2005); they are "providers of services to our communities" (Anderson 1994: 3); they "enrich the quality of individual lives" (Weil 1999: 255); and they promote "social justice" (O'Neill 2006). Museums are indeed moving to adopt the definition now espoused by the International Council of Museums, the organization that represents the global museum profession:

> A museum is a non-profit making, permanent institution *in the service of society and of its development*, and open to the public, which acquires, conserves, researches, communicates, and exhibits, for purposes of study, education and enjoyment, material evidence of people and their environment.
>
> (ICOM 2001, italics added)

At their very core, museums today are institutions of social service.

Critics and concerns

Not everyone supports these changes. In 1991, museum expert Elaine Heumann Gurian correctly predicted both an increase in "museums that provide social service and community support as integral parts of their work" (2006a: 86) and the kind of arguments that would be leveled against such efforts. Critics have indeed argued that a focus on social service is dangerous for museums themselves since it renders them "no longer museums as such" (Moore 1997: 22) and "distorts the very basis of the institution" (Appleton 2001: 4). Museum director James Cuno cited "the emerging 'consensus' among politicians, community activists, funding sources, and engaged academics that the art museum is first and foremost a social institution ... with a mandate to encourage therapeutic social perspectives" as "the biggest problem facing art museums today – and the gravest threat to the quality of their scholarship" (Cuno 1997: 7).

Others question the effectiveness and impact of museums' social service. According to David A. Tucker, the idea that museums "really make a difference to their subjects is a delusion, and moreover, an insult to real social workers, police officers, teachers and housing officers who strive to make a material contribution to the quality of people's lives" (1993: 7). As scholar Kevin Moore has warned, museums' misguided efforts may actually cause harm by masking real problems, patronizing people, or diverting financial and human resources from more effective service vehicles (1997: 22).

In addition to critics are those with compelling practical concerns. Some directors and board members may consider the idea far afield of their institution's stated missions. Some rank other priorities much higher, particularly when resources are scarce. Recognizing that museum workers may well lack the necessary skills and knowledge for such work, many question their museum's capabilities for engaging in social service. Deep inside, even the most well-meaning professionals may harbor prejudice, stereotypes, and fears about dealing with people who face serious challenges or who seem different from themselves. For some practitioners, these points alone justify distance from social service work, especially as visions of practical risk such as public protests, lawsuits, and funding withdrawal come all too clearly to mind. For others, more intrigued than daunted by the continuing transformation of the museum field, these concerns mark key areas where information and guidance is sorely needed in order to move forward.

Despite such criticism and concerns, museums' social service is proliferating worldwide. In the last decade or so, government agencies and professional organizations such as the United Kingdom's Group for Large Local Authority Museums (GLLAM) and the American Association of Museums (AAM) have helped fuel museums' pursuit of expanded social roles with field-wide calls for such work (e.g., GLLAM 2000; AAM 2002; Hirzy 2002). All over the world, museums are generating a variety of offerings and approaches for serving as agents of well-being and as vehicles for social change, and case examples abound (e.g., Sandell 2002; Janes and Conaty 2005). More scholars, like Carol Scott (2006) and Lynda Kelly (2006) in Australia, are undertaking valuable empirical research on the social benefits and public value of museums. The field has launched new journals like *museum and society* in Britain and *Museums & Social Issues* in the United States. Even mainstream news media and the Internet are spreading word daily of new initiatives. By the time this book is published, there will be much more to digest.

Goals and structure of this book

As the work grows, so does the urgent need for a meaningful synthesis of this diverse body of knowledge and practice. How do we explain the nature of museums' service to society? Uniting advocates, critics, and the undecided alike are several pressing questions. First of all, why *are* so many museums embracing social service? What has led to this moment? A look to the past is essential to provide context for the present. Second, what theoretical perspectives are useful for understanding and organizing this work? What framework can illuminate its collective significance? It is alarming to recognize that museum professionals may be engaging in the complex realm of social service with outdated views and inadequate preparation. Third, what exactly are museums doing in the name of social service, how, for whom, in what circumstances, and to what effect? An integrative survey of recent work is long overdue, as relevant research, successful trends, and compelling examples are currently scattered around the globe. Without assembling a foundation on which to build, it is difficult to chart a meaningful future. Fourth, to what extent have museums reached their potential as agents of well-being and social change? What challenges and possibilities have yet to be addressed? If museums' social service is meant to advance further, the field will need a clear and informed sense of direction. These are the pressing questions *The Social Work of Museums* aims to answer so that all readers may make knowledgeable decisions, arguments, and actions about museums and their evolving service to society.

There is, however, a fifth set of questions glaringly absent from the museum literature to date that we will address throughout this book. What is social work? How do social work perspectives, methods, and practitioners bring museums to their potential? As we will see, the global profession that specializes in social service can help provide clear answers to the questions museums now face and illuminate a compelling vision for the future.

Our journey for answers will unfold over seven chapters. This chapter describes two key factors that fuel and support the current social service focus: museum history and museum theory. Chapter 2 examines the social work profession and some of its history and theory, and explains how social work perspectives complement and expand current museum thinking. The chapter then presents a key set of questions based on these social work perspectives as a framework for synthesizing relevant research, international trends, and compelling examples. Chapters 3 through 6 apply that framework to survey four different types of important human relationships and the ways in which museums are used to benefit them. Chapter 3 explores the self; Chapter 4 examines close pairs; Chapter 5 studies families; and Chapter 6 addresses groups. In conclusion, Chapter 7 reflects on the significance of this work, and the challenges and promise of the future. Let us now consider the current foundations of museums' social service.

Only yesterday? A brief history of museums as social service

Despite the relatively recent shifts in professional thinking and practice toward a definition of museums as social service institutions, that notion is far from novel. It is as old as museums themselves. While a comprehensive international history of museums is beyond the scope of this book, even a brief account of five key milestones in museum history reveals that the idea of museums as agents of well-being and social change has ancient and enduring roots. Each of these five major museum forms has involved a core expectation of positive outcome for those who engage with them and their artifacts: 1) mouseoins; 2) cabinets of curiosities; 3) public museums and settlement house museums; 4) traveling exhibits; and 5) integrated museums, ecomuseums, and neighborhood museums. The positive outcomes wrought by these types of museums have nearly always been social in nature, benefiting individuals, pairs, families, and/or groups. Social problems and social conditions have been addressed, and social change pursued. Even a cursory look back begins to reveal an essential tradition of museum social service that strongly pervades the present.

Mouseions

The mouseion of classical times, often the starting point for museum history, was essentially a temple for the Muses, those mythical goddesses who inspired human thought, creativity, and action, particularly in the arts and humanities. In the mouseion, shown proper respect, the unpredictable Muses might grace their human subjects with insight, ideas, and abilities. In short, the museum began as a site devoted to transformation.

Founded in Egypt in the third century BCE, the Great Museum of Alexandria, the most famous mouseion, resembled a contemporary university even more than a temple. Complete with lecture halls, observatories, and a hugely famous library (Forster 1982), it was designed to foster social exchange among its denizens and "included accommodations for some 30 members of an academic community, with rooms and colonnades for lectures, thought, and conversation" (Simpson 2000: 29) as well as facilities for communal dining. Also housed in the Great Museum were "statues of thinkers, astronomical and surgical instruments, elephant trunks and animal hides, and a botanical and zoological park" (Alexander and Alexander 2008: 3), provocative objects that likely honored the Muses and primed reflection and conversation among the scholars. If the Muses cooperated, the residents of the Great Museum such as Euclid, Archimedes, and Erathosthenes (Alexander and Alexander 2008) experienced transformations in thought and action that led them to produce great works of scholarship and philosophy, transformations that benefitted the scholars as well as society at large.

At first glance, the mouseion of ancient times seems far removed from the twenty-first-century museum. With a closer look, however, it is hard to imagine a more prescient blueprint. In a poetic and visionary analysis of the "Alexandrian Paradigm" of museum history, scholar Thomas K. Simpson (2000) identifies several "insights concerning the nature of the museum itself, on which we might ground ... inquiry into the museum in our own time." Five of these insights foreshadow key defining components of museums as social agents. First, Simpson notes that the museum is a sacred space, in which "something fundamental ... is summoned, inducing fresh production, a new and unpredictable life of the spirit to arise." Whether credited to the Muses, God, grace, or human will, museums today continue to be places where people can experience the power to change. Second, observes Simpson, "The museum is a fellowship." From elite scholars to residents of the local nursing home, museums still facilitate social interaction among groups of people. Third, Simpson contends, "the museum is universal ... its work ... undertaken on behalf of mankind, deeply and fundamentally addressing our common humanity." From the Great Museum of Alexandria to the children's museum, museums indeed seek to serve society and address universal human concerns. Fourth, Simpson notes, "the museum is political ... it is of the essence of the museum to *be* political." Despite some who still believe it to be a matter of conscious choice, museums today increasingly embrace their role as political institutions that can impact social conditions. Fifth, Simpson observes, "The museum is a place of collection," which includes "conservation, preservation,

Halle in der Alexandrinischen Bibliothek.

Figure 1.2 Inside the library of the Great Museum of Alexandria, Egypt, third century BCE. Artistic rendering by O. Von Corven. Mary Evans Picture Library.

and display, and interpretation of the world's treasures" (2000: 29–30). From the Mouseion of Alexandria to the museums of today, collections of artifacts, broadly defined, are still more often than not the fundamental resources that enable museums to do their work. As places of human transformation, universal work, and political work, through collections and social interaction, museums in their *earliest* iteration as mouseions laid a clear foundation for providing social service.

Cabinets of curiosities

As European explorers and scientists of the 1500s and later opened up literal and figurative new worlds, those with means and time sought to acquire the physical symbols of such expansion (Impey and MacGregor 2001; Mueller 2001). In a special room or a lighted hallway, often in one's own residence, many a well-to-do collector in sixteenth- and seventeenth-century Western Europe presided over a cabinet of curiosity, a carefully arranged personal display of unique and unusual artifacts considered to be the "true prototype of the modern museum" (Stocking Jr. 1988: 6). Based on whim, the cabinet might be enjoyed by its creator in contemplative solitude or shared with select members of his circle who were close, lucky, or important enough to be invited. In this popular European iteration of the museum, the activities of collection and display took center stage. Although not yet public in nature, as vehicles for self-development, communication, and relationship building, these museums unquestionably served social purposes.

Viewed through the lens of contemporary research on collecting, cabinets of curiosities were indeed no frivolous indulgence. As scholars now recognize, collecting is a nearly universal behavior by which one makes sense of the world, one's relationship to it, and one's sense of self (Cameron 1972; Clifford 1988; Pearce 1995): a collector's assemblage becomes "a non-verbal reality model which will express his dreams and aspirations, the answer to his search for identity" (Cameron 1972: 193). As vehicles of social interaction and relationship, cabinets of curiosity helped their keepers, and to some extent their viewers, to influence their identity, image, and reputation (Olmi 2001; Turner 2001), communicate prestige and status (Bennett 1995; Olmi 2001), and forge social bonds of affiliation, respect, and friendship (ibid.). Although benefiting just the narrow group of cabinet owners and their selected guests, the "prototype of the modern museum" (Stocking Jr. 1988) existed to foster self-development and relationship building – key aspects of social service – through the collection and display of artifacts.

Public museums and settlement house museums

In the late eighteenth and nineteenth centuries, the United Kingdom and the United States wrestled with negative effects of industrialization like poverty, overcrowding, and disease. Against this backdrop, the truly public museum emerged, opening its collections to others than scholars and the wealthy (Ripley 1969; Bennett 1995; Lowry 2004). Around this time the first settlement house also appeared, a community-based social service in which students, clergy, activists, and artists "settled" in order to interact with, learn from, and assist people who were poor (Kirst-Ashman 2003). Widely considered one of the foundations of the modern social work profession, the settlement house will be the subject of more detailed discussion in Chapter 2. It is worth noting here that the settlement house and the public museum shared intriguing commonalities and intimate links at the time of their inception.

Motivated by a desire to improve the conditions of industrial society and a particular concern for working-class and immigrant individuals and families, an increasing number of museums, like settlement houses, aimed to combat poverty, alcoholism, and social unrest (Choate 1917; Ripley 1969; Bennett 1995; Skramstad 1999; Schwarzer 2006; Woodson-Boulton 2007). Leaders in both worlds drew inspiration from a common source – the ideas of philosophers such as John Ruskin, William Morris, and others who espoused the transforming power of art and culture (Waterfield and Smith 1994; Woodson-Boulton 2007). These leaders included no less than Sir Henry Cole, founder of the South Kensington Art Museum (later the Victoria and Albert Museum); Joseph Choate, an early trustee of the Metropolitan Museum of Art in New York; and two foundational figures of social work: Vicar Samuel Augustus Barnett, who founded Toynbee Hall, the first settlement house in London, in 1884; and Jane Addams, founder in 1889 of Hull House, the best-known settlement house in America.

Some settlement houses, such as Toynbee Hall and Hull House, developed and operated their own museums as part of their work. At least one museum, the Ancoats Hall Art Museum, invited the local Manchester University Settlement to "settle" within its complex and eventually merged with it to become the Manchester Art Museum and University Settlement (Harrison 1993; Rose 1993). In instances like these, the "common ground" of early social work and early public museums became a physical reality.

Further linking several public museums and settlement houses at the time was the belief shared by their leaders that the unique environment of the museum and the medium of the exhibition were powerful tools for social service, particularly with families. In England, for example, the notion that the museum provided the working-class man with an opportunity for beneficial family leisure as an alternative to drinking was a compelling argument for extending the hours of the South Kensington Museum. As founder Henry Cole suggested,

> Open all museums of Science and Art after the hours of Divine service; let the working man get his refreshment there in company with his wife and children, rather than leave him to booze away from them in the Public-house and Gin Palace. The Museum will certainly lead him to wisdom and gentleness, and to Heaven, whilst the latter will lead him to brutality and perdition.
>
> (Cole et al. 1884: 368)

In America, as Jane Addams explained, "An overmastering desire to reveal the humbler immigrant parents to their own children lay at the base of what has come to be called the Hull-House Labor Museum" (Addams 1910: 235). Developed with input from John Dewey, the Labor Museum exhibits, an early form of living history with a social work purpose, featured neighborhood immigrants from various countries actively demonstrating their craft skills, an exercise aimed explicitly at improving self-esteem and relationships within families. Representative of those affected by the exhibits was Angelina, an Italian girl who came to perceive her immigrant mother as "the best stick-spindle spinner in America" (Addams 1910: 244). She consequently "allowed her mother to pull out of the big box under the bed the beautiful homespun garments which had been previously hidden away as uncouth" (Addams 1910: 245).

In addition to serving families, some public museums and settlement house museums believed that their environments and exhibitions could help to serve local groups and society at large by bringing disparate people together to interact, learn from each other, and perhaps bridge their differences, most notably differences in social class. Exhibitions such as St. Jude's, a program of Toynbee Hall that later

Figure 1.3 At the Hull-House Labor Museum in nineteenth-century Chicago, mothers demonstrate their spinning skills as their children play nearby. Jane Addams Memorial Collection (JAMC_0000_0177_0475), Special Collections and University Archives Department, University of Illinois at Chicago Library.

evolved into the Whitechapel Free Art Gallery, were considered to be vehicles "through which misunderstanding and hatred between rich and poor could be translated into mutual appreciation for the transcendent truths and beauties of art" and "lead to political, social and economic solidarity" (Koven 1994: 24). Some contemporary writers characterize these late-nineteenth- and early-twentieth-century efforts as patronizing attempts to teach lower classes the ways of the elite that did little to change prevailing class and power differences (e.g., Bennett 1995; Schwarzer 2006). However, many positive benefits did result, such as increased interaction across class lines, improvement in the lives of some individuals and families, and an expansion of the public that attended museums (Koven 1994; Waterfield and Smith 1994). Although still controlled by the elite and middle classes, public museums and settlement house museums quite intentionally aimed to apply their unique resources to benefit those whose lives were negatively affected by social conditions. Thus, for the first time in the evolution of museums, the institution was used consciously as a social work tool.

Temporary traveling exhibits

Museums developed further as public forums in relation to a number of other "exhibitionary" institutions, including fairs, national exhibitions, and international expositions (Bennett 1995), many of which aimed to influence the knowledge, attitudes, and behavior of their viewers. Institutions of all kinds saw that an exhibit could be assembled nearly anywhere, preferably close to its desired audience, and thus the temporary traveling exhibit was born, a portable display that could help "to make cultural values more readily accessible to all, without regard to social distinction or geographic isolation" (Osborn 1953: 12). Being mobile, the traveling exhibit could reach diverse populations across great distances (Ambrose and Paine 1993) as well as confined communities such as hospitals and prisons (Bose 1983). As a visual medium, it could transcend language barriers, including illiteracy (Osborn 1953; Alexander and Alexander 2008). Given these strengths, the traveling exhibit developed a significant and enduring use as a means to mobilize people and improve social conditions. This use has spanned decades as well as continents.

In 1899, yet another foundational institution of the modern profession of social work, the Charity Organization Society, demonstrated how a temporary exhibit could inform all citizens about a social problem, rally public protest, and assert political pressure to impressive ends. Seeking reform of the appalling slum housing problem in New York City, social reformer Lawrence Veiller and a volunteer committee created *The Tenement-House Exhibition of 1899*, a display of more than a thousand compelling photographs, models, illustrations, and facts that was housed for two weeks in an old Fifth Avenue building. Impressively, the exhibit mobilized citizens who were not themselves directly affected by the problem as well as those who were. "Rich and poor came to see that speaking record of a city's sorry plight, and at last we all understood" (Riis 1902: 143). Widely attributed to the exhibit was the generation of plans for more humane housing as well as the passage of the New York State Tenement House Law, credited to Veiller as the exhibit organizer (ibid.).

The 1950s and 1960s saw the frequent use of traveling exhibits to deliver public health and social welfare campaigns and empower citizens to help themselves, particularly in developing countries where basic needs were great. As world leaders proclaimed the singular importance of science as a solution to social problems of the day, science exhibits developed by the United Nations Educational, Scientific and Cultural Organization and outfitted on buses, trains, and trucks traveled throughout Asia, Africa, and India to show citizens how to improve their sanitation, economy, and welfare (Daifuku 1965; Bose 1983). In a later program across India headed by Saroj Ghose, professional social workers familiar with the area were part of the design team: exhibits encouraged irrigation and water purification procedures and promoted the raising of more crops to address the growing problem of food scarcity (Bose 1983).

Traveling exhibits have also been used to educate people about the experiences of different groups in efforts to reduce stigma and bias. A leader in this work has been Riksutstallningar, a highly successful state-run exhibit organization in Sweden devoted to "geographical justice and social justice" (Hjorth 1994: 99). In a display about life for people with physical disabilities, for example, created in collaboration with members of the disability community, visitors navigated in wheelchairs to experience firsthand the challenges of insensitive design. The exhibit also included a section where local officials were asked to explain how they had met the needs of people with disabilities (Westerlund and Knuthammar 1981). Museums found they could greatly increase their ability to advocate for social action and improve social conditions through traveling exhibits addressing the social problems of vulnerable groups. In addition to museum workers, these efforts increasingly involved a broadening array of people, including citizen volunteers, social workers, and members of the groups of concern.

Integrated museums, ecomuseums, and neighborhood museums

In many parts of the world, the late 1960s and 1970s saw profound social movement that took such forms as civil rights, minority liberation, and a growing respect for group identity, all of which influenced museums (de Varine 2005). New kinds of institutions began to emerge in both theory and practice – among them the integrated museum in Latin America, the ecomuseum in France, and the neighborhood museum in the United States. This "revolution" in museum work, often hailed as the "new museology" (van Mensch 1995; de Varine 2005), featured the museum itself, embedded within its specific community, operating as a powerful tool for development and social change (van Mensch 1995; Davis 2004). These museum forms were not just for the people but tools of the people.

Key to this new wave was the idea that a museum should interpret and address the complex environments in which people live. In 1972, at a historic meeting in Chile called the *Round Table on the Development and the Role of Museums in the Contemporary World*, museum workers from all over Latin America gathered to discuss ways to tackle rural, agricultural, and urban challenges in the region. Mario Teruggi of Argentina outlined one approach, the "integrated museum" that would link directly to its community and, in particular, to "the most urgent problems faced by inhabitants." These problems, Teruggi proposed, "might then form the main theme of exhibitions which would place them within their economic, social, ecological and anthropological context" (in Guido 1973: 12) and ultimately "create wider awareness of … problems" (ibid.: 35). Widely discussed and disseminated, the concept of the integrated museum and other resolutions from the meeting inspired the museum field in Latin America and well beyond (Davis 2004; de Varine 2005).

Considered by many to be fundamental to these new museum forms was the deep involvement of the community itself in every aspect of museum operation. Perhaps no kind of museum in history has demonstrated this involvement more clearly than the ecomuseum, which originated in France. Although ecomuseum experiments involving the French Regional Nature Parks began in the late 1960s (Hubert 1985), the years 1971–4 saw the creation of the defining project, the ecomuseum of the community of Le Creusot-Montceau-les-Mines, pioneered by Marcel Evrard and

Georges Henri Riviere (Poulet 1994). Interpreting the people and industry of the region, Le Creusot defined community holistically as a broad environment made up of people, places, ways of life, and meanings. Like many subsequent ecomuseums, Le Creusot empowered its involved citizens themselves to shape and present their identity and to utilize heritage and cultural resources for development and change (Poulet 1994). Since Le Creusot, ecomuseum theory and practice has expanded in many directions and numerous countries (Davis 2005).

Breadth of community involvement was also a key feature of this new museology. Never before had the actual operation of museums involved such a diverse range of groups, a feature well exemplified by the Anacostia Neighborhood Museum in the United States. Founded in the late 1960s in a low-income inner-city area of Washington DC, this unique collaboration between the Smithsonian Institution, a local neighborhood organization, and Director John Kinard, a pastor and experienced community organizer, ultimately engaged community groups of all kinds, including teen organizations, church groups, and social clubs, in such matters as administrative decisions, design of exhibits addressing local problems, and exhibit installation (James 2005). To Kinard, "the 'community' included the Nation of Islam, anti-methadone organizations, a group called the Inner Voices of Lorton Reformatory, bands and dance groups needing rehearsal space" (Kernan 1996: 29). All contributed to shaping a neighborhood museum widely esteemed for its groundbreaking "work to improve the quality of life for the people within its reach" (Kinard 1985: 223). Together, the neighborhood museum, the ecomuseum, and the integrated museum demonstrate the ability of a museum to empower a place-based community, engage its diverse groups, and seek solutions to its own problems.

Toward the social work of museums

The complete international history of museums as social service deserves a book of its own, as many other museums, leaders, and trends rightfully belong in the fuller, more detailed story. It is obviously a history still in the making. Yet even this selective review illuminates an essential fact: museums have *always* been institutions of social service. For countless years and all around the world, museums have both intentionally and unintentionally facilitated the expression and transformation of individuals and their sense of identity and contributed to the development and maintenance of friendship, family, and other important social bonds. They have fostered solidarity among people with commonalities and facilitated interaction among people with differences. Museums have also aimed to influence public knowledge, attitudes, and behavior; deliver public health and social welfare campaigns; reduce stigma and bias; empower citizens and communities; and mobilize other forms of social action and social change. As we will see in Chapter 2, museums have long used their unique resources to pursue the same basic goals that define the profession of social work: "helping individuals, groups, or communities enhance or restore their capacity for social functioning and creating social conditions favorable to this goal" (National Association of Social Workers 1973: 4–5).

Unquestionably, the past has provided much of the groundwork for the present: museums engage in social service today in large part because they have *always* done so and because effective approaches, techniques, and applications are accessible in the history of museums. Indeed the work of museums past is clearly reflected in contemporary practice. As the climate of accountability worldwide has pressured museums to justify their worth, it is not surprising, but rather inevitable, that they are acting upon a growing awareness of their broadest potential: what we might call the social work of museums.

Explaining tomorrow: theories about museums, visitors, and society

Thanks to the work of many different museum scholars and visitor studies specialists, contemporary policymakers and practitioners now have ways to imagine, understand, and even predict how and why museums can provide social service. Along with museum history, these theories help to inspire and justify the growth of museum social service initiatives. Presently, the professional literature does not contain a single comprehensive theory that explains the social work of museums. However, it does contain several perspectives that shed some light on how museums foster social functioning and favorable social conditions. Once again, a review of all relevant theories is beyond our scope here, but even a brief sampling of eight perspectives provides valuable insight: 1) interactive experience and social relationships; 2) communication as meaning-making; 3) the meaning of things; 4) human needs; 5) outcomes and changes; 6) relationship benefits and social capital; 7) social change; and 8) culture change. Together these illuminate the mechanics of the social work of museums as presently understood in the museum field.

Interactive experience and social relationships

To begin, what is a museum experience? Who or what will typically be involved? What is the setting for museums' social service? Taking a systems theory approach, John Falk and Lynn Dierking's interactive experience model (1992) offers a useful sketch of museum experience as a social endeavor that takes place in the context of *relationships*. While usually used to explain an actual visit to a physical museum, the model also applies to virtual museum experiences, outreach, and any other instances where museum resources and people come together. Even when there is but a single person physically involved in the encounter, his or her experience will be the product of many social relationships that are activated and implicated in the process.

As Falk and Dierking (1992) explain, factors and variables from three different contexts will interact to constitute and shape a person's museum experience: the physical, the personal, and the social. Physical factors include the museum environment itself, the exhibits, and the objects. Many of these factors are created by and therefore represent other people such as the museum staff, artists, or even society at large. Personal factors include all that a particular visitor brings, such as previous experiences and memories that are likely to reflect important relationships in the visitor's life. Social factors include the companions, if any, with whom one visits the museum, as well as others encountered there – either real, such as a docent, or implied, such as other visitors whose remarks can be read in a comment book. During a museum experience, a visitor therefore engages with many other people, real or symbolic, including museum staff, family and significant others, strangers, and even society at large. From this perspective, the museum experience is surely "social" work: by definition it constitutes relationships and interaction through which, as we will see later, growth and development may occur.

Communication as meaning-making

What predictably ensues when museum resources, individuals, and groups come together? Throughout the history of museums, the answer is clear: processes of communication will take place. From conveying self-image through a cabinet of curiosity, to working with others to design an exhibit, to viewing a museum Web site, people in interaction with museum resources and with each other will create, exchange, and share information and meaning – in real or virtual time and space. How does this work? For years, the museum field subscribed to a linear "transmission" model of communication that posited museum professionals as the "senders" of intended information, messages, and significance through media such as exhibits, programs, and other museum fare to visitor "receivers." Consequently, many museums examined the efficacy of this transfer, as well as the manipulation of variables such as exhibit content and format that might help insure visitors would "get the message" intended by the senders. In the last few decades, in light of broad paradigm shifts in communication theory as well as empirical studies that revealed museum visitors to be actively involved in making sense of what they encounter, the field has moved to a more contemporary model of communication known as meaning-making (e.g., Silverman 1990; Silverman 1991; Hooper-Greenhill 1992; Roberts 1997; Silverman 1999a; Hooper-Greenhill 2000). From this perspective, it is now understood that the "product" of communication is not receipt of a message, but rather the creation of meaning, which occurs through the interaction of those who create museum fare, the visitor, and the fare itself, which provides the resources used in the process (Sandell 2007). As understood in later sections of this review, the creation of meaning in museums is significant in a number of ways to individuals, groups, and society.

The perspective of meaning-making in communication explains several key mechanisms of the social work of museums. First, when making meaning in a museum, visitors indeed bring to bear a variety of personal frames of reference, including their experiences, emotions, memories, background, and previous knowledge (Silverman 1990; Perin 1992; Doering and Pekarik 1997), in short, their self, life, and relationships. Thus, personal connection and reflection is activated in the museum environment. Second, research has also shown that when encountering museum fare, visitors will likely consider and value not only the messages and meanings intended by educators, exhibit designers, artifact makers, or artists, they will also value, sometimes equally or more, the personal or affective meanings they create themselves as they connect what they encounter to their own lives and relationships (Silverman 1990). Thus, meaning can result from the various relationships activated within the museum experience. Third, the meaning-making model reveals how fluid and socially dependent meaning is. Indeed, the meaning of museum objects, exhibits, messages, and experiences is a constant negotiation within those relationships. It therefore follows that museums are places where meanings can be considered, shared, affirmed, contested, discarded, or changed (Hooper-Greenhill 1992) – and individuals, groups, and even society may change as well.

The meaning of things

Fueling the meaning-making process is a unique relationship between people and objects. This relationship constitutes the heart of museum communication. As the interactive experience model suggests, any aspect of the physical context of a museum experience might engage visitors, including the surroundings, the gift shop, and the museum building itself. Yet central to most communication in museums are the objects on display. This is not just because the museum is known as a place for encountering and reflecting upon material culture. It is also because people throughout history and the world find objects, whether natural or human-made, powerfully provocative. Objects "embody human purposes and experiences, and they invite us to act towards them in ways which may give us what we desire" (Pearce 1995: 166).

As many scholars agree, museum objects elicit a variety of responses that constitute evidence of meaning-making in action (e.g., Silverman 1990 and 2002b; Maines and Glynn 1993; O'Neill 1995; Kavanaugh 2000; Morrissey 2002; Scott 2002). Emotions, opinions, reflections, recollections, and debate are evoked whether objects are presented with minimal interpretation or placed within the interpretive context of such hallmark museum media as exhibits, programs, Web sites, activities, and tours. As visitor conversations indicate, objects function as symbols of identity, relationship, and social group; as reminders of lived experience; as beacons of possible futures; and as symbols of nature, society, and the divine (e.g., Csikszentmihalyi and Rochberg-Halton 1981; Csikszentmihalyi 1993; Pearce 1995) – even when on display in museums. Thus we begin to see that by making meaning of objects, people in museums are actually developing – and sometimes even changing – meanings and aspects of themselves, their relationships, and the society in which they live. In other words, meaning-making in museums yields beneficial consequences, rendered more concrete through the perspectives of human needs, outcomes and changes, relationship benefits and social capital, social change, and culture change.

Human needs

Theorists agree that museums offer an environment in which people can meet specific, predictable *human needs*. Early proponents of this view focused on three types of experience that people require and that museums can provide: 1) educational experience; 2) associational experience, opportunities to connect and share with others; and 3) reverential experience, a connection with something bigger than oneself and/or awe-inspiring (Annis 1974; Graburn 1977). More recently, others have posited that museums can help people in their search to satisfy the hierarchy of fundamental human needs outlined by humanistic psychologist Abraham Maslow in 1943 (Knudson et al. 1995; Silverman 1999b). Considered essential to human health and prerequisites for creativity, contribution, and community, these sequential human needs range from the most basic physiological and safety issues, such as the need for food and shelter and freedom from fear and anxiety; to social and relationship needs; followed by ego and self-esteem needs; and culminating in the need for self-actualization, including creativity and the achievement of potential (Maslow 1943). Clearly, all of these levels of need require interaction in order to be met. Significantly, the human needs perspective suggests that by meeting certain universal needs common to all people, museums benefit individuals, groups, and society at large.

Outcomes and changes

As recent models demonstrate, museum communication can also result in positive *outcomes or changes* for people (Sandell 2002; Scott 2002; Hooper-Greenhill et al. 2003; Museums, Libraries and Archives Council 2004; Scott 2006; Worts 2006a; Institute of Museum and Library Services 2007). Many of these models have emerged in response to government mandates requiring publicly funded agencies, including museums, to demonstrate their value and fiscal accountability in measurable terms (Dilevko and Gottlieb 2004; Scott 2006). In the United Kingdom, for example, a model advocated by the Museums, Libraries and Archives Council (MLA) in 2004 has been widely used by museums to document occurrences of and increases in five "generic learning outcomes" for people: 1) knowledge and understanding; 2) skills; 3) attitudes and values; 4) enjoyment, inspiration, creativity; and 5) activity, behavior, progression (Hooper-Greenhill et al. 2003; MLA 2004). In the United States, the Institute of Museum and Library Services (IMLS), a federal grant-making agency, requires its grantee museums to utilize a model of outcome-based evaluation to measure and document "achievements or changes in skill, knowledge, attitude, behavior, condition, or life status for program participants" (IMLS 2007). This model was adapted from one developed by the United Way, a major social service umbrella organization (United Way of America 1996; Sheppard 2000).

In addition to models that conceptualize and measure change for individuals and groups of museum participants, other models suggest that positive outcomes attributable to museums can also occur within broader collectives (e.g., Sandell 2002; Scott 2006; Worts 2006a). As suggested by the frameworks developed in Canada by the Working Group on Museums and Sustainable Communities, for example, changes can occur not only within individuals, but within communities and within museums themselves (Worts 2006a), while Scott's (2006) work demonstrates the long-term impacts of museums on the economy and society at large. Reflecting years of collective visitor research results, the outcomes and change lens begins to organize what is known about specific ways in which museums can help facilitate transformation. The social work of museums takes place at multiple levels.

Relationship benefits and social capital

As we have seen, the museum experience itself activates relationship and interaction. It is therefore not surprising that meaning-making in museums can also yield growth and development in a range of social relationships, perhaps the most obvious dimension of the "social" work of museums. It has long been known that museums provide valued opportunities for leisure experience, social interaction, and communication within pre-existing relationships, usually visitor groups consisting of family members and/or friends (e.g., Cone and Kendall 1978; Hilke 1989; Hood 1989; Silverman 1990). Through interaction in museums, family members can better understand themselves, each other, and their family unit (Silverman 1989), and pairs of visitors, including long-standing intimate partners as well as new friends can evaluate, build, and express their relationships (Silverman 1990). Since museums are perceived as safe places for congregant behavior and public forum (Gurian 1995a and 2006b), they can also bring together for interaction and discussion larger groups who may not know each

Figure 1.4 Visitors interact with the museum environment and each other in *Scotland's Wildlife*, one of twenty-two new displays at the Kelvingrove Art Gallery and Museum, Glasgow. Photo courtesy of Culture and Sport Glasgow (Museums).

other well. Through collections and collaborations (Janes 2007) as well as exhibits, outreach programs, and other means (Silverman 2002b; Newman and McLean 2004), museums help link community members and encourage the formation of groups (Daly 2005; Scott 2006), build networks (Newman and McLean 2004), and decrease social isolation (Silverman 2002b). Museums can also help combat prejudice (Sandell 2007).

A number of museum theorists believe that museums facilitate the building of social capital, an extremely popular concept from political science that is compelling, challenging to measure, and defined in the museum literature in two subtly different ways. Echoing the work of political scientist Robert Putnam (1995; 2000), some view social capital as the development of actual trusting relationships that link people, build society, and undergird the market economy (Newman and McLean 2004; Janes and Conaty 2005; Janes 2007). Others follow the perspective of political economist Francis Fukayama (1999; 2002) in viewing social capital as the shared norms, values, and experiences that enable cooperation and action, such as community organization and political protest (Scott 2006). Research suggests that social capital is linked to health, happiness, democracy, and a civil society (Putnam 2000). Both views add to the growing understanding of the museum as a social agent.

Social change

As museum leader Mark O'Neill has observed, "Museums can only be as good as their analysis of society and their awareness of the reality of people's lives" (2006: 111). Museums are beginning to recognize the complex social problems and inequalities that affect people's existence and diminish their ability to experience the benefits offered by museums. Perhaps most frequently, they are responding by promoting social change through exhibits, educational programs, special events, and other efforts that raise public awareness of social issues and encourage effective action (Scottish Museums Council 2000; Hein 2005). From HIV/AIDS to global warming, such work in museums is rapidly increasing worldwide. As outcomes and change models demonstrate, museum communication has the potential to alter people's attitudes, values, knowledge, and behavior. When successful on a collective level relative to a social issue, a museum operates as an agent of social change.

As advocated by the UK government in recent years, many museums have turned their attention to combating social exclusion, a broad concept that John Vincent has defined as "the process of being shut out, fully or partially, from ... political, social, cultural or economic systems" (in Burns Owens Partnership 2005: 13). Many museums work directly with people whose lives are negatively affected by social problems and inequalities and often collaborate with other social agencies to devise strategies for meeting consequent needs (Department for Culture, Media and Sport 2000) and fostering desirable changes (e.g., Silverman 2002b; Newman and McLean 2004).

Citing cultural exclusion as "the arena in which museums and galleries are most readily able to engage," museums in Scotland have focused attention on addressing exclusion as a means to social change. Defining cultural exclusion as "the process by which people encounter barriers to participating in and being represented in the cultural sphere" (Scottish Museums Council 2000: 6), this strategy posits the engagement of people with history, heritage, science, and the arts as a route to "changing their lives and tackling problems" (ibid.: 4). To mitigate cultural exclusion, Scottish museums are working to identify and remove the barriers that prevent equal participation and representation in culture (ibid.). Acknowledging the contention that museums wittingly or unwittingly help create and preserve the dominance of certain social groups (Bennett 1995; Duncan 1995), other museums are examining and rectifying their own problematic practices (Hein 2005). For example, since objects constitute the raw material of museum communication, decisions about whose objects are collected and how they are displayed and interpreted become a powerful means of cultural inclusion or exclusion (Karp and Lavine 1991; Hooper-Greenhill 2000) that "can open up or close down historical, social and cultural possibilities" (Sandell 2002: 8). Increasingly, museums are turning their social activism inward to effect much needed change by redressing the exclusion and/or misrepresentation of historically excluded groups like people with disabilities (Delin 2002; Sandell 2007) and lesbians and gay men (Vanegas 2002).

Altering the very perspectives from which museum professionals approach their work can be seen as an important strategy for addressing cultural and social exclusion. As Mark O'Neill points out, the majority of the world's museum visitors still reflects the more educated and well off in society. While many professionals do not view this as a problem, others, like O'Neill, consider it evidence of the "unequal distribution of the good" of museums that can only be redressed by adopting a new view of museums that involves a theory of justice (O'Neill 2006: 100).

Culture change

Viewed from the widest angle lens, the social work of museums involves nothing less than the making and changing of culture. As LeVine (1973) and Ogbu (1995) have suggested, culture consists of the shared ways of doing things that enable human beings to live together, what Douglas Worts has called the "foundation blocks" of society (2006b: 128). As we have seen, visitors in museums are actively involved in creating and altering many aspects of culture that shape our lives, including identity, relationships, and shared values, attitudes, and behavior. From this perspective, it is clearly essential that all people have equal opportunity to participate in museum communication (O'Neill 2006).

As a product of human interaction, culture can and does change. Because the ways of a society are thus always open to the possibility of transformation, museums possess what Eilean Hooper-Greenhill has called their "radical potential":

> As long as museums and galleries remain the repositories of artefacts and specimens, new relationships can always be built, new meanings can always be discovered, new interpretations with new relevances can be found, new codes and new rules can be written.
>
> (Hooper-Greenhill 1992: 215)

Increasingly, museums are taking intentional aim at cultural change. For example, a group in Canada has been studying and implementing approaches for museums to promote the value of sustainability, critical to our future (Sutter and Worts 2005). Through museum communication, human beings can work to change their culture and their society, including "themselves, each other, and the world" (Worts 2006b: 128).

In the service of society

Understanding precisely how museums foster social functioning, human well-being, favorable social conditions, and social change is an ongoing process. New ideas will develop, new data will confirm or challenge existing perspectives, additional links will be broken, made, and explained, and, true to its nature, theory – itself an aspect of culture – will evolve and change. Yet, from this selective review of theoretical perspectives from the museum literature, a preliminary model of the social work of museums as presently understood emerges to explain what occurs when people, objects, and museums come together.

Fundamentally, museums offer interactive social experiences of communication in which relationships are activated and people make meaning of objects. This communication yields beneficial consequences: people may meet fundamental human needs like the need for self-esteem and self-actualization; achieve change in essential areas such as knowledge, skills, values, and behavior; build and strengthen social connections and relationships, including social capital; address social problems; and promote social justice and equality. The consequences may involve and/or benefit individuals, groups, and society at large. In effect, through museum communication, people enact, share, and alter key elements of *culture* that shape the very operation, quality, and experience of social life. This includes not only our selves, relationships, social problems, and social structure, but also the understandings, solutions, and broader vision that inform our daily lives as well as our individual and shared futures. It also includes our museums.

This is but one way to link some of the most useful current theories to begin to form a comprehensive explanation of the social work of museums. In sum or in part, the development and availability of these theories, along with museum history, has provided both roots and wings for museums' growing embrace of social service. But are current perspectives sufficient for understanding what museums are and could be doing? What *is* social work, and how can the social work profession move museums toward their potential? These are the questions we turn to next.

Figure 2.1 Social Work: Making a Difference. Photo by Wendy Bush, inspired by Janet Fletcher R.S.W. and Good Shepherd Women's and Children's Services, Hamilton, Ontario.

Chapter 2

Social work perspectives

Those who move mountains begin by carrying small stones.
Confucius

As long as public museums have existed, so has an entire profession devoted to the service of society and its development. For more than one hundred years, as the museum field inched toward declaring a prevailing concern for the public good, the profession of social work actively fostered the well-being of individuals, groups, and society, while refining theories and methods for doing so. Luckily, museums value interdisciplinary knowledge, professional development, and productive partnership. From the fields of education and communication, for example, museums have adopted important concepts and techniques. It is from the field of social work that museums have, intentionally and unintentionally, garnered both essential approaches and practical guidance to inform many of their social service efforts to date. Increasingly, museums are engaging in social work. It is therefore not only professionally wise but ethically necessary for museums to deepen their relationship with this essential global profession. What *is* social work, and how do its fundamental perspectives further advance museum theory and practice? Let's briefly return to our scenes of change in museums for a closer look at social work in action.

Relationships of change

For many of the nursing home residents who participated in the museum tour arranged by the agency's social worker, the encounter with art, a lively guide, and each other stimulated body, mind, and spirit. For the woman with the long, grey hair and the tall, slender man, the experience also started a friendship. Back at the nursing home, the two now sit together at meals, sometimes talking about art, other times in silence. While self-esteem and social needs are considered basic to all humans (Maslow 1943), research demonstrates that friends and social networks not only offer support, increase self-confidence, and ease depression, they help people over 70 years of age to live longer (Giles et al. 2005). Coping with the onset of dementia, these two have many reasons to appreciate their new connection, which the social worker takes care to encourage.

In the children's museum, the ten-year-old boy and his father, a prisoner nearing the end of his sentence, are enjoying each other's company. With guidance from the museum social worker, the hands-on music exhibit and other museum activities also provide them with opportunities to practice essential family interaction skills like patience, listening, and cooperation. Through this program, the boy and his father have become less fearful and more hopeful about their eventual reunification. While functional family bonds are essential for most people, the re-establishment of this family promises specific benefits for a parent and a child facing particular risks. As research indicates, successful reintegration of former prisoners into family life is associated with lower recidivism rates (Petersilia 2003) as well as more positive outcomes for their children (Boswell and Wedge 2002; Travis and Waul 2004).

As the group of neighbors working to create a museum recall in amazement, their effort began as a conversation among three people. Before long they had recruited others with a variety of skills, including a teacher, a politician, and a social worker with community organization experience. Their differences serve the group well: as research shows, the success of community action to prevent future violence is significantly enhanced when the planning and implementation team is diverse (National Youth Violence Prevention Resource Center 2007). Yet, as the social worker knows, the group's ability to transcend their differences is equally essential, and not just for the good of the project. Through the mutual aid possible in a supportive group, people can help each other to heal, even from trauma and loss (Gitterman 2004; Yalom 2005).

Social work and relationships

What is social work? As different as they are, each of these scenes of change provides an answer. A social worker at a local nursing home helps residents cope with the challenges of illness and aging. Another helps a family lay the groundwork for their future. A group united by tragedy works to foster change in their community as well as in themselves. Present in some form in every country in the world, social work today is an endeavor as diverse and multifaceted as the people it involves, the contexts in which they live, and the specific goals they pursue. As defined inclusively by the International Federation of Social Workers (IFSW), the organization that serves more than eighty-six member countries,

> the social work profession promotes social change, problem solving in human relationships, and the empowerment and liberation of people to enhance well-being. Utilising theories of human behaviour and social systems, social work intervenes at the points where people interact with their environments. Principles of human rights and social justice are fundamental to social work.
>
> (IFSW 2000)

Despite different settings, goals, and methods, each of these scenes also demonstrates the common core of social work. The elderly man and woman meet basic needs and find meaning in their fledgling friendship. The boy and his father realize new benefits as a family. The neighbors wield far more impact on their community as a group than any of its members could alone. Fundamental to social work is the recognition that human beings survive, live meaningfully, and achieve fulfillment through *relationships* (Schriver 2004; Netting et al. 2004; Jordan 2007), especially, the self, the close pair, the family, and the group (Schriver 2004). It is therefore "social work's primary activity" (Hare 2004: 411) and "chief contribution" (Jordan 2007: 11) to foster and improve relationships, for they are the agents of well-being (Schriver 2004; Jordan 2007).

As research demonstrates, robust human relationships are also the critical ingredient of nearly every aspect of a healthy, well-functioning society. Essential to collective happiness and well-being (Putnam 2000), relationships are the vehicles by which people meet needs, solve social problems, and transform cultures (Netting et al. 2004; Jordan 2007). Of particular interest to social workers, effective relationships are key to the achievement of human rights, equality, and social justice (Kirst-Ashman 2003; Jordan 2007). Relationships are the agents of social change (Kirst-Ashman 2003).

Social workers know that creating and maintaining effective, beneficial relationships is a challenging endeavor, more complex than popular theories of social capital might suggest. From a social work perspective, relationships are more than a stockpile of favors or a collection of shared ways of thinking, they are living systems that grow and change (Schriver 2004) and sometimes require assistance and support. Therefore, social workers engage in the "professional activity of helping individuals, groups, or communities enhance or restore their capacity for social functioning and creating societal conditions favorable to this goal" (National Association of Social Workers 1973: 4–5). In short, social work serves relationships, the vehicles of well-being and social change.

"Much maligned and misunderstood"

As countries and communities around the world struggle to achieve peace and sustainable futures, the profession of social work has never before seemed so essential. Increasingly, social workers are called to the table to provide their perspectives on personal, local, and global issues. Yet, despite its relevance and an impressive record of contribution and impact around the world, there is another side to social work. To the great chagrin of many practitioners, "social work is a much maligned and misunderstood profession defined all too often by negative news coverage and out-dated stereotypes" (Social-Work.co.uk 2006). In the public mind, social work frequently conjures images of stern matrons, inefficient clerks, burnt-out caseworkers, and worse. Involved at times in high-risk situations such as violence, addiction, or abuse, social workers' missteps can have dramatic consequences, deemed far more newsworthy in today's media culture than their many everyday victories.

Radical views contend that the maligning of social work has deep historical roots that in fact demonstrate the power of the profession and the highly charged, politicized nature of its work. In many places and times, social workers have been or are resented for challenging or altering the status quo (Haynes and Mickelson 2003). Negative attitudes reflect thinly veiled discomfort with the "undesirable" circumstances and people that social workers historically assist (DeLauro 2005). Often, social workers aim to foster changes that are not welcomed or desired by all, especially those with vested interests in "business as usual."

Compounding its image problem is the scope of social work today; "the range of activity, variety of employment settings, and diversity of clients all contribute to an indistinct and often distorted professional representation" (DeLauro 2005: 18). Informed by a host of other fields, including psychology, psychiatry, and counseling, social work is frequently confused with these, although some studies have shown that the public views social work as the most valued and needed of these professions (Sharpley 1986; LeCroy and Stinson 2004). Still it appears that the public would benefit from better information about the social work profession (LeCroy and Stinson 2004). Like the museum field, social work struggles to convey its true nature and public value clearly.

Social work ... and museums?

Why would museums adopt perspectives of the "much maligned and misunderstood" profession of social work, so characterized by challenge? From fighting politicized battles to contesting the status quo to working with "undesirable people," museums themselves have, throughout their history, ventured into social work both knowingly and unknowingly. Serving as a rarely acknowledged mentor, the social work profession has often informed these efforts. Its principles have filtered into museum literature, and its practitioners, clients, and agencies have frequently served as partners, collaborators, and leaders in socially oriented museum initiatives. A connection was forged long ago, when the first public museums, settlement houses, and Charity Organization Societies began.

Now, as museums grow aware of and committed to their potential as agents of human well-being and social change, a deepened and purposeful bond between these two kindred fields has never been more essential. To translate their potential into effective action, museums have much more to learn from and about professional social work. At this juncture, museums are in dire need of a more informed conception of the social work they have been doing and a meaningful framework with which to organize, integrate, and analyze how they are doing it, with whom, where, and to what effect. Such systematic integration and analysis will provide a foundation for their evolving future as agents of relationship and social change. To these ends, we will first consider a brief history of the social work profession, examine some of the fundamental theoretical perspectives of social work, and identify how each perspective complements and expands prevailing museum theory. Then, we'll articulate an expanded vision of the social work of museums and a framework of subsequent questions for surveying existing knowledge and practice.

Social work begins: development of the relationship profession

Throughout history, societies have had various means of assisting their members with the challenges of living. Social work as a profession, however, emerged in England and the United States at the turn of the nineteenth century from the same context and influences as the first public museums. During this period of rapid industrialization, cities on both sides of the Atlantic experienced unprecedented growth and potential, as well as unprecedented social ills like overcrowding, poverty, disease, and crime. Life for many, especially the immigrants and their families who settled in teeming urban centers, was fraught with problems and discontent.

Alongside museums, two unique institutions developed to provide social service. The Charity Organization Society was founded in London in 1869, and Toynbee Hall, the first settlement house, was founded in 1884 in the same city. Less than ten years later, each had its counterpart in the United States, and together they served as prototypes for many similar institutions. Their methods and philosophies soon provided the basis for training programs to prepare a new type of professional. The Charity Organization Society (COS) movement and the Settlement House movement focused on different but ultimately inseparable goals. The former aimed to help individuals better themselves and their lives, while the latter worked to address social problems and problematic conditions in neighborhoods, communities, and society at large. Together, these pursuits form the foundations of the social work profession to this day.

Concentrating on the challenges of poverty, the COS movement believed that individuals and families were responsible for meeting their own needs, solving their own problems, and overcoming obstacles to well-being. Yet individuals and families could be helped to help themselves, especially through the attention, support, and knowledge of a "friendly visitor," an agency representative trained in approaches to problem solving and knowledgeable about available charities and resources (Kirst-Ashman 2003). For example, in order to make positive changes, an immigrant family with no income might need referral to language classes, assistance in securing employment, and encouragement to boost morale. Drawing upon an emerging science of helping and human change as well as moral principles, the friendly visitor assisted family members by means of the very relationship she developed with them.

Over time, many of the original COS agencies disbanded or changed focus, but their fundamental approach continued as one of two basic types of modern social work, now known by many different names, including casework, clinical practice, social care, care management, direct service, therapy, micro practice (with individuals), and mezzo practice (with families or small groups). Implemented around the world in institutional, private, and informal settings, this type of social work features a worker, informed by theory and experience, engaged in a purposeful relationship with an individual, family, or group to help explore issues and problems, facilitate changes, forge links to resources, and enhance and promote effective relationships. Like the friendly visitor of the past, a social worker today might still assist an immigrant family

Figure 2.2 A "friendly visitor" meets with a poor family in the winter of 1888. Mary Evans Picture Library/*Illustrated London News*.

with no income by emphasizing their strengths, referring them to a language class, and connecting them with employment agencies and resources. Informed by an expanded professional literature, the contemporary social worker understands from a foundation of theory and practice which approaches are helpful and why.

The Settlement House movement of the nineteenth century espoused a different approach to the challenges of urban life. Its adherents believed that people's problems and obstacles to well-being were in fact attributable to society, not the particular individual or family. Since society at large caused the problems, the appropriate focus of scrutiny and change was society itself. However, individuals, families, and groups could themselves become the vehicles for change through such means as advocacy, community organization, and social action (ibid.). Thus, settlement house workers fostered effective, beneficial relationships at many different levels. Settlement houses established unique communities in which people with intense need and others who wished to assist them would engage together in a range of educational, social, and cultural activities to mutual benefit. Frequently, settlement workers functioned as advocates for, or partners with, people in need by helping to empower them to recognize their authority and capability to effect change and influence social problems. For example, families in a troubled neighborhood, sharing concern for their sick, overworked children, banded together with settlement house workers to advocate for a new child labor law. Drawing upon experience and passion, settlement workers mobilized groups and assisted them in creating societal change, once again through the vehicle of relationships.

The Settlement House approach has evolved into the second basic type of modern social work, known today as community work, social and political action, policy practice, community activism, social reform, social development, and macro practice (Gray and Fook 2004; Hare 2004). Implemented around the world in a range of settings, this type of social work involves a practitioner engaged in purposeful relationships with communities, institutions, and other collectives to alleviate problems, foster beneficial relationships, and promote well-being through societal change. Like the settlement house worker of the past, the social worker today might still help families in a troubled neighborhood to mobilize, join together, and mount an initiative for a new law to improve those families' lives and the well-being of the entire neighborhood. While never far away from its grassroots heritage, macro social work practice in many parts of the world today has grown increasingly sophisticated and theory based.

The Charity Organization Society and the Settlement House movements of nineteenth-century Britain and the United States decisively shaped the social work profession. While the former recognized that individuals, families, and small groups could effect changes in themselves in order to meet needs, solve problems, and improve lives, the latter argued that human well-being was also dependent upon meeting needs, making changes, and solving problems at other levels of social relationship, including neighborhoods, communities, and society at large. Together the movements merged into a single field devoted to human well-being through relationships and change.

By the twentieth century, social work had spread from England and the United States to many other parts of the world (Weiss 2005). While much of global social work began by using Western ideas and approaches (Midgely 1981), many social workers have more recently focused on developing approaches and practices indigenous to their country's needs, values, and ideologies (Healy 2001). For example, social work in South Africa has emphasized "social development and social action models capable of addressing *inter alia* mass poverty, gross inequality, growing unemployment, and HIV/AIDS" (Gray and Fook 2004: 630). This differs from Australia, where critical and feminist approaches to social work are on the rise, or Singapore, where agency-based case management appears to predominate and practitioners are working together (ibid.; Weiss 2005; Singapore Association of Social Workers 2008). Social work is truly a "contextual profession, strongly influenced by its social environment and by the political and economic context within which it is practiced" (Healy 2004: 592).

Despite its contextual nature, social work in much of the world today reflects a relatively unified set of key theoretical perspectives that inform social work practice.

Figure 2.3 On 20 January 2007, more than 500 social workers and their families gathered for Singapore's first ever Social Workers' Day, now an annual event. Photo courtesy of Lynette Yeo Balota.

As we will soon see, many of these social work views already exist in some form within the theories of museums. Taken together, these perspectives can provide a new way to think about the social work of museums and a framework of basic questions with which to organize and synthesize its currently scattered body of knowledge and practice, the project we will pursue in Chapters 3 to 6. First, let us consider these fundamental perspectives of social work and how they apply to museums.

Social work views: insight for museums

Like any field, the social work profession draws on many different theories to explain and inform its practice. Eight of these are especially relevant: 1) the planned change process; 2) the client-centered empowering relationship; 3) people-in-environments and close relationship systems; 4) relationship needs; 5) people at risk and altered needs; 6) interventions; 7) human rights and social justice; and 8) culture in relationships. What do these perspectives contend, and how do they expand the ways that museums conceptualize what they do? We will now consider each in turn.

The planned change process

First of all, what is a social work experience? Who or what is typically involved? Social work is usefully viewed as a process of planned change – an intentional effort by a social worker and client(s) to influence "some specified condition, pattern of behavior, or set of circumstances that affects [the client(s)'] social functioning" (Sheafor et al. 2000: 119). Although context-dependent, this planned change process usually involves some combination of six major activities that may take place over a period of visits: engagement, assessment, planning, implementation, evaluation, and termination (Kirst-Ashman 2003; Netting et al. 2004). Early on, the social worker and client(s) will likely meet and talk to establish rapport and begin to develop their relationship. The social worker will gather information about the client(s)' situations, concerns, relationships, and other relevant issues. With this information, the social worker and client(s) will develop plans for their work together, including decisions about specific goals and strategies for pursuing them. Over time, they will implement these plans, evaluate their experience and progress, and make changes as needed. When the work is done, this special relationship will end with care and preparation for all involved. Each of these activities is integral to the process of planned change.

The experience of social work is not always so neat and linear as the planned change process might suggest. Sometimes, goals are "clear at the outset; at other times, goals and processes emerge as the interaction progresses" (Plath 2006: 60). Real-life factors, like insufficient resources or emergency situations, frequently dictate what happens in a particular experience, such as which activities of the planned change process will occur, in what order, and for how long. Some social work and social change happens slowly, over many years. Often, changes and benefits occur that are not intended or expected. In general, however, social work practice is as intentional and systematic as possible.

Like social work, most museum work today is typically implemented through intentional, systematic processes made up of discrete but related activities that very often aim to foster planned change of some kind in visitors or users of museum resources. From exhibit design to fund-raising, most aspects of museum work routinely include the activities of planning, implementation, and some kind of evaluation. What they sometimes, but do not always, include are the activities of engagement, assessment, or termination, parts of the planned change process of social work that signal its most important ingredient: a sustained relationship between social worker and client. Viewed through the social work lens, museums and museum workers may well have significantly more work to do to establish, deepen, and foster sustained relationships between themselves and those they wish to serve.

The client-centered empowering relationship

True to its most fundamental principle, social work itself begins with and depends upon the development and implementation of an effective relationship. Despite stereotypes that may suggest otherwise, social workers today strive to cultivate a client-centered personal relationship with each of their clients, a unique bond of trust and caring. Of short or long duration, this relationship is typically intimate and individualized. More often than not, social work engages areas of people's lives that matter deeply. Social workers uphold the fundamental principle of every person's right to self-determination, to make one's own decisions in life, including what changes to pursue. Focusing on clients' strengths and talents rather than limitations and weaknesses, the social work relationship is especially concerned with empowering clients – increasing their power and influence upon their lives and the world around them (Saleebey 2002).

As research shows, even social work with involuntary clients like prisoners or court-ordered participants yields more positive results when individuals are active agents in the process, especially in defining problems, developing goals, and choosing solution strategies (Trotter 2006; Rooney 2009). Social workers contribute to the relationship their knowledge and experience about human needs, relationships, behavior, and processes of change, while clients bring their expertise on their lives, situations, and selves. The social work model fosters change through the client-centered empowering relationships social workers and clients build with each other.

Many museums already operate from a client-centered vantage point, and a collaborative one at that. Thanks to the growing practice of visitor studies, museums in many countries pay close attention to and aim to meet the interests, needs, desires, and experiences of those they seek to serve. Having adopted the meaning-making approach to communication, museums as a field have, at least in theory, come to appreciate that visitors often value most their own ideas, points of view, and goals although they are generally quite open to, and interested in, the views and expertise that museums provide. At the broad conceptual level, museums often relate to their visitors from a client-centered perspective. Yet frequently, the practical "brass ring" for which they strive is repeat visitation – a potential basis for a relationship, but not necessarily one of much breadth or depth.

Less frequently developed is the ability of museums to engage in the sort of personal, sustained, empowering relationships that social work requires. Increasingly, however, museums show both talent and interest in doing so. As their efforts have turned toward social service, museums have employed methods for fostering more personal relationships with specific communities, neighborhoods, and groups through town meetings, focus group series, planning teams, and the use of community advisors. These kinds of activities can be empowering for participants. In some of their most explicit social service endeavors to date, museums have fostered deeper and more sustained relationships by working in partnership with social workers and social service agencies, in long-term partnership with community groups, and in teams that include social workers, community members, and clients. Viewed from the social work perspective, such approaches and relationships are essential to the social work of museums. Museums must continue to strengthen their own relationships and relationship-building capabilities and strive toward actions and activities that empower visitors and other users.

People-in-environments and close relationship systems

No one is an island; rather, we are "people-in-environments," operating within many relationships, or systems, at the same time. From this systems theory view in social work, people are not only individuals, or micro systems, but are also members of close relationships, or mezzo systems, like friendships or families, as well as members of meaningful collectives, or macro systems, such as religious groups, neighborhoods, and cultural communities. Each system is replete with potential influences, including biological, physical, social, political, spiritual, and cultural factors (Robbins et al. 2006). People and relationships are clearly affected by the broader social environment of the interrelated systems of which they are a part. People and relationships can also affect those systems and the broader social environment as well (Hare 2004: 410). Distinguishing social work from most other helping professions, social work uniquely recognizes that problems – and their solutions – exist within systems, not solely with individuals. Social workers therefore help people strengthen their important and influential relationships. Most often, this means our closest relationships – self, close pairs, family, and face-to-face groups – the fundamental agents of human well-being and social change (Schriver 2004).

Systems theory is familiar in the museum field, notably through the interactive experience model (Falk and Dierking 1992), which offers a kind of person-in-environment view of the museum experience and highlights the importance of physical, social, and personal factors. Moving us deeper into systems theory, the explicit social work perspective of people-in-environments and close relationships as systems provides three expanded ways to think. First, it suggests that a museum experience involves a number of other important factors besides the personal, social, and physical. Also critical are biological, geographic, political, spiritual, and cultural factors that are likely to influence museum users as well as museum workers. Second, it takes into account the fact that such factors and influences occur through the particular set of interrelated systems or relationships to which a person or relationship belongs and thus provides museums with a more complete and holistic way to understand human beings than existing approaches to visitor studies have allowed. Third, and most importantly, prevailing theory has long viewed the museum experience as a highly social endeavor that can yield a range of benefits for visitors and their closest human relationships. From the social work perspective, this is indeed museums' most essential service to society.

Relationship needs

Whatever our background or circumstances, all people have needs – "physical, psychological, economic, cultural, and social requirements for survival, well-being, and fulfillment" (Barker 2003: 291). From health to intimacy, needs motivate us and are usefully understood within social work as universal themes of human concern and experience. Although individual needs are important, relationships also have basic needs that must be met in order for self, close pairs, families, and groups to function and thrive (e.g., Bowen 1991; Kilpatrick 2003; Kumashiro et al. 2008; Logan et al. 2008). These needs typically provide the basis for specific goals that clients and social workers pursue in their efforts together (e.g., Bowen and Kilpatrick 1995; Kilpatrick 2003; Schriver 2004). Social work helps people meet the needs of their most important relationships, removes barriers to them, and improves situations related to them.

Aspects of the social work perspective on relationship needs finds parallels in museum theory, but only thus far as separate ideas. Scholars do contend that museums can meet individual human needs and can benefit relationships, but they have not considered how the two intersect. From the social work perspective of relationship needs, it becomes clear that museums can serve people of all kinds by helping them meet their basic relationship needs. Since this amounts to nothing less than the essential requirements of human well-being and fulfillment, it is imperative that museums understand more fully how best to do such critical human work.

People at risk and altered needs

While people and their relationships have fundamental needs, those needs are all too easily altered or intensified for people at risk, i.e., those for whom "some identifiable characteristic ... places them at greater risk of social and economic deprivation and oppression than the general mainstream of society" (Kirst-Ashman 2003: 51). From age to illness to life circumstance, many characteristics are routinely rendered "problematic" by unsupportive and damaging social attitudes and other societal factors seemingly beyond one's control. A clear demonstration of person-in-environment in action, the at-risk perspective reveals how easily needs are affected because of influences in the broader social world. Social workers take care to examine how such factors may be affecting clients' needs.

Since its start, the social work profession has devoted particular attention to serving individuals and relationships at risk (Hare 2004: 413) – oppressed, vulnerable, or already socially excluded. At the same time, social work recognizes that, as a social creation, the at-risk experience implicates everyone, for we are all interconnected and interdependent. Some people have unquestionably experienced long-term, deeply entrenched oppression and social exclusion. However, everyone is at risk from social and economic deprivation and oppression at times. While many people experience this chronically or constantly, others experience it temporarily. Social workers therefore pursue two interrelated goals. First, they assist and empower persons at risk by helping them to cope with challenges. Second, whenever possible, they also seek to right deprivation, halt oppression, and otherwise change offending circumstances within the broader social environment.

Many museums have long recognized and sought to engage individuals and groups with accessibility needs and/or minority status. Increasingly, museums are exploring ways they can assist people at risk for social and economic deprivation and oppression to adjust to and thrive in the face of challenging social circumstances. Museums are also recognizing their ability to empower people to tackle the root causes of social circumstances like prejudice and ignorance. The social work perspective toward people at risk illuminates two new possibilities for museums. First, moving beyond simplistic views that actually maintain social inequalities, museums can view the experience of being at risk as a shared social problem, and not just a shorthand for subgroups of visitors or nonvisitors to whom special programs are marketed. Second, this perspective helps museums recognize the need to address two major systems for change – people at risk and the social conditions that create and contribute to such risk. Both systems involve us all.

Interventions

Whether aiming for planned change in individuals, relationships, or society, social workers and clients choose specific "activities to solve or prevent problems or achieve goals" (Barker 2003: 227). While some contend that social work interventions are "rarely discretely defined and labelled" (Plath 2006: 60), they typically involve a number of tacit or explicit practice decisions, including what interventions seem appropriate in a given situation, likely to foster a specific goal, and why. Among the general activities or tools of the trade available are "psychotherapy, advocacy, mediation, social planning, community organization, finding and developing resources, and many other activities" (Barker 2003: 227). Intervention also involves the knowledge of one or more guiding theories that explain and support the intervention choice(s). As the social work literature demonstrates, a wide range of theories informs social work intervention, including ecological systems theory, cognitive theory, feminism, and radical casework theory (Schriver 2004; Robbins et al. 2006), and many social workers advocate the use of integrative perspectives that blend more than one theory (Trotter 2006). Intervention also includes evaluating the effectiveness of the chosen activities. To this end, social work employs a diversity of methods, including outcomes and evidence-based approaches as well as more holistic, interactional techniques that stress participants' feelings, meanings, relationships, and quality of life (Cheetham 1992; Sheldon 2001; Plath 2006). Social workers recognize that even evaluation and research are tools of relationship building, advocacy, and social change.

The social work principle of intervention as applied to museums offers exciting promise for both fields. At the broadest level, intervention reframes museum activities and museum fare like exhibits, programs, or the building of a new museum as "activities to solve or prevent problems or achieve goals" (Barker 2003: 227), including those that foster the needs of relationships. More specifically, particular museum experiences can and do offer interesting techniques and mechanisms for "psychotherapy, advocacy, mediation, social planning, community organization, finding and developing resources, and many other activities" (ibid.). Social work theories that inform intervention, such as cognitive theory, radical casework theory, and others, can also offer museums exciting new ways to approach their work and, in turn, theories about museums and museum objects, such as meaning-making and objects as symbols, can also point out new directions for social work practice. Developing, evaluating, and advancing the use of museums and their resources as social work interventions is a collaborative endeavor of tremendous promise for both professions and the people they seek to serve.

Human rights and social justice

In 1948, the General Assembly of the United Nations created the Universal Declaration of Human Rights, a document describing the basic rights that should be considered inalienable, including the right to liberty and security, the right to form a family, the right to equal pay for equal work, and the right to community and cultural participation (General Assembly of the United Nations 1948). As a profession, social work has always aimed to uphold these human rights, along with social justice, a related principle defined as "an ideal condition in which all members of a society have the same basic rights, protection, opportunities, obligations, and social benefits" (Barker 2003: 404). Of particular importance in social work, human rights and social justice includes the right of all people to satisfy their needs (Hare 2004). From this fundamental perspective, being at risk is unacceptable; its remedy necessitates the pursuit of changes in social conditions. Through its commitment to these principles, social work fosters the well-being of all people.

Social workers around the world abide by a core set of professional values and ethics that translate the profession's fundamental concern for human rights and social justice into guidelines for practice, although its interpretation and application may vary by country (National Association of Social Workers 1996; Healy 2001; Weiss 2005). Codified by the *Ethics in Social Work, Statement of Principles*, a joint statement of the International Federation of Social Workers (IFSW) and the International Association of Schools of Social Work (IASSW), these guidelines include the charge to identify

Figure 2.4 Marchers from Centro Presente, a member-driven Latin American immigrant organization in Massachusetts, take a stand for social work values. Photo courtesy of Centro Presente.

and develop peoples' strengths, recognize diversity, and challenge discrimination, as well as to uphold principles of professional conduct (IFSW and IASSW 2004). This values and ethics base not only provides a critical tool for navigating the sometimes rocky course of social work practice, it also inspires the strong activist orientation of many practitioners. With its commitment to the Universal Declaration of Human Rights (General Assembly of the United Nations 1948) and related documents, social work does ultimately "reject a purely relativist stance" (Healy 2001: 166) and works to protect human rights and promote cultural change as needed.

Over a decade ago, Carol Stapp, Director of the Museum Education Program at The George Washington University urged museum professionals to "own up to the fact that museums *never* present value-free exhibits or programs" (1998: 231). These days, an increasing number of museums are recognizing their capacity to work on behalf of human rights and social justice. As we saw in Chapter 1, some are aiming to improve social conditions through education, advocacy, the redressing of historical exclusions and misrepresentations, and the promotion of cultural inclusion. Currently, many of the museums that engage in such work do so in relative isolation from each other and with no clear statement of the fundamental principles that justify and motivate such action. Inspiring exceptions are those historic sites and museums that make up the International Coalition of Sites of Conscience, now linked together in a broad global endeavor (Abram 2005). Some leaders are calling for museums to incorporate a theory of justice into their thinking in order to help redress inequity both within and beyond museums (O'Neill 2006), and to adopt a "non-negotiable, institutional commitment to the importance of equality for all and a due respect for difference" (Sandell 2007: 196). Social work, with its field-wide, fundamental emphasis on human rights and social justice, provides a model for doing so and a perspective that demonstrates how museums can be of service to all people, including, but not limited to, those in circumstances of intensified need.

Like social work, the global museum field maintains and adheres to its own set of ethical principles, articulated in the *Code of Ethics for Museums* of the International Council of Museums (2006).While highly regarded by museums around the world, the current code emphasizes the care of collections rather than of people, with only one of eight sections devoted to issues of community. From the perspective of social work, it becomes clear that museums must expand or revise their existing code or move swiftly to adopt or develop related documents that are appropriate for the social work in which they have been engaged. The Universal Declaration of Human Rights is one appropriate resource (Silverman and O'Neill 2004). Such field-wide commitment to relevant values and ethics is an essential component of all social work practice.

Culture in relationships

From the social work perspective, culture is far more than one or more dominant sets of rules or ways of guiding society. Within social work, culture is viewed as a fundamental aspect of every relationship or system, at every social level (Robbins et al. 2006). In other words, culture is the "ideas, images, and meanings" (Jordan 2007: xiv) as well as "customs, habits, skills, technology, arts, values, ideology, science and … behavior of a group of people in a specific time period" (Barker 2003: 105) that defines a particular relationship. Changing the world, or even a dominant culture, requires changing "how things are done," one relationship at a time.

With increasing frequency, museums are taking aim at aspects of the dominant cultures in which they exist by targeting issues like values and equal access to cultural experience for all people. While these efforts are admirable, the social work perspective provides a practical view of culture that illuminates a different and more direct approach to cultural change. Coming full circle to the fundamental core of social work, relationships are once again what matter most. Culture exists not just theoretically in the world, but visibly every day in the workings of self, close pairs, families, and groups. It is here that museums, like social work, can most readily make their mark.

In sum: broader vision

A detailed picture of social work emerges from this review of important theoretical perspectives. Social work is a process of planned change in which a social worker and client(s) develop and implement a close, empowering relationship that enhances the client(s)' well-being, social functioning, and personal influence. Since human relationships are the fundamental agents of well-being and social change, social work strengthens our closest, most influential relationships – especially the self, pair, family, and group. To this end, social workers help clients address the needs of their close relationships, which typically provide the basis for the specific planned change goals they pursue. Since people exist within multiple relationship systems, their relationship concerns or problems – and lasting solutions – may in fact require changes at the societal level. Social work is especially concerned with people and relationships that experience altered or intensified needs because of oppression, discrimination, and other problematic social conditions and factors. Whether aiming for planned change in relationships or society, social workers and clients implement interventions that they believe are best suited for their goals. Motivating social workers is a field-wide commitment to human rights and social justice and other relevant values and ethics. Ultimately, social work aims to foster beneficial, positive culture within every relationship system.

The eight theoretical perspectives discussed here offer museums much food for thought. Not only does each view apply to and enhance current museum thinking, they collectively illuminate a vision of the social work of museums that is grounded in the knowledge and experience of the social work profession. In this expanded vision, museums' most essential social service is to foster close relationships, the agents of well-being and social change. In particular, museums can serve all people by helping them meet their basic relationship needs.

All human beings, including actual or potential visitors and other clients, are members of sets of interrelated relationship systems and subject to a host of factors that may help or hinder their success in meeting relationship needs. Factors within the broader social environment can easily create at-risk experiences in which those needs become altered or intensified. Museums can respond to these shared social problems by helping people cope with and adjust to challenges as well as by fostering needed change within society. Museums achieve this through a process of planned change in which a museum and client(s) develop and implement a close, empowering relationship that enhances client(s) well-being, social functioning, and influence. Museum resources, media, and experiences provide meaningful interventions, i.e., "activities to solve or prevent problems or achieve goals" (Barker 2003: 227) at multiple system levels. Justifying and motivating museums in their efforts is a field-wide, explicit commitment to the basic principles of human rights and social justice and other relevant values and ethics. Through these efforts, museums help foster beneficial, positive culture within every relationship system.

Taking stock: toward an integrative survey

Is this enhanced vision of the social work of museums a remote fantasy or an emerging reality? To what extent have museums achieved their full potential as agents of well-being and social change? To answer these questions, among others, it is long past time for museums to survey, organize, and integrate systematically from a theoretically grounded social work perspective the growing body of museum knowledge and practice currently scattered around the globe. Only with an informed understanding of what they have been doing can museums chart a wise course for the future.

Following from the social work perspectives presented in this chapter are several key questions that form a useful framework for this essential integrative survey. First are questions about relationships. How does social work understand self, pair, family, and group relationships, the key vehicles of well-being and social change? What needs are fundamental to these relationships? Next are questions about relationship needs and museums. What relationship needs, if any, are museums serving, through what interventions, for whom, where, and in what circumstances? What theory or evidence, if any, supports these efforts? Third are questions about museums and society. How, if at all, are museums intervening at the societal or macro level to address social factors and conditions that affect relationship needs and social functioning? Fourth and finally, what conclusions can be drawn from integrating relevant visitor studies, international practice trends, and representative examples culled from the burgeoning literature? These are the questions we will now consider as we assemble a much-needed foundation for the evolving social work of museums. Let us now begin stocktaking in true social work fashion, one relationship at a time.

Figure 3.1 Night Mask, Kavat. Photo by David Hassell. With the kind consideration of the Indiana University Art Museum.

Chapter 3

From body to soul

Every blade of grass has its angel that stands over it and whispers, Grow! Grow!
Talmud

Of all human relationships, perhaps none evokes more awe than the one we have with our own existence, otherwise known as the self. Remarkably, through a lifetime of social interaction, each of us becomes an entity that is both similar to and different from all others. For this journey, humans have long found support and inspiration in diverse sources, from religion to poetry to science. In the twenty-first century, service to the self is also plentiful in museums.

How do museums serve the self? As visitors flocked to the Metropolitan Museum of Art in New York in the weeks following the 2001 World Trade Center attacks, director Philippe de Montebello proffered a bold possibility: "Hospitals are open. They're around to fix the body. We're here to fix the soul" (in Kimmelman 2001). In fact, from London to Japan, empirical evidence demonstrates that museums also offer physical benefits like lowered stress hormone levels (Clow and Fredhoi 2006) and increased brain activity (Sone et al. 2007). From Australia to Canada, museums are helping people develop skills, acquire jobs, and express identity. From South Africa to Oklahoma, museums are aiding individuals as they grapple with difficult experiences. Taken together, these initiatives tell a compelling story: museums serve key needs of the self relationship, even in circumstances of risk, and subtly influence relevant social conditions as well. To understand this first realm of the social work of museums, let's start with a closer look at the self.

Understanding the self

No group today can rightfully claim more intimate understanding of the self than social workers, who routinely tend to individuals in need and to "the deepest parts of ourselves that make us fully human" (Furman and Langer 2006: 2). First and most simply, social work defines the self as the fundamental building block of all social relationships, the means by which you and I are able to participate in partnerships, families, and groups of all kinds. From this perspective, the health of our dearest connections depends in large part on the health of the self. Social workers therefore help individuals to understand, develop, and transform the self in order to promote effective relationships.

Influenced by social psychology theory, social work also maintains the slippery view that the self is, by definition, already a relationship: between a person and the divine, a person and other people, and a person and his or her experiences. Demonstrating the field's spiritual and religious roots, social work asserts that some form of connection to the universe, God, or a divine force, however understood, is necessary for human life. Relationships with others, which shape and define the self, also begin immediately: "from the moment of birth ... self ... is in active interchange with other selves" (Miller 1991: 14). Relationship with one's own set of unique experiences helps tell the self "who I am" in the world. This perspective directs social workers to help individuals strengthen the connections that sustain the self relationship.

To get to know clients, contemporary social workers often use some version of a checklist of essential questions widely known as a bio/psycho/social/spiritual assessment. This interdisciplinary approach to understanding a person demonstrates the third and perhaps most practical definition of self utilized in social work: the self is a system, consisting of four major subsystems, or aspects of a person: 1) biology, including physiology, chemistry, and physical functioning; 2) psychology, including cognitions, emotions, attitudes, and behaviors; 3) sociology, including the nature of bonds with others and with the broader social environment; and 4) spirituality, including connection with the divine, God, and/or the universe. In other words, the self involves the workings of body, mind, social relationships, and soul. From this perspective, social workers strive to promote effective functioning of the entire self system, to identify what subsystems might be enriched in a client's life, and to understand where and how to intervene to target planned change. To do so effectively, social workers must consider client needs.

Like all human relationships, the self has "requirements for survival, well-being, and fulfillment" (Barker 2003: 291). While no single, definitive checklist of these essential elements exists within the field, social workers draw from humanistic psychology, social psychology, and other disciplines to describe the basic tasks of being a self or social creature. While some needs vary by culture, social science demonstrates that many are in fact universal (Deci and Ryan 2000; Sheldon et al. 2001; Sedikides et al. 2003).

As social workers know, needs of the self are often the reasons why people seek or require social services. During a bio/psycho/social/spiritual assessment, a client's story of his or her situation will typically suggest self needs that have been frustrated, altered, or perhaps never met. For example, a person struggling with an alcohol addiction may find her current situation meaningfully understood as a health need, impacted by factors such as a lack of knowledge about treatment options and an absence of social support. Assessing needs is essential for determining fruitful ways to facilitate change.

As the macro side of social work practice reminds us, meeting the needs of self is not just an individual task; it is a social issue of the broadest cultural significance.

Without meeting these needs, there can be no effective relationships and hence no effective society. Yet, without conducive social conditions, self needs will not be met or met equitably for all people. Social conditions influence the needs of the self in many ways by creating or intensifying them, obscuring less pressing ones, and maintaining barriers. For example, the person with an alcohol addiction deals not only with her body and soul, but with the social pressure to "meet at the pub" after work each Friday, the steady stream of popular media messages equating drinks with glamour, and the seemingly contradictory social stigma of addiction. Fostering the needs of the self means examining society and when necessary, fostering social change.

What, then, are the universal needs of the self that we all must meet for our individual and collective good? How do these needs intensify in circumstances of risk, and what social issues are especially relevant? Where do museums fit in? While the project of cataloging all possible self needs is beyond the scope of this book, four in particular share something remarkable. Health, competence, identity, and transcendence are needs of the self that museums serve. How, and for whom? To understand museums and the self, from body to soul, we begin with health.

Health

Every self requires health, defined in ideal terms by the World Health Organization as "a state of complete physical, social, and mental well-being and not merely the absence of disease or infirmary" (1946). Health involves both feeling and function (Scottish Public Health Observatory 2008), subjective experiences like outlook and mood as well as the operation of physiological and biological systems. Influencing each other, feeling and function are inseparable elements of health.

It is unfortunately easy to be at risk for ill health either temporarily or chronically. Around the world, common risk factors include family history and genetics, environmental conditions, and poverty. Also at risk for further decline are individuals who already live with illness or disability. Poor health often brings additional challenges, including the negative attitudes of others. The need for health is a social issue, supported or thwarted by public health concerns, social policies, and the availability of appropriate care.

Museums contribute to the self's pursuit of health in at least five major ways. Museums can promote relaxation, an immediate intervention of beneficial change in physiology, emotions, or both. They also encourage introspection, a process of understanding one's feelings and thoughts that is essential to mental health. Museums foster health education that helps equip individuals to care for themselves. They address broader social conditions related to health through public health advocacy and by enhancing healthcare environments.

Relaxation

In our fast-paced world, museums foster health by providing relief from physical tension and mental anxiety. As research demonstrates, many individuals seek out and value museums for relaxation and restoration (e.g., Packer 2006 and 2008; Clow and Fredhoi 2006). In a unique study conducted at the Guildhall Art Gallery in London, even a brief lunchtime visit appeared to produce a "rapid and substantial" reduction in levels of the stress hormone cortisol as well as in self-reported levels of stress among local office workers who chose to participate (ibid.). According to the attention restoration theory of psychologists Rachel and Stephen Kaplan, museums can remedy "directed attention fatigue," that familiar form of mental exhaustion that results from prolonged focus or work, because they meet four conditions of a "restorative environment" (Kaplan and Talbot 1983; Kaplan and Kaplan 1989; Kaplan et al. 1993): they fascinate, or "engage without effort" (Packer 2008); they are away, separate from one's usual environment and everyday concerns; they offer extent, the perception of a place that one can explore for a long time; and they afford compatibility, support for one's purposes at the time (Kaplan 1983). Museums of art, history, natural history, and living things naturally meet these conditions and benefit many visitors (Fischer and Glennon 1993; Kaplan et al. 1993; Scopelliti and Giuliani 2005; Packer 2006; Packer 2008). According to clinical psychologist Ester Shaler Buchholz, museums may also restore one's sociability by providing opportunities for "alonetime" or positive solitude that can recalibrate the mind, body, and ability to interact with others (2000). Many museums are embracing their capacity to foster relaxation in innovative ways. From reflective imaging exercises at the Art Gallery of Ontario (Worts 1995) to yoga and meditation classes in the galleries of the Munson-Williams-Proctor Arts Institute in New York and the Trammell and Margaret Crow Collection of Asian Art in Dallas (Stapleton 2006), mental and physical refreshment is abundantly available in museums.

Physiological conditions as well as life circumstances can easily intensify one's need for relaxation and restoration; museums can help. For example, individuals in a counselor-led anger management program offered by the Florida social service agency Let's Grow Well Together found visits to the Morikami Museum and Japanese Gardens to be a valuable tool for stress relief (Patel 2008). In countless hospitals, where fears and anxiety run high, patients of all ages are calmed by museum programs that offer soothing and diversionary objects and collection-related activities. In Athens, Greece, for example, the Hellenic Children's Museum, Agia Sofia Children's Hospital, and PISTI, an association of parents with ill children, joined forces to offer object-based play opportunities led by museum staff for hospitalized children and their families (Kalessopoulou 2002). The McMullen Art Gallery, located within the University of Alberta Hospital in Canada, one of many museum–hospital collaborations to offer an *Artists-on-the-Wards* program, engages adults as well as children in bedside arts activities with practicing artists (Pointe 2005). As reflective evaluations suggest, two factors appear essential to such programs: a focus on collections-related activities such as a garden walk or object-based play and the involvement of a specially trained facilitator sensitive to both the common and particular needs of participants (Kalessopoulou 2002; Pointe 2005).

Those who work in health care settings and other caregivers face particular risks for directed attention fatigue and reduced opportunity for alone time. When daily environments are especially demanding, museum resources can provide welcome restoration opportunities. This was the case for a fifty-five-year-old nurse of five years' experience at Indiana's busy Columbus Regional Hospital. She experienced respite in *Serenity Cove*, a pilot interactive exhibit booth designed by a collaborative team of hospital professionals and a museum specialist to foster staff rejuvenation while on the job. Using the private booth with its closeable curtain, comfortable chair, headphones with music, and soothing nature scenes, she found, "it comforted me to have a place to go on our unit even for a few minutes to get refreshed and calm down … helping to calm staff has a positive effect on patients, too" (in Silverman 2007). As an evaluation study demonstrated, many hospital staff members who used *Serenity Cove* felt similarly (ibid.).

Introspection

Museums and their contents regularly elicit affective as well as cognitive responses. Studies demonstrate that visitors use and appreciate museums for the experience of introspection (Pekarik et al. 1999; Packer 2008), defined as turning "inward, to feelings and experiences that are essentially private, usually triggered by an object or a setting in the museum" (Pekarik et al. 1999: 158). As social work defines it, introspection is a critical component of mental health and a process that involves identifying, reflection upon, and understanding one's own feelings, experiences, and thoughts. Indeed, studies demonstrate that visitors naturally engage in both personal meaning-making and self-exploration in museums by contemplating what they encounter and/or discussing it with others (Silverman 1990; Williams 1994; Silverman 1995; Paris and Mercer 2002; McCaffrey 2007).

For individuals coping with challenge or needing to make changes in their lives, introspection is an essential activity. Though some people in need may find it uncomfortable or difficult, introspection is an important tool in social work and counseling. It is therefore not surprising that different kinds of care workers – including family therapists, art therapists, and social workers – advocate the usefulness of museums for this purpose (Silverman 1989; Winn 2000; Treadon et al. 2006). The partnership of museums and art therapy is particularly fruitful. In addition to stimulating individuals' feelings and insights about themselves and their lives through artifacts, art, and exhibits, museums can also promote introspection by providing opportunities for art making, such as drawing, painting, sculpture, and collage. Many effective programs developed and/or led jointly by museum staff and art therapists involve both viewing and doing art, like those at the McMichael Canadian Art Collection for troubled youth and individuals with life-threatening illness (McMichael Canadian Art Collection 1996; Deane et al. 2000), the *Arts for Health* gallery-based art therapy program at the National Gallery of Australia for people with chronic illnesses (Winn 2000), and programs for teens through the Museum of Tolerance in Los Angeles (Linesch 2004) and Florida State University Museum of Fine Arts (Treadon et al. 2006). Evaluations show that participants in such programs have gained new insights about themselves and their lives (Deane et al. 2000) and enjoyed high levels of satisfaction with the experience (Winn 2000).

Health education

In addition to serving as agents of immediate effect on function and feeling, many museums foster the knowledge, understanding, and behavior that helps equip individuals to care for themselves. From the Deutsches Hygiene Museum in Dresden, Germany, to the Hu Qing Yu Tang Museum of Traditional Chinese Medicine in Hangzhou, China, hundreds of health and medical museums around the world stimulate curiosity and provide information simply by displaying compelling artifacts like antiquated tools or medicinal recipes. Even art collections enlighten people about health issues: for example, *Melancholy: Genius and Insanity in the Western World*, a sweeping exhibition of more than three hundred artworks first mounted at the Grand Palais of Paris in 2005, effectively conveyed the nature of malaise, depression, and mental illness through images rather than words. In the New York–New Jersey metropolitan area, where death rates from heart disease are among the highest in the United States (Fessenden 2005), the Liberty Science Center has pioneered the use of interactive videoconferencing technology for innovative and relevant "real-time" museum interpretation. Their award-winning *Live From …* programs enable local and distant viewers alike to observe surgeries in progress and interact with medical professionals about many health issues (Koster and Baumann 2005).

Since 1995, many museums around the world have fostered health education in an especially profound and controversial way by hosting the wildly popular traveling exhibition series *Body Worlds* by German anatomist Gunther von Hagens. These displays feature cadavers turned compelling artistic sculptures through a process called plastination that replaces body fluids with colored polymers to reveal inner structures. Viewed by more than twenty-five million people in over eight countries, *Body Worlds* and similar exhibitions aim to educate people and to promote better health choices (Leiberich et al. 2006). According to exit studies, the majority of *Body Worlds* viewers reported learning about their bodies, and about half left the exhibits resolved to take better care of their physical health (Institute for Plastination 2006; Leiberich et al. 2006). Regardless of their apparent impact, some people, among them some museum professionals, consider the *Body Worlds* exhibits to be distasteful, disrespectful of human life, immoral, and/or exploitative. As discussed by ethicist Lucia Tanassi (2007), the exhibits have especially raised questions about the origin, self-determination, and consent of the body "donors," since many were unclaimed bodies like those frequently obtained for medical school dissections that tend to be those of poor, homeless, imprisoned, and other socially excluded individuals. In some countries, including England, Scotland, and the United States, new legislation regulating such exhibits has been developed as a result. While museums foster health education in a range of ways, the clear consent of interpretive participants is essential.

For symptomatic individuals or those recently diagnosed, health information and guidance can become an urgent priority. Museums contribute significantly by encouraging referrals to other institutions for additional support and care. For example, *Take a Positive Step*, an interactive exhibit about HIV/AIDS at the Kenya National Museum in Nairobi, included specific guidance about antiretroviral therapy, nutrition, and ways of treating other infections. The exhibit also provided computers with links to major organizations like Family Health International and the World Health Organization that could provide further assistance (Dadian 2005). At the John P. McGovern Museum of Health and Medical Science in Houston, the exhibit entitled *Depression: More Than Just the Blues* offered brochures as well as phone numbers of local and national crisis hotlines, social service agencies, and support groups, in addition to interpreting aspects of mental illness (Bender 2003). For many individuals in the beginning stages of illness, linkage to helpful resources is a critical first step in self-care.

Museums, health, and society

Health is obviously a social issue: a shared pursuit supported or thwarted by many social factors, including government policy, prevailing attitudes, and the nature and availability of appropriate care. Lasting change in individual health often requires intervention at the societal level. Museums serve the health needs of the self by fostering relaxation, introspection, and health education. They also take aim at social conditions in two valuable ways. Museums serve as agents of public health mobilization and they enhance health care environments.

Public health mobilization

Museums are important institutions for raising public awareness of the social dimensions of key health issues and promoting relevant prevention behavior. For example, in Berkeley, California's Hall of Health, a well-evaluated field trip program armed fifth- through eighth-grade student participants with approaches for responding to peer pressure to take drugs and drink alcohol (Cartmill and Day 1997). The program, consisting of a docent-led presentation, a film, and hands-on exhibits, facilitated an immediate decrease in students' stated intentions to use drugs and alcohol, still present for most of the drugs two weeks later. As the study authors concluded, "If one museum field trip can impact students' intentions to use drugs, the effect of several such trips over a period of years could be both significant and lasting" (ibid.: 209). In Puerto Rico, where control of the viral disease dengue spread by mosquitoes is a serious health concern, the popular Museo del Niño Puerto Rico mounted a hands-on exhibit for children featuring live mosquitoes in larval habitats, a video presentation, and a museum interpreter showing children how and why to collect larvae from water. An evaluation study conducted in collaboration with staff from the Centers for Disease Control and Prevention found that the exhibit effectively increased dengue-related knowledge and understanding among participants (Winch et al. 2002). As these examples suggest, museums have a role to play as agents of public health mobilization.

Enhancement of health care environments

Health care needs are often served through special institutions such as hospitals, rehabilitation centers, and long-term care facilities. These environments can be intimidating and unfriendly. Museums and museum professionals are part of a growing worldwide movement to integrate the arts into health care and, in particular, to help health care environments become more pleasant, relaxing, and engaging. Research demonstrates that art displays and other environmental enhancements in hospitals and health care facilities positively affect the health and well-being of patients and staff alike (Staricoff 2004; Wikoff 2004; Daykin et al. 2008). From art and artifacts in patients' rooms to hands-on activities in waiting rooms and staff lounges, nearly every major museum medium is being used to these ends. At Columbus Regional Hospital in Indiana, a small display of staff members' most treasured possessions and their stories, entitled *Window of Joy* and located at the nurses' station in the hectic Cardiovascular Unit, jumpstarted conversations among patients, families, and staff (Silverman 2007). A collaboration between the Maritime Aquarium at Norwalk and the Maria Fereri Children's Hospital in Connecticut even brings bed-bound patients to the museum – virtually that is – using distance-learning technology and live-feed video cameras. Museum resources appear particularly useful for making health care environments more social. Subtly but surely, museums are helping to foster positive change in the nature and culture of health care itself.

Competence

We all seek competence, "the acquired mastery of ... skills necessary to exist as a member of human society" (Barker 2003: 402). Involving both the command of ability and the feeling of being capable, the need for competence spans all cultures (Sheldon et al. 2001). From speaking a language to plying a trade, everyone needs to be effective at the things they aim to do.

Some people master skills easily or with a bit of effort and persistence. For others, however, the achievement of competence is complicated by individual difference, social exclusion, and/or limited opportunity. As a social construct, competence often lies in the eyes of the beholder – a fact that can work against a person with a developmental disability, a non-native speaker of an official language, or anyone who looks or acts "differently." From poverty to cultural tradition, social factors can also limit access to the very experiences that facilitate and sustain competence, such as advanced education and employment.

As educational institutions, museums help visitors of all kinds to gain and hone many abilities, from self-care to art making. In particular, as Andrew Newman has observed,

> There is also a tradition of ... projects based in museums, galleries and heritage organizations which aim to provide participants with useful skills. These mainly

focus upon social and personal development, but also might provide participants with skills that may facilitate individuals obtaining employment.

(Newman 2005a: 230).

Indeed, museums perhaps best facilitate two specific areas of competence essential to the twenty-first century self: communication and work. They do so by helping individuals exercise and develop important skills and by providing unique vocational experiences in which to apply them. Museums also tackle social conditions pertinent to competence of the self by fighting unemployment and enhancing public service.

Communication

Museums are places devoted to communication: through objects, exhibits, film, and other media, they facilitate the exchange of information and meaning. In response to museum fare, visitors exercise their own communication skills, including observation, reading, and speaking, as they make meaning themselves and with companions, museum staff, and other visitors. To foster visitor communication, many museums provide opportunities such as feedback boards, comment books, video recording booths, interactive Web sites, and blogs for individuals' use. Increasing numbers of museums also offer exhibits and programs that aim to develop specific communication skills, from basic reading and writing to mass media production. In the National Museums of Scotland project *Creating the Past*, for example, workshops based on the intensive study of Celtic and Pictish stones and objects developed observation skills in teens and offered opportunities to exercise their drawing, recording, describing, and storytelling abilities (McLean 2002). As part of its *Free Spirit: Stories of You, Me, and BC* initiative, the British Columbia Royal Museum provided on-line resources for video production to help students and community members create and contribute their own video stories of life, legacy, and meaningful possessions. In initiatives such as these, evocative cultural artifacts owned by museums or by individuals frequently provide the stimuli for developing communication skills.

While communication competence is essential for everyone, some individuals may be at risk for its development because they lack access to relevant opportunities. Others may find themselves facing a new environment with insufficient skills. Even in such cases, museums are making positive contributions. For example, through the *Refugee Heritage Project* of the London Museums Hub, a four-year collaborative project of refugees, museums, and refugee community organizations, individuals who fled to England from other countries have learned to record and communicate their Kurdish, African, Somali, and Afghan heritage through exhibits, films, and other museum media. Reflecting upon her participation in a public museum event, one young woman remarked, "I was embarrassed … to go out to the front, and do the explaining. But at the end, I feel so good about myself, for doing it, and people liked it so I must have done a really good job" (in Morris et al. 2007: 21). According to project staff, she indeed "emerged as a vital community worker" (ibid.: 16). As

Figure 3.2 Many participants in the *Refugee Heritage Project* of the London Museums Hub, like this woman from Somalia, developed communication skills and pride through the program. Somali Refugee Heritage Project in partnership with Ocean Somali Community Association and Ragged School Museum, London. Photography: Anna Griffith. Copyright: London Museums Hub.

the project evaluation demonstrated, 89 percent of all participants acquired valuable new abilities like filmmaking, interviewing, presentation, and language skills, as well as a strong sense of achievement and pride in their work (Davison and Orchard 2008). Using museum collections as stimuli to teach interpretive techniques, museums provide individuals at risk with enjoyable ways to develop communication competence and increase their self-esteem in the process.

Work

Central to the well-being and healthy functioning of the self is work, a "major source of actual and perceived competence" (Hazan and Shaver 1990: 271). From making a chair to leading an archaeological dig, work takes many forms; through them all, the self expresses valued skills, earns wages, and, ideally, experiences satisfaction and a sense of contributing to society. Since their earliest days, museums have inspired individuals in their work pursuits. From study collections and museum art schools to internships and employment opportunities, museums help foster the development and expression of knowledge and abilities in key disciplines like craft, technology, and science. In museums around the world, specialists of all kinds find opportunities to learn and practice their talents.

Museums also play a growing role in the training of some of society's most essential service professionals. Doctors, for example, must possess finely honed skills of observation, description, and interpretation in order to diagnose and treat patients, skills that "are also the special province of the visual arts" (Bardes et al. 2001). Recognizing this potential, nearly half of all U.S. medical schools now incorporate the arts into their required or elective coursework, many through an "art of observation" course or activity developed in partnership with a museum (Rodenhauser et al. 2004). In a collaboration of the Yale Center for British Art and Yale University School of Medicine in 1998, for example, first-year medical students were trained to observe and describe the visual evidence in unfamiliar representational paintings through a curator-led discussion program. Evaluation revealed statistically significant increases in participants' observational skills (Dolev et al. 2001). In another successful partnership, the Department of Family Medicine at the University of Cincinnati and the Cincinnati Art Museum created an entire elective course for second-year medical students that combined sessions and exercises in the museum, discussions at the university, and clinical training with practicing doctors. Qualitative evaluation demonstrated positive impact on the targeted skills of most participants, as well as the importance of immediately applying those skills to the clinical encounter to facilitate learning (Elder et al. 2006).

Doctors are not the only service professionals whose competence is being fostered by museums: police officers, investigators, soldiers, lawyers, and court judges are also reaping benefits. After several years of successful collaboration with the Weill Cornell Medical School in New York, the Frick Collection has partnered with the New York Police Department, the U.S. Federal Bureau of Investigations, and the U. S. National Guard to use museum art to sharpen their members' observation and communication skills. Evaluations have demonstrated that the programs are successful and deeply appreciated by participants (Herman 2007). Through partnerships with the Anti-Defamation League, police departments, and judiciary organizations, the United States Holocaust Memorial Museum uses its exhibits and Holocaust history to provide police recruits, chief justices, and other professionals with ethics-based programs that, according to evaluations, routinely cause participants to "reexamine the decisions they make on a daily basis and their role in society" (Appelbaum 2009). Although these diverse training programs vary in format, length, and profession, two common factors appear key to their success. First, museum artifacts and exhibits are essential teaching tools, be they historical photographs, paintings of doctors and patients together (Reilly, Ring, and Duke 2005), art that depicts death and dying (Bertman 1991), or fossils and dinosaur bones (Lagiovane 2006). Second, the partnership of museum staff and representatives of the participating profession is critical to insure effective program design. Through such partnerships, museums are learning how their resources can best be used to help prepare more effective service workers.

While some people develop careers in highly respected professions, others struggle to get and keep a minimum-wage job. Although meaningful vocational activity is important for everyone, those at risk for unemployment may lack advanced skills or previous experience, or fall short of an employer's expectations because of chronic symptoms or other recurring problems. For some people, the solution lies not in trying harder, but in securing an alternative form of work opportunity, either temporary or long-term, such as sheltered employment, transitional employment, or supported employment. Interestingly, all three of these alternative work models, originally developed and widely utilized in social work and vocational rehabilitation, are possible through museums.

In sheltered employment, individuals who are incapable of working competitively in the larger community instead work in a segregated vocational setting (Kregel and Dean 2002). While research suggests this is not the most beneficial solution for some people with cognitive disabilities (ibid.) or mental illness (Pratt et al. 2002), it is desirable in some circumstances. A sheltered employment program at the Niger National Museum of Niamey in Africa, first described in 1976, proved successful for individuals with blindness and other physical disabilities who would otherwise have been begging for money to live. Museum staff provided participants with food, transportation, clothing, and training in the leatherwork trade, followed by the opportunity to ply their new craft in a dedicated workshop on the museum premises; their work yielded profits for themselves and also helped sustain the program (Saley 1976).

In 1981, Johannes Sivesind, then director of the Borgasyseel Museum, an outdoor museum of living history, rural technology, and traditions located in Sarpsborg, Norway, described his pioneering approach to sheltered employment for persons with disabilities. While "sheltered" in the unique, understanding museum environment, program participants were guided back to their previous occupations through engagement as fully integrated members of the museum staff. One of the participants, a restorer who faced personal challenges as he prepared to return to open employment, found the attitudes of respect and mutuality among all staff were especially helpful:

> At the Sarpsborg Local Community Museum … nobody is branded or classified as a rehabilitation case. On the contrary, each person works on the same footing as all the other members of the staff. The expectations they have of him have a positive effect.
>
> (in Sivesind 1981: 150)

As Sivesind observed,

> Work involving conservation of our cultural and historical heritage is well suited as therapy for people who do not fit into the system and are suffering from stress. The work surroundings are restful, and contact with objects dating back to long before our stress-laden age provides a steady anchor in the hectic rush of modern life.
>
> (ibid.)

In the alternative work model known as transitional employment, a segregated work setting is not a final destination, but rather an intermediate step that helps equip individuals with the training, skills, and experience to succeed in competitive employment in the community (Kregel and Dean 2002). With government funding, the Margrove Café of the Margrove Heritage Centre in England, a museum of geology, archaeology, and heritage no longer in existence, operated for several years as just such a "supportive training environment" (Heritage Lottery Fund 2004: 39). There, participants dealing with mental health issues learned to serve the café's many customers. In an evaluative research project, program staff described the changes wrought in participants' lives as "difficult to quantify" yet noted with confidence "that many people have moved on from their café experience to gain full-time employment and that everyone feels they have benefited from the project" (Research Centre for Museums and Galleries 2001: 7).

Supportive employment, considered the most beneficial model of employment for many people at risk, posits everyone as capable of competitive employment in an integrated setting, given enough support and a good match between the job and an individual's preferences, skills, and interests (Pratt et al. 2002). In an inspiring, 20-year-old initiative that applies these principles, *The East Sussex Archaeology and Museums Project* in England has provided long-term unemployed people with archaeology, environmental management, and museum training through careful placements in museum and community heritage work (Bennett and Bareham 2005). Considered the "most successful Government-supported training programme for the long-term unemployed of its kind in the southeast" (East Sussex County Council 2004), the program has nearly doubled the local average for getting such jobs among those who completed the training. According to project pioneer and manager Tristan Bareham, one of the keys to the project's effectiveness is the close relationships between project staff and participants that enable highly personalized experiences. Another is the participants' involvement in real work with practicing professionals that promotes understanding of work requirements (Bennett and Bareham 2005).

Museums, competence, and society

Competence in communication and work are not only needs of the self, they are requirements for a functional society. Museums benefit both individuals and the world in which we live by helping people to develop relevant skills and to apply them in vocational opportunities. Through such efforts, museums subtly influence social conditions related to competence in two essential ways: they fight unemployment and enhance public service.

Fighting unemployment

Unemployment, the condition of being without a job and subsequent income to meet one's economic needs, is a chronic and rampant problem in many countries and a major factor in poverty (Karger and Stoesz 2002). It is also an issue of social justice:

as Article 23 of the Universal Declaration of Human Rights states, "Everyone has the right to work ... and to protection against unemployment" (General Assembly of the United Nations 1948). Through training initiatives, employment opportunities, and alternative work models like those described, museums take aim at this worldwide issue. By employing people with varying abilities and offering different kinds of work, museums help broaden employment opportunities for individuals at risk. In these ways, however small, museums demonstrate advocacy and social responsibility regarding unemployment.

Enhancement of public service

Many of our individual and social needs are served by specially trained public service professionals, including doctors and police officers. Since the well-being of both individuals and communities are affected by the actions of such professionals, their training is truly a social issue of significant impact. As tragic news stories suggest, doctors who view humans as predictable machines or police officers who respond defensively to unusual behavior sometimes misjudge individuals. By promoting the refinement of observation and communication skills in such professionals, museums help enhance public service for us all, especially those at risk of misunderstanding and maltreatment. As the Frick Collection–Weill Cornell Medical College project team members have proposed, "By engaging with works of art, students may learn a broader concept of human-ness, one that incorporates both objective and subjective domains" (Bardes et al. 2001: 1161). By fostering positive change in individual public service professionals as well as expectations and norms for their training, museums enhance the cultures of medicine and law enforcement, among other professions, and the very delivery of public service.

Identity

Every individual seeks identity: the defining of self that tells us and others who and where we are in the social world. In social work, identity consists of three related needs: to find belonging and affiliation with other people, or social identity; to experience uniqueness and autonomy from others, or personal identity; and to evaluate and view oneself positively, or self-esteem. Over a lifetime, the self works to develop a stable core, as well as the ability to alter it as desired (Rounds 2006). In sum, identity is the ongoing effort to assert, affirm, and modify our similarities to and differences from others.

Although identity may seem like a given, its pursuit may be challenged in circumstances of risk. Any individual can become a minority and face struggles for belonging and affiliation when surrounded by others who are different. A natural disaster or economic depression can hinder individual autonomy by making people unduly dependent. From lack of opportunities to negative stereotypes, roadblocks to self-esteem are frequent in life. Maintaining a consistent identity or instigating desired change can often be affected by social factors beyond one's control.

How do museums contribute to identity needs of the self? As a growing body of scholarship attests, museums foster the fulfillment of social identity, personal identity, and self-esteem (e.g., Worts 1990; Silverman 1995; Paris and Mercer 2002; Leinhardt and Knutson 2004; Falk 2006; Newman and McLean 2006; Rounds 2006; Kelly 2007; Falk, et al. 2008). They do so by providing five key opportunities: group affiliation and membership, role enactment, personal meaning-making, storytelling, and exhibit making. Museums also support self-identity at the societal level by fostering stability and providing support for change.

Affiliation and membership

By birth, circumstance, or choice, every self is a member of various groups that help to shape identity and foster a sense of pride and self-esteem; museums provide resources for this. From the flag of one's country to a ritual object revered by one's religion, museum artifacts communicate shared meanings among group members. By viewing or discussing such objects, people can learn, remember, or affirm their sense of affiliation and membership, a frequent museum experience (Silverman 1995; Worts 1995; Research Centre for Museums and Galleries 2001; Paris and Mercer 2002; Newman and McLean 2006). On a larger scale, topical exhibits and devoted institutions like museums of ethnicity, race, or nation present information and identity resources like group history, norms, beliefs, and folkways. They also provide opportunities for selves to express group affiliation through active museum involvement, from simply visiting a given museum (Newman 2005a) to volunteering, becoming a member, or donating goods or money. Through special programs, tours, lectures, and other events, museums also convene individuals of similar background to meet, interact, and learn from each other. In these ways, among others, museums foster group affiliation and membership.

When fellow members are scattered or scarce, as in the case of minority groups, refugees, or those who are or have been persecuted, securing a sense of belonging and similarity may be easier said than done. Political and social oppression can further reduce opportunities for affiliation and the expression of group membership. In such circumstances, museums can play a particularly profound role by educating people about the groups to which they belong, affirming their identity, and fostering self-esteem through engagement with collections, exhibits, mass media, and other means. For Litvaks, Jewish people of Lithuanian descent, for example, the Vilna Gaon Jewish State Museum in Vilnius helps serve these purposes (Vilna Gaon Jewish State Museum 2006). As the museum's comment books, Web site guestbook, and visitor records attest, the museum symbolically unites a large diasporic group of devoted supporters, including a small number of Holocaust survivors still living in Lithuania today as well as Litvaks and their descendents around the globe.

Role enactment

Each of us operates in the social world through a variety of roles – distinct, recognizable relationships and/or social positions with culturally determined expectations and behaviors (Karls and Wandrei 1994). Fulfilling those expectations is a common source of self-esteem. Interacting with museum objects, other people, and the museum environment, selves find opportunities to express and affirm key roles and develop new ones (Silverman 1995; Falk 2006; Rounds 2006). For example, discussing museum artifacts that evoke memories of past good times can affirm the role of *friend*, while sharing knowledge about a particular painting may bolster one's position as *expert*. Simply taking your children to a museum can affirm you as a *good parent*. In addition to such essential daily roles, museums also provide opportunities to enact roles that appear specific to the museum setting: the curious *explorer*, the companion-oriented *facilitator*, the information-seeing *professional/hobbyist*, the driven *experience seeker*, and the reverential *spiritual pilgrim* (Falk 2006; Falk et al. 2008). Research and observation suggest that the museum's unique environment and the specific objects found there enable the enactment of such roles.

Complicated by factors like poverty or a lack of models, successful enactment of an important social role like parent does not come easily for some. Negative life circumstances can also lead to the experience of role engulfment, in which being a *cancer patient* or *unemployed person*, for example, comes to dominate identity and impair self-esteem. Museums can serve the role enactment needs of people at risk in two ways: role development and social role valorization. For example, in the highly successful *YouthALIVE!* initiative in the United States, "girls, minorities, and adolescents who, because of low-income status, have had limited opportunities to explore science" (Beane and Pope 2002: 327) were trained to become *science doers*, mentors and teachers of other children, respected roles that help foster self-esteem and empowerment. As discussed in greater detail later in this book, several children's museums have pioneered programs that use museum activities to boost confidence and role enactment ability in those who are young, poor, homeless, and/or dealing with other risks by fostering their parenting skills. Many museum projects like these also foster social role valorization – the opportunity to fulfill roles that are respected by society rather than devalued, stigmatized, and engulfing. In the *Museums as Therapeutic Agents* project, a collaborative of museums, social service agencies, and their clients, individuals whose identities were consumed by the role of *sick person* found pleasure, therapeutic benefit, and enhanced self-esteem in learning and enacting "normal" roles made possible in museums, like *museum visitor*, *exhibit contributor*, and *museum interpreter* (Silverman 1998; Silverman and McCormick 2001).

Personal meaning-making

In addition to group membership and social roles, identity involves one's sense of uniqueness in relation to other people – the self's distinct personality with its special mix of idiosyncrasies. In museums, visitors experience and express their individuality though personal meaning-making, those subjective responses like opinions, evaluations, feelings, imagination, and memories that arise when they encounter museum objects and exhibits (Silverman 1995). From private thoughts to spontaneous comments to creative expressions such as poetry, drawing, and painting, personal meaning-making can take many forms. As we've seen, personal meaning-making can lead to introspection, an important health intervention for everyone.

While museum professionals have long viewed such idiosyncratic responses as naïve, uniformed, and inappropriate (O'Neill 1995), a more positive interpretation now prevails. Personal meaning-making is a natural and essential means of engagement with museum fare that is worthy of facilitation and support. For a 20-year-old student from Vancouver, British Columbia, completing a *Share Your Reaction* card provided by the Art Gallery of Ontario was an opportunity to feel and express her unique moving response to a painting of Glace Bay (Worts 1995). As she wrote,

> My paternal Grandmother was born in Glace Bay. For my entire life i have wondered what her childhood was like. Until very recently, i have been able only to communicate with her in shouts & sign language. She is 92. She will die soon. But now, now i have seen her home. Now the words are not as necessary. Thank-you.
>
> (in Worts 1995: 176)

At the Ackland Art Museum in Chapel Hill, North Carolina and the Harvard Art Museum, *Personal Highlights* tours created by educator Ray Williams to encourage visitors' personal reactions proved effective in helping new residents of a retirement community, hospice caregivers, and students find and express connections between museum objects and their own life experiences, emotions, and hopes (Williams 1994; Williams 2008). As the *Share Your Reaction* cards and *Personal Highlights* tours demonstrate, art and objects can foster not only identity affirmation and meaningful self-expression, but also imagination, an essential precursor to self-change (Bedford 2004; Rounds 2006).

Personal storytelling

While individuals express personal meaning in a variety of ways, we are by nature storytelling creatures (Bruner 1990). From past experiences to dreams for the future, our personal stories, as scholar Charlotte Linde believes, are "among the most important social resource for creating and maintaining personal identity" (1993: 98). Museum visitors frequently express personal meaning-making in narrative form, spontaneously telling stories to companions that link events in sequence and reveal aspects of who they were, are, or could be (Paris and Mercer 2002). As research indicates, museum objects often provide stimuli, illustrations, and triggers for the telling of such stories (Silverman 1990; Bedford 2001; Paris and Mercer 2002; Newman and McLean 2006).

Some people can no longer take their storytelling abilities for granted because of illness or disability. Others may find their need to tell personal stories intensified by a desire to influence the perceptions of others. Even in such circumstances, museums can help. In a study of community projects in Scottish museums, scholars Andrew Newman and Fiona McLean found that socially excluded program participants used their memories, contributed artifacts, and personal stories to selectively make, remake, and present aspects of their personal identity (2006). They used museum resources to emphasize their links to groups and significant people instead of sharing more troubling aspects of their pasts. On the other hand, museums can also help when the goal is to share rather than avoid painful experiences and aspects of identity. Staff social workers, recreation therapists, and volunteers created a powerful project with resident Holocaust survivors in mind at the Baycrest Centre for Geriatric Care, a comprehensive social service facility for older adults in Toronto, Canada, with its own museum. Workers helped community members share their personal stories, along with artwork, photographs, and memorabilia for inclusion in *A Tribute to Courage: Stories of Survival*, a moving exhibit for the entire Baycrest Centre community. As documented in a reflective evaluation, the project had many educational and therapeutic effects. Especially important for many survivor participants was the "reaffirmation of the person they were and still are inside" (David et al. 2001).

Exhibit making

As the Baycrest Centre project demonstrates, museums can, if they choose, offer individuals a unique opportunity to contribute to and/or participate in the creation of displays and exhibits for the public. While personal storytelling and self-expression is beneficial in its own right, research indicates that sharing one's personal meanings, stories, artifacts, and creations through museum exhibits can build confidence and self-esteem (Silverman 1998; David et al. 2001; Dodd and Sandell 2001; Dodd et al. 2002; Research Centre for Museums and Galleries 2001; Davison and Orchard 2008). For some participants, this appears to result from the exhibit "process": in developing new skills and competencies related to exhibits, participants do things they never thought they could or would and exceed their own expectations (Research Centre for Museums and Galleries 2001; Dodd et al. 2002). For others, self-esteem is also linked to the exhibit product: seeing their contributions displayed and valued by museum staff and other people boosts confidence, a sense of achievement, and pride (Dodd 2002; Davison and Orchard 2008).

As social workers witness daily, self-esteem significantly impacts the self one is and dares to be. Linked to coping ability and goal setting, the self-esteem essential for one's present and future is vulnerable in times of change, loss, or other challenge. Many museums have successfully offered exhibit participation opportunities for individuals at risk of social exclusion, including refugees, older adults, and individuals with mental illness. Notably, research suggests that the self-esteem benefits experienced by participants at risk involved in exhibit-making projects may have a lasting effect. For example, the *Keeping Cultures Project* of the London Museums Hub found that a quarter of all refugee participants still felt a sense of pride in their contributions a year later (Davison and Orchard 2008). Through exhibit participation opportunities, museums can increase the self-esteem that paves the way for further identity development.

Museums, identity, and society

As Andrew Newman and Fiona McLean point out, identity is necessary for social inclusion (2004). Yet without society, there would be no self (Hewitt 1997). Identity is therefore a social issue: societal factors support as well as deter us along the way. In his compelling essay "Doing Identity Work in Museums," Jay Rounds described the many characteristics of the museum that make it a "good tool for identity work" (2006: 139). Viewed from a social work perspective, Rounds's analysis provides a framework for understanding how, as cultural institutions, museums symbolize and promote stability as well as change at the macro, or societal level.

Promotion of stability

Museums serve society by fostering stability in a number of ways. Most obviously, they collect, preserve, and quite literally stabilize the important material culture of society. As Rounds suggests, the ordered and logical nature of museum exhibits and their display of relationships among objects make them valuable cultural mechanisms for fostering ontological security: the feeling "that life makes sense, that things happen according to some meaningful principle, that there are reasons why things happen the way they do" (ibid.: 140). Exhibits also help promote ontological security, consistency, and stability through stories and explanations about cultural traditions, enduring human traits, and repeating history. By returning to their favorite objects and displays repeatedly over a lifetime or during times of social unrest and insecurity, visitors show they value the stable nature of museums. Indeed, the soul-fixing that Philippe de Montebello observed in museums following the September 2001 terrorist attacks in America (Kimmelman 2001) may well have been rooted in museums' ability to promote stability, one-half the social foundation of identity.

Support for change

Contrary to traditional belief, museums today are not just institutions of preservation, they also symbolize and support the human capacity for change. Though exhibits and stories, museums have always provided society with tales of human creativity, invention, motivation, hope, triumph, and inspiration. Museums also offer visitors what Rounds has called "a whole smorgasbord of exotic ways of perceiving the world, and of living in the world" and "a first step toward imagining the possibility that you might be different" (Rounds 2006: 146). As institutions of lifelong informal learning, museums contribute to the development of knowledge and understanding. As institutions of social service, they support change in individuals, relationships, and society. Museums provide inspiration, motivation, and resources for change, the other half of the social foundation of identity.

Transcendence

There is more to the self than meets the eye: there is also the life of the soul. To survive as well as thrive, every self needs transcendence – three kinds of expansion that characterize human existence. First, transcendence involves spiritual connection, movement past time and space to relationship with God, the divine, or animating universal force. Second, transcendence refers to personal transformation, what social workers call resilience, the remarkable experience of movement past real or perceived limitations to healing, integration, and growth. Third, transcendence means compassion, movement past concern for oneself to concern for all, particularly those who suffer. Social workers are reminded daily that all three kinds of transcendence are intimately related, sometimes in unexplainable ways. Together, they foster the achievement of the "highest" or most authentic self: a fully functioning member of the interconnected web that is the universe.

From birth to death, the predictable challenges of living test everyone, even those who are healthy, employed, and loved by family and friends. Still, many people face additional risks for meeting transcendence needs. Religious persecution or oppressive customs can impede an individual's sense of positive spiritual connection. Lack of social support, positive role models, or financial resources can thwart resilience (Fraser 2004). Direct experience of discrimination or violence can adversely affect one's compassion.

In 1977, anthropologist Nelson Graburn noted that a museum can meet one's need for "a personal experience with something higher, more sacred, and out-of-the-ordinary than home and work are able to supply" (1977: 180). Evidence has flourished ever since (e.g., Perkarik et al. 1999; Falk et al. 2008). Museums today serve transcendence needs of the self through spiritual encounters, transformative meaning-making, and social consciousness. Museums also support transcendence at the societal level by promoting religious and spiritual tolerance and providing resources for public healing.

Spiritual encounter

For some people, museums can foster a direct experience of connection to God, the divine, or animating force that is characterized by a distinct yet temporary shift in consciousness or state of being. Like any spiritual encounter, one that involves museum resources may occur within the context of a religious education initiative or arise in seemingly random circumstances. While deconstructing spiritual mystery may be a fruitless exercise, evidence suggests three elements frequently involved in spiritual museum encounters. For some, a singular object appears to be key, such as the painting entitled *Nachi Waterfall* at the Nezu Institute of Fine Arts in Tokyo that has moved visitors to tears and the sense that they had encountered God (Elkins

2001) or a statue of the Hindu god Shiva at St. Mungo's Museum of Religion in Glasgow that has evoked devotional behavior in the gallery. For others, a transcendent shift accompanies museum-related ritual activities – a pilgrimage to a well-known cultural shrine like the Louvre or Vatican or the practice of meditation or Chinese vibrational therapy in the presence of art at the Isabella Stewart Gardner Museum in Boston. Still others find that a created museum environment transports them toward transcendence. For example, *From the Verandah: Art, Buddhism, Presence,* a 6,400 square foot installation at the University of California Los Angeles' Fowler Museum of Cultural History, offered visitors a spiritual setting featuring a translucent white scrim wall, sunken garden areas, and a centerpiece sculpture of unpolished white marble entitled *Rice House* by German artist Wolfgang Laib. Embodying basic Buddhist principles such as suspension of ego, impermanence, and cultivation and focus of attention, the installation was used extensively during its three-month run (Berns 2006).

In the face of challenge or change, the need for spiritual encounter can become particularly profound. For some people, a sense of connection to God or a higher power provides strength, comfort, and healing. When selves feel the loss of soul, museums and their resources can be an avenue for spiritual reconnection. During wartime in England and the United States for example, individuals of many faiths residing in terrorized cities sought spiritual connection in museums, noting their remarkable capacity to provide "comfort, replenishment, beauty" as well as restoration of a sense

Figure 3.3 A visitor seeks the sacred in *From the Verandah*, Fowler Museum at the University of California, Los Angeles. Photo by Farshid Assassi, courtesy of the Fowler Museum.

of "love, compassion" (Kimmelman 2001). In La Jolla, California, on the grounds of the Scripps McDonald Center of Scripps Memorial Hospital, a drug and alcohol treatment center, *The Serenity Garden* uses museum elements to provide a restorative, immersive environment based on the Twelve Steps of Alcoholics Anonymous. In the garden, each of the twelve spiritually based principles is represented with compelling rock sculpture, original artwork, and inspiring words. Here, individuals facing the challenges of drug rehabilitation find a sacred space for meditation, prayer, and spiritual connection in a time of heightened need. Hospital staff and visitors use it as well.

Transformative meaning-making

As observed by influential psychiatrist Viktor Frankl, nothing motivates human beings more than the search for meaning in life (1981). With a sense of perspective and significance, even suffering and challenge may become endurable, and the self can transcend its limitations. Museums specialize in opportunities for meaning-making. This includes opportunities for "those elusive moments of insight, transformation, and deep significance – that help us to see the purpose and reasons for living" (Silverman 2002a: 7). As artist and visionary Suzy Gablik would say, in our overly rational world, such moments offer the kind of magic and enchantment necessary to restore the soul (Gablik 1991). Like spiritual encounters, occasions of magic or transformation in museums are difficult to analyze yet increasingly noted by museum writers (Toon 2000; Bedford 2001; Bedford 2004; Carr 2006). Two mechanisms seem clear. First, by providing opportunities for comparison, insight, and reframing, exhibits and other interpretive fare can link the self to others in different times and places who have dealt with similar circumstances; for example, a tired mother may indeed find a new perspective on her own situation in viewing an exhibit about motherhood around the world. Second, artifacts of overwhelming beauty or human ingenuity can remind a person of the power of human creativity and possibility. Museums and their artifacts have long been used for inspiration.

When one cannot find meaning or significance in a painful situation, emotional crisis can ensue. Those who are socially isolated because of physiological or legal reasons are at extra risk since they lack opportunities to gain perspective or new views. Through collaboration with social service agencies, museums can provide individuals at risk with interpretations of and perspectives on challenging life experiences. For example, in a therapeutic museum visit program for clients with HIV/AIDS and their caregivers at Wylie House Museum in Bloomington, Indiana, created as part of the *Museums as Therapeutic Agents* project discussed earlier in this chapter, individuals coping with life-threatening illness and their companions took private guided tours of the historic house with a specially trained docent. These included visits to and discussion about the Wylie "sick room" for ailing family members and the experience of diseases such as tuberculosis in the nineteenth century. For many participants, the sick room and its contents prompted meaningful comparison to their own circumstances and a sense of historical connection (Silverman 1998; Silverman

2002b). In a partnership between the Philadelphia Museum of Art and the State Correctional Institution at Frankville, Pennsylvania, an art program featuring art slides, a devoted teacher, and art making in a group setting provided inspiring art instruction and creative opportunities for prisoners. In the words of one participant, "The program has opened doors to a host of possibilities, encouraging me to make profound modifications in my attitude, behavior and primary objectives, a new lease on life" (in Wisker 1997: 235). Museum artifacts and activities can indeed spark opportunities for transformative meaning-making in some particularly challenging circumstances.

Social consciousness

Transcendence can be fueled by social consciousness, defined in social work as the self's "awareness of the needs and values of other people and of society in general, often accompanied by actions to meet those needs and enhance those values" (Barker 2003: 402). Learning about the dire social problems of the world and/or acting to help can well move the self toward connection with God, personal resilience, and compassion for others. With increasing frequency, dedicated exhibits, programs, and new institutions are informing people about pressing issues such as conservation, sustainability, and hunger, fostering individual action. As Nina Simon (2007) has observed, the most effective of these efforts link two key factors: clear, compelling presentation about a social issue and a vehicle for an individual to act immediately to affect the situation, such as an opportunity to sign a petition or donate money while in the museum. At the Monterey Bay Aquarium, for example, an informative and dramatic exhibit on the importance of marine protection complete with a live letter writing campaign yielded ten thousand postcards to the state governor to urge marine protection legislation that he subsequently supported (Simon 2007). The innovative Action Center to End World Hunger, a unique collaboration between Mercy Corps, a global relief and development agency and MSI, a museum/interactive space design firm, has made such social consciousness work its mission. With museums in New York and Portland, Oregon, the Action Center offers interactive exhibits, computer technology, and a variety of programs to help "people to take immediate and longterm steps to aid the fight against poverty and hunger around the globe" (Mercy Corps 2008). By increasing awareness of suffering in the world and how to help, museums foster transcendence that benefits the self as well as society.

When one is or has been hurt, helping someone else may seem impossible. Yet, belief that one's difficult experience might somehow benefit others can give meaning and purpose to suffering and foster transcendence. For Richard Williams, assistant manager of the Alfred P. Murrah Federal Building in Oklahoma and survivor of its 1995 bombing, working with the Oklahoma City National Memorial & Museum has been a remarkable opportunity to heal and serve. When the truck bomb exploded, Williams endured a fractured skull, severed ear, crushed hand, and months of surgery and rehabilitation, not to mention the loss of many dear friends and colleagues (Siebert 2001). Shortly thereafter, Williams became deeply involved in the formation of the museum, and along with other survivors, also became a docent to share his story and teach others about domestic terrorism. Describing what they do as "cathartic," "like therapy," and the source of a "strange peace" for themselves, these survivor docents provide profound interpretive experiences for visitors and continue their own transformative meaning-making in the process (Crow 2001). As Richard Williams has explained, "I can stand there and talk and come home feeling good ... maybe that's healing – just being able to tell people how I got to where I am today. Not just that I survived, but that I'm O.K." (in Crow 2001). From the Robben Island Museum off the coast of Cape Town, South Africa, to the Pacific Tsunami Museum in Hawaii, many museums around the world facilitate this blend of transformative meaning-making and social consciousness by engaging individuals who have lived through particular traumatic events as consultants, contributors, lecturers, and/or guides.

Museums, transcendence, and society

Since transcendence refers to the interconnectedness of all beings, it is indeed a social issue. In addition to fostering spiritual encounter, transformative meaning-making, and social consciousness, museums serve the transcendence needs of the self through two interventions at the societal level. Museums serve as agents of religious and spiritual tolerance, and they provide public resources for healing.

Religious and spiritual tolerance

Throughout history and around the world, individuals all too frequently encounter intolerance, discrimination, and violence because of their religious and spiritual beliefs and practices. While some people suffer directly because of it, religious and spiritual intolerance involves us all. As institutions of spirit and ritual, museums affirm the universal importance of sacred experience. From the Museum of World Religions, in Taipei, Taiwan, to the Museum of Islamic History in Cairo, Egypt, museums collect and interpret the material culture of a variety of religions and promote respect for diversity of faith. Many general museums of art and culture use parts of their collections in creative ways to engage visitors directly with religious principles and practices. Through their educational efforts, museums help fight negative social attitudes by working to replace fear and misunderstanding with knowledge. In these ways, museums help foster religious and spiritual tolerance.

Public healing resources

From tsunamis to school shootings, events that intensify the transcendence needs of individuals often affect many people at once. Although resilience is a personal journey, it occurs in a social context and can be served by public means of support. From makeshift exhibits at trauma sites to the development of memorial institutions, museums provide resources for healing at the macro or societal level. As the expanding number of memorial museums and sites of conscience worldwide suggests, museums provide lasting touchstones for the validation of human tragedy, suffering, integration, and resilience. Through commemorations, rituals, exhibits, and other means, museums provide resources for interpretation and collective meaning-making, as well as opportunities for individuals with similar transcendence needs to link together for solidarity and support. In cases where the need for transcendence has been intensified by government, politics, war, and other social forces that place individuals at risk, museums provide societies with vehicles for public acknowledgement, memory, retribution, and transformation.

As we move beyond the self, keep in mind the foundation we have seen. Museums serve the self by fostering the essential needs of health, competence, identity, and transcendence. In so doing, they equip and sustain us for the most essential human social work possible – the making of close pairs, families, and groups. Through these relationships, all things become possible.

Figure 4.1 Magnetic Sculpture. Photo by Kevin Atkins (www.KevinAtkins.org). With the kind consideration of WonderLab Museum, Bloomington, Indiana.

Chapter 4

Solve et coagula

When two … combine, both are altered.

Carl Jung

From the moment of birth, we seek someone who will care. Hardwired to unite, humans partner for countless reasons, like comfort, attraction, convenience, support, and procreation. What amazing alchemy turns strangers into friends, selves into lovers, and back again? It's all on display in museums, where close pair relationships are built, sustained, and changed.

How do museums benefit close pairs? It seems no coincidence that some of the earliest philosophers who aimed to make gold from base metal through the alchemical arts of *solve et coagula* – Latin for "separate and join together" – made discoveries and shared secrets in the Great Museum of Alexandria. For centuries since, pairs of many kinds have been doing likewise in museums. Today, the children of enemies in Ireland and in Israel, divided by religious difference, are finding common ground for fledging friendships through lively museum activities. Caregivers and their spouses in Finland and in New York are enjoying more meaningful conversation together because of art museum programs. Gay, lesbian, bisexual, transgendered, and heterosexual couples in Australia and Oregon are affirming their bonds by sharing their love stories in exhibits. Heartbroken lovers in Croatia and army widows in California are facing the loss of their beloved partners with support from museums. Together, this varied evidence yields an exciting conclusion: museums serve essential needs of close pairs, even in cases of risk. They also influence several key social issues pertinent to partnership. Exactly how are museums engaging in social work with close pairs? We start this part of our survey by considering the nature of pairs.

Understanding the close pair

Whether friendship, romantic partnership, or marriage, a close pair is a purposeful union of two individuals created through interaction over time and characterized by intimacy. Found in every culture, close pairs are essential to human development and well-being, and can even extend our years (Pearlin and Johnson 1977; Bersheid and Reis 1998; Ornish 1998; Ryff and Singer 2001; Maccio 2008). Not only do close pairs provide the immediate context for many people's daily lives, they enable individual and social change. Fostering close pair health is therefore one of social work's most important endeavors.

In serving a close pair, a social worker will carefully acknowledge the uniqueness of each individual. However, since their union creates a new system greater than the sum of its parts, the pair relationship, rather than either individual, becomes the "primary unit of attention" in social work practice (Bowen and Kilpatrick 1995: 166). Although it's a challenging process at times, social workers help to move pairs from a "me" to a "we" perspective. This requires identifying the shared goals that best serve the relationship and promoting its effective functioning.

At the most practical level, a close pair is also a communication dyad: a relationship of two that is literally created anew each day through repeated patterns of interaction. From this perspective, it is clear that meeting relationship goals and maintaining couple health depends in large part upon the pair's ways of speaking, thinking, feeling, and behaving with each other and with others in their environment (e.g., Kaslow 1987). From education programs to sex therapy, many social work strategies exist for helping couples prevent problems and work through issues. Central to most of them is a focus on helping close pairs understand and, if necessary, change their interaction patterns to meet their needs effectively.

Close pair members share many basic human needs that can only be satisfied in relationships, like affection, belonging, and love (Kumashiro et al. 2008). Yet, close pair relationships also have requirements that must be met or they will not develop or endure (ibid.; Bowen 1991). When a couple seeks the aid of a social worker to deal with a conflict, there is typically one or more close pair needs at its root. For example, partners suspecting each other of infidelity may find their crisis more collaboratively viewed as a need for greater intimacy in the relationship. Mindful of the "we," social workers choose intervention strategies "on the basis of the couple's needs" (Bowen and Kilpatrick 1995: 1667).

From a macro perspective, meeting close pair needs involves more than just two partners, it concerns the entire collective. Biologically speaking, pairs are necessary to populate society. Yet, it is that very society that "informs and shapes the values, expectations, and beliefs of the partners and constrains their patterns of interaction and transaction as a couple system" (ibid.: 1671). For example, same-sex couples often face discrimination, hostility, and limited legal options – obstacles which can intensify their need for emotional support (ibid.). Facilitating the needs of close pairs can require change in society rather than change in partners.

Research demonstrates that many different individuals seek fundamentally similar aims in their close personal relationships (Argyle et al. 1986; Burleson 2003). While every pair is unique, all close pairs share several essential needs even across cultures and pair types. Although the basic needs of close pairs are many, four are especially noteworthy: companionship, intimacy, interdependence, and separation are needs that museums serve. Let us now consider each in turn with attention to its nature and the promising role of museums. To understand museums and close pairs, both *solve et coagula,* we begin with companionship.

Companionship

Companionship, or the experience of being with a person you like while engaged in enjoyable activity, is a need of every individual and a basic requirement of close pair relationships. Ironically, it is both a state we strive for and a means to get there. Simply put, time together having fun is a basic ingredient of friendship and romance. It is often how a close pair begins and usually a factor in the development and life of close pairs.

If you've ever felt lonely, you know that companionship does not always come easily. Finding a desirable companion can be a challenge, further complicated by issues of opportunity, culture, and the attitudes of others. At risk for companionship are people labeled "different," both as individuals and as pairs. Some lack settings in which to spend time together comfortably without feeling fearful or judged. While companionship seems like the natural state for humans, its achievement is frequently thwarted by social factors.

Museums contribute to the close pair's pursuit of companionship in at least five ways. First, museums provide social connection opportunities for potentially like-minded strangers to meet. Second, museums offer both fledgling and established pairs enjoyable leisure activity to share. Third, museum contents stimulate conversation, which, along with activity, is a key means through which potential pairs assess compatibility and established pairs affirm their bonds. Museums also address broader social conditions that support companionship by combating prejudice and discrimination and by promoting common ground.

Social connection

As public places, museums are often full of people – those we know and those we don't – at least not yet. While we may think of museums as social settings enjoyed by established close pairs, they are also settings in which uncoupled individuals can meet potential acquaintances, friends, or romantic partners. As a host of studies suggest, visitors in museums notice, watch, and spontaneously communicate with others whom they do not know (Falk and Dierking 1992; Bitgood 1993; vom Lehn et al. 2001; vom Lehn 2006). Some use museums quite intentionally to meet like-minded strangers, as demonstrated by more than ninety Internet-based *Museum MeetUp* groups in Japan, Austria, and six other countries that organize face-to-face meetings in museums. Casual observation, empirical study, and even popular movies agree that close pair relationships can begin in museums (Spousta 2005). As *New York Times* writer Lily Koppel has pointed out, "Museums allow people to explore, looking for something, or someone, that moves them" (2008: B3).

In our couples-oriented world, some people may consider being alone or uncoupled an at-risk condition. Searching for companions in on-line chat rooms, bars, and other stereotypical meet-up places can be emotionally and even physically risky. Embracing their ability to foster alternative meeting opportunities, many museums offer singles nights that feature music, dancing, food, and cocktails, as well as encounters with art and culture (Spousta 2005). For example, "Sex, Sake, and Sushi" at San Francisco's Asian Art Museum provided a "chance to meet others interested in Asian Art" (in Spousta 2005) while "Gay, Lesbian, Transgender and Bisexual Singles Night" at Liverpool's Merseyside Maritime Museum was for many "a fabulous opportunity for gay, lesbian, transgender, and bisexual singles to soak up culture while meeting new people" (National Museums Liverpool 2006). Through such increasingly popular events, museums harness their image as relatively safe public places to meet a potential companion who is cultured, curious, and desirable.

Shared activity

From being together to doing together, companionship requires shared activity. Be it napping or rock climbing, activity provides the context for time spent with each other and the mutual experience through which pair bonds develop and strengthen. As studies demonstrate, museums offer a range of pleasant leisure activities enjoyed by potential or actual close pairs that indeed benefit relationship development (Silverman 1990; Falk and Dierking 1992; Debenedetti 2003). From exhibit viewing to art making to shopping, museums foster companionship by providing the setting and opportunity for enjoyable, meaningful activities that two can share. Research as well as casual observation reveals that many pairs need little or no prompting to use museums for shared activity (Silverman 1990; Debenedetti 2003).While some museums advertise their "romantic" nature or market special couples' getaways and programs, they seem to have simply caught up with a phenomenon that has long been in place.

In times of grief or other impairment, shared activity may present a frustrating paradox. While the need may intensify, desire and ability may diminish. Even in such circumstances, museums can provide the fuel for companionship. This was surely true for Bill McLaughlin and Dick Hughes of Pennsylvania, two World War II veterans and fellow church members in their eighties. As Bill withdrew from life, despondent with grief over his wife's death, acquaintance Dick invited him out for a visit to the nearby Academy of Sciences in Philadelphia; the following week, for a trip to the Battleship New Jersey. Over the next three years, Dick and Bill explored every museum within fifty miles of Philadelphia – 203 to be exact – and in the process, Bill not only healed from his loss but the two became best friends, "too close to stop getting together" (Vitez 2008: A1). They even devised their own special activity: recording their reactions and critiques to create *Travels with Dick and Bill,* a modestly priced museum guide sold to benefit their church, St. Paul's Episcopal in Chestnut Hill, Pennsylvania (ibid.). As Dick and Bill discovered, museums are flexible environments that accommodate changing needs.

Others at great risk for the shared activity of companionship are people who have learned to view each other as enemies. Around the world, seemingly insurmountable differences between groups easily manifest as prejudice, mistrust, and hatred between individuals and prevent the very companionship that might break down such barriers.

Some remarkable museums in places of intense social conflict have offered programs that bring enemies together to participate in enjoyable museum activities. For example, the Ulster Folk and Transport Museum's Educational Residential Centre, now a part of the National Museum and Galleries of Northern Ireland, developed one-day and residential programs to introduce Catholic and Protestant children. Often these children "grow to adulthood without meeting, much less forming friendships with, anyone from the 'other' community" (Speers et al. 1994: 11). As an evaluation study demonstrated, the program of games, role playing, and art making provided a chance for fun as well as hope for the future: as summed up by a participating teacher from one of the worst sections of Belfast, "If you can accept a person as a friend, then the labels Catholic and Protestant are unimportant, the friendships can grow, the labels can be forgotten" (in Speers et al. 1994: 12). At the Bible Lands Museum of Jerusalem, a coexistence program called *The Image of Abraham* used museum tours, races, and joint projects to help nine- and ten-year-old Palestinian and Jewish children and their parents interact and identify common elements in their cultures and themselves. While some parents believed the four-week program was not enough time to change anything, the museum learned that several cross-cultural friendships were formed and sustained well beyond the four-week program (Gaouette 2003). Although extensive study of such programs is definitely warranted, two important elements seem clear. First, shared museum activities provide a relatively safe and low-risk way for enemies to come together, enjoy each other's company, and observe their similarities. As research indicates, similar interests and shared leisure preferences make powerful fodder for friendship development (e.g., Fehr 2000; Fehr 2004). Second, the presence of teachers, parents, and other significant adults who model positive interaction with enemies may well help children feel safe and less fearful, while benefiting the adults as well.

Conversation

While companions often enjoy silence together, they are usually not quiet for long. Essential to companionship is conversation, the exchange of ideas that not only conveys information but helps maintain social bonds (Stubbs 1983). In museums, artifacts and activities are powerful stimuli for conversation, with important consequences. Through museum conversation, individuals express interests, preferences, and knowledge that enable pair members to learn about each other, assess their compatibility, affirm their ongoing connections, and simply enjoy each other (Cone and Kendall 1978; Draper 1984; Silverman 1990). Recognizing this, some museums intentionally support and promote companion conversation through accommodating spaces, read-aloud labels, and familiar objects (Morrissey 2002), as well as handheld electronic guidebooks designed for two (Aoki et al. 2002).

Enemies, strangers, or pairs who haven't known each other long may find it difficult to converse in many settings. Fear, cultural etiquette, or lack of shared history can impede the very exchange that might spark a new relationship. Museums provide natural opportunities for pairs to talk with relatively little emotional risk. By comparing their reactions to museum objects and exhibits, pairs subtly glean information about their similarities and differences. In museums with historical items, for example, pairs frequently indicate which objects they recognize or remember and on that basis draw conclusions about their compatibility in terms of age, background, and upbringing (Silverman 1990). In response to art, pair members often state what they like, dislike, and why. Equating artistic taste with personality traits, people judge how they'd get along on the basis of each other's responses to images (ibid.). Some pairs do this with little guidance. For those unable or unwilling to come together on their own, a structured program with a museum facilitator, like the examples in Northern Ireland and Israel, can guide potential pairs into conversation about artifacts that identifies differences, similarities, and compatibility.

Social distance is not the only factor that puts pairs at risk for conversation. Disease or trauma, often accompanied by depression, can render one companion nonresponsive and the other exhausted, like long-time couples in which one member has assumed care of the other. Through guided tour programs developed especially for patient–caregiver pairs, art museums have been notably effective at restoring conversations (Shaw 2006) and enhancing relationships by providing opportunities for "talking about the art they have seen together" (Belgorod in Fackelmann 2007). For example, *The Memory Lane Project* in Finland, created by staff at the Ateneum Art Museum in cooperation with the Alzheimer's Society, has offered Alzheimer patient–caregiver pairs an interactive multisensory museum tour in which the "art can create a new degree of interaction between the patient and caregiver" (Itkonen 2008: 1). Such programs need not be limited to art museums. Given the variety of museum collections and the personal responses they generate, the use of museums to facilitate conversation among pairs at risk is a ripe area for further development.

Museums, companionship, and society

With whom and how you spend your time may seem like a personal choice; it is also a social issue. A host of societal factors shape our search for companionship, including family and cultural norms, social attitudes, and power issues. In addition to fostering social connection, shared activity, and conversation – means to the assessment of compatibility and the affirmation of connections – museums address social conditions relating to companionship in two key ways. They fight against intergroup prejudice and discrimination and help build common social ground.

Fighting prejudice and discrimination

Given the infinite possibilities of human difference, it's a wonder close pairs exist at all. Yet, the true social threats to relationship are not differences, but the destructive, tenacious ways that humans collectively manage them, including prejudice, stereotypes, and discrimination. As commonly understood, prejudice refers to usually negative beliefs held about an individual or group, often related to stereotypes – labels for people based on simplified traits. These lead to discrimination – the unequal or unfair treatment of people based on such categorizations (Kirst-Ashman 2003). As Richard Sandell explains, prejudice, stereotypes, and discrimination are not only what individuals think and do, they are structural features of society that maintain inequality (2007: 29). As social workers see daily, these negative features affect companionship in a range of ways, from the realities of who we do or do not spend time with to the reasons why. Museums clearly have roles to play in combating prejudice and discrimination in society (Sandell 2007). One of the most important is simply to foster contact among people who are different from each other.

Building common ground

Richard Sandell has demonstrated that museums contribute to a more equitable society because they "can enable and facilitate conversations about difference, providing a forum (and one with unique qualities) in which disputes, arising from the conflicting values held by different communities, can be addressed and explored" (2007: 26). At the same time, museums can also enable and facilitate conversations about similarity and provide forums in which agreement, arising from common interests, concerns, and values, can be addressed and explored. While people may well need more practice and support when it comes to dealing with differences, the realm of similarities is equally essential to a healthy society. From accumulating social capital to resolving conflict, the ability to connect with others and build common ground is a huge part of what unites and moves pairs, groups, and societies to action. In so many ways, museums help people recognize their common humanity, often one pair at a time. From the strangers on singles night who like the same paintings to the lifelong friends who love to visit and chat, museums help foster companionship by building common ground.

Intimacy

Centuries of love songs suggest that the most celebrated need of close pairs may well be intimacy, that "strong sense of physical and emotional closeness, empathy, and attachment" (Barker 2003: 227) conjured through verbal and nonverbal exchange. Research bears out the popular idea that intimacy involves both physical and emotional dimensions for pairs of all kinds, including friends, patient–caregivers, and pairs who are sexually involved (Adams and Plaut 2003). Through intimacy, pair members meet needs for belonging and affection as they deepen and sustain their relationship.

Even in an established close pair, intimacy can be fleeting or lost. Intimacy requires trust that can be difficult to maintain. Poverty, hunger, and the search for paying work can render intimacy a distant dream. On the other hand, pairs encountering sexism, homophobia, or racism on a daily basis may find their need for intimacy intensified.

Museums contribute to the close pair's need for intimacy in many notable ways. Museums help close pairs exercise and develop empathy, a necessary ingredient of intimacy. They also foster mutual disclosure, one of the fastest routes to emotional closeness. In the physical realm, museums promote nonverbal involvement behavior, and they provide sex education. They also support intimacy at the societal level by breaking taboos and fighting against sexual violence.

Empathy

Intimacy is fueled by empathy, or "perceiving, understanding, experiencing, and responding to the emotional state and ideas of another" (Barker 2003: 141). Essential to relationship satisfaction and longevity (Hendrix 2007), empathy is a learnable skill set, and museums provide pairs with opportunities to exercise and develop empathy.

From considering a companion's opinion of an artwork to imagining the life of a couple in a photograph, pairs in museums routinely practice interpersonal perspective-taking and respectful response. History museums and historical sites are especially effective at fostering visitor empathy with others across time and distance, since empathy is critical for historical understanding (Davis Jr. 2001). Through evaluation studies at many significant sites, researcher Randi Korn and her associates have documented museums' ability to foster empathy among present-day museum visitors of different ages and backgrounds for Holocaust victims, European immigrants to Ellis Island, and turn-of-the-century tenement dwellers (Randi Korn & Associates, Inc. 1999, 2007a, 2007b, and 2007c). Korn's studies empirically demonstrate that the authentic places, actual artifacts, and stories of real people unique to museums are keys to historical empathy. These same resources also act as conduits for empathy when partners exchange personal perspectives in museums.

While all close pairs require empathy, some may find it especially critical. For example, pairs in which one partner is dependent upon another for care require a great deal of emotional sensitivity, while troubled pairs may find that empathy can prevent break-up (Hendrix 2007). With help from social workers, many close pairs at risk have strengthened their relationships through empathy training programs and empathy-oriented counseling techniques in which participants practice essential skills like listening, paraphrasing, and validating (ibid.; Angera and Long 2006). Given their power to stimulate personal meaning-making and pair conversation, museums are an untapped and innovative venue for empathy training interventions. Together, social workers and museum educators could develop creative new forms of empathy intervention that use the unique museum resources of real places, artifacts, and stories to benefit close pairs.

Mutual disclosure

Nothing fuels intimacy more than mutual disclosure, the exchange of personal information with another that generates positive feelings for both (Prager 2000; Morry 2005). Mutual disclosure involves two skills: self-expression and the ability to respond with interest, understanding, and empathy. Since objects and exhibits elicit emotions, transformative meaning-making, and conversation, it is no wonder that museums provide a conducive setting for mutual disclosure. As studies of visitor conversations demonstrate, some close pairs share nothing less than their heartaches, hopes, and dreams while strolling amidst the world's finest treasures in museums (Silverman 1990).

Mutual disclosure asks much of a pair: to bare their deepest selves and still affirm each other. Such profound exchange seems unlikely between strangers or those who view each other with limiting assumptions. This might have been what participants thought when they first joined the *Vital Visionaries Collaboration,* a unique project of the National Institute on Aging, the Johns Hopkins School of Medicine, the American Visionary Art Museum, and the Academy for Education Development that partnered young first-year medical students like Nivee Amin with older adults like Sol Goodman. Yet, the remarkable four-session program of disclosure-inspiring, facilitator-led activities met its stated aims of promoting better "understanding and appreciation of older people by medical students and awaken[ing] older people to their creative possibilities" (McManus 2004; National Institute on Aging 2004; Semmes 2005) as unlikely pairs like Nivee and Sol expressed and affirmed their way to special friendship.

Among the ways that Sol and Nivee got to know each other was a staff-guided "stranded on a desert island" exercise, in which they asked each other ten questions that revealed their personal tastes and values, as well as the remarkable coincidence that they lived in the same building. Through a session that invited participants to share their own creative work, Nivee learned more about Sol as he read *Trilogy,* a group of his original poems. Another day, led by museum staff, they enjoyed a "superhero" activity that beautifully evoked the two skills of mutual disclosure. Exercising self-expression, they first answered questions about what sort of superhero they would be by defining what unique powers, mission, tool, and name they would have. Then, demonstrating the ability to respond with understanding and empathy, they rendered *each other's* vision using cardboard, foil, feathers, and stars, and explained the superheroes to the group (National Institute on Aging 2004). In an evaluation of the program, the young students showed a statistically significant improvement in their attitudes toward aging and older people, while the elders explored their creative sides (ibid.). Clearly, the innovative efforts that fostered mutual disclosure between Sol and Nivee have broad applicability for many other pairs at risk in their pursuit of intimacy.

Figure 4.2 Sol Goodman and Nivee Amin show off their superhero creations during the *Vital Visionaries Collaboration*. Photo courtesy of National Institute on Aging, Bethesda, MD.

Nonverbal involvement behavior

Museums are public spaces, but they invite personal behavior. In particular, they elicit what social psychologists call "nonverbal involvement behavior," physical actions that quietly convey attention, interest, and concern as they build and sustain intimacy (Prager 1995 and 2000). Scholars have noted a variety of nonverbal involvement behaviors within pairs in museums, like moving in similar ways, touching each other unconsciously, and looking at the same things (McManus 1988; vom Lehn et al. 2001). These intimacy-building behaviors are supported by the free-choice museum setting, its exhibits, and even the intimate interactions of other visitors.

Not every pair will readily display physical connection behavior in the museum. Some gay, lesbian, and bisexual couples edit their nonverbal involvement in museums because they don't want to endure negative or aggressive responses from other visitors (Heimlich and Koke 2008). Other pairs, like those in the midst of conflict, may simply prefer some physical distance from each other. Interpretive techniques that provide options for individual as well as shared use, like electronic guidebooks and hands-on exhibits, may provide some pairs at risk with a valued sense of control. For others, feeling comfortable to express physical affection together might require museums to make institutional changes like posting antiharassment policies and providing domestic partner/couple membership benefits (ibid.).

Sex education

From surprisingly erotic ancient artifacts to contemporary nude photography, sex "appears in some form in the collection of almost every museum," as John Fraser and Joe Heimlich have noted (2008: 6). As a result, museums foster the intimacy needs of pairs through intentional and unintentional sex education. In growing numbers, dedicated museums like the Asia Eros Museum of Seoul and the China Sex Museum, popular among women and couples, provide information and guidance about sexual intimacy, sexually transmitted disease (STD), and family planning. For those who prefer a hip, populist approach, Amora promotes itself not as a museum but an "academy of sex and relationships" and a "social experience and lifestyle brand that celebrates the essence of sensual pleasure" (Amora 2007): its debut ten-month incarnation in Piccadilly, London, featured hands-on exhibits about being a better lover, fetishes, and sexual diversity and attracted over 300,000 visitors, between 60 and 75 percent of them couples (Letts 2007; Rayner 2008). Amused, aroused, or intrigued, close pairs in museums can find resources for their most physically intimate interaction.

As too many pairs know from experience, the most blissful of human experiences can turn tragic. Sexual intimacy entails significant risks, like the possibility of disease or an unwanted or complicated pregnancy. Museums around the world are taking an active role in the promotion of safe(r) sex to prevent infection as well as conception. For example, at the Universum, the Science Museum of the Autonomous University of Mexico, an exhibit entitled *Why Talk about AIDS?* and related conferences and workshops on healthy sexual behavior, have attracted more than 200,000 visitors per year. Evaluation showed that the museums' efforts led 60 percent of visitors to seek additional information and significantly increased their knowledge of sexual health practices (Carles 2002).

Some couples find their sexual intimacy at risk because of delicate issues such as sexual dysfunction. Others may want privacy in their search for help because their sexual preferences are stigmatized or misunderstood. The creators of Amora, who included counselors and therapists, rightfully recognized that personalized interventions would be preferred by some pairs. To this end, Amora provided on-site sex therapists to speak with couples privately as well as to run specialized workshops like *Gays Guide to Great Sex* described in *Gay Community News* as "not for the faint-hearted" (Wilson 2007: 29).

In many countries, sex is a taboo subject, like some of the couples who engage in it. The Antarang Museum, originally located in Mumbai, India, offered an inspiring model of sex education for some uniquely high-risk pairs. Opened in 2003 in Kamathipura, a stigmatized red light district of the country's biggest city by a collaboration of the Brihanmumbai Municipal Corporation, Mumbai District AIDS Control Society, and doctor/artist Prakash Sarang, the free Antarang Museum taught local school groups and married couples about STDs, conception, and safe sex. With thanks to local health workers who facilitated the visits, the museum also "became popular among prostitutes and some of their clients" who developed "close relationships and sometimes visit[ed] the museum together" (Mukherjee 2007: 1). According to many sex workers in Mumbai, the museum "changed their lives" and their pair relationships (ibid.). In 2008, the Antarang Museum planned to open in a new location to attract a wider audience (Coelho 2008). From a social work perspective, the Antarang Museum was quite successful as a powerful model of multipartner collaboration on behalf of pairs at risk.

Museums, intimacy, and society

Intimacy is a need of close pairs that helps to create society. At the same time, the most private interactions of two are shaped by that broader world. Museums serve pairs by fostering empathy, mutual self-disclosure, nonverbal physical behavior, and sex education. They also support intimacy through two societal interventions: breaking taboos and advocating against sexual violence.

Breaking taboos

Intimacy is fraught with taboos – social bans against "offensive" behavior, presumably for good. Yet, taboos that persist inappropriately are damaging as well as offensive – causing silence instead of sexual health policy in countries where HIV/AIDS rages or continued discrimination against interracial or interethnic couples for no good reason. Around the world, museums help to break destructive intimacy taboos. For example, an exhibition entitled *Against Nature* at the Oslo Natural History Museum in Norway presented evidence of homosexuality in numerous animal species in a planned effort to "reject the all too well known argument that homosexual behaviour is a crime against nature" (Oslo Natural History Museum in BBC News 2006). Through displays and workshops on "better loving," museums like Amora empower people to break their own intimacy taboos. As respected cultural institutions, museums can introduce and demystify "off-limits" subjects to the public, convey pro-social messages, and model positive attitudes and behaviors. In these ways, they chip away at damaging norms that negatively influence pair intimacy.

Sexual violence

Physical intimacy by coercion is a profound global problem and human rights abuse (Harvey et al. 2007). By current estimates, between one-quarter and one-half of all women *in the world* have been abused by an intimate partner, and between 40 and 70 percent of all female murder victims were killed by a lover or spouse (Advocates for Human Rights 2006). Museums are taking aim at this overwhelming phenomenon through a variety of international and local interventions. These range from Amnesty International's *Imagine a World*, a traveling exhibition of contemporary global art meant to promote dialogue about violence against women, to an Internet-based course that teaches domestic violence prevention techniques to teenage boys in tribal communities, developed by a partnership of the California Indian Museum and Cultural Center and the National Indian Justice Center with funding from Verizon Communications, Incorporated.

Addressing the abhorrent reality of state-supported sexual violence during war, two unique initiatives offer important examples of museum activism. The Women's Active Museum on War and Peace (WAM) in Tokyo, proposed by Japanese civil rights leader Yayori Matsui before her untimely death in 2002, now serves as an action center and institutional witness to help eliminate violence against women. In particular, WAM works to urge the Japanese government to accept responsibility for the "comfort women" system of military sexual slavery perpetrated before and during World War II (Women's Active Museum on War and Peace 2006) and to continue the efforts of the Women's International War Crimes Tribunal on Japan's Military Sexual Slavery held in 2000 to this end (Chinkin 2001). WAM pursues these goals through traveling exhibits, publications, activist speakers and seminars, information hotlines, rallies, and active research. On another continent, the United States Holocaust Memorial Museum reports and maps recent experiences of crimes against humanity like sexual violence against women in the Democratic Republic of Congo through its *World Is Witness* geoblog. Blog writers include Holocaust museum staff members who travel to meet victims in various countries and, with the help of translators, gather and post their stories. Museums like these demonstrate inspiring commitment to the fight against the abuses of intimacy.

Interdependence

As pairs grow close, they need interdependence, "the sharing of responsibilities and benefits that are required for survival or well-being" (Barker 2003: 222). On a practical level, interdependence is demonstrated by the stable patterns of interchange that enable two to function as "we" in society – from pet names to argument styles, divisions of labor to holiday rituals (Backman 1990). Through interdependence, close pairs create nothing less than the culture of their relationship, including their pair identity and the nature of their life together (Burleson et al. 2000).

Achieving interdependence is easier said than done. Some close pairs never develop stable patterns of sharing because of commitment phobia, lack of trust, or value differences. Many more pairs evolve unhealthy patterns, like ineffective conflict resolution and oppressive norms, which harm partners as well as their relationship. In many parts of the world, pervasive social problems like insufficient health care and poverty foster situations of codependence, tolerance of abuse, and despair. Like other pair needs, healthy interdependence requires change in society as well as in relationships.

Museums provide close pairs with opportunities to express, examine, and alter their patterns of exchange. These interventions involve some that serve the self's need for identity, like role enactment, meaning-making, and storytelling. Yet, as partners engage in them together, they work to serve the pair. Museums address interdependence needs through opportunities for communication norms, role complementarity, couple language, love stories, and museum contributions. Museums also support close pair interdependence at the societal level through gender equity advocacy and the commemoration of marriage laws.

Communication norms

Every close pair develops communication norms, unspoken guidelines for interaction. Norms that promote respectful and affectionate exchange are especially critical for a pair's ability to work through inevitable conflict and for the overall health of a relationship (Gottman 1999; Burelson et al. 2000). In museums, couples demonstrate many of their communication norms, such as how they make decisions, speak to each other, and solve small challenges (Silverman 1989; vom Lehn et al. 2001). In theory, museums provide close pairs with a low-risk setting in which they might examine, understand, and even change communication patterns and norms.

Consider, for example, an intriguing yet typical scene described by Dirk vom Lehn and his colleagues in their compelling video-based field study of companion interaction in several English museums. At a small science center in Nottingham, a male and female pair approached a hands-on 3-D puzzle:

> The man stretched with his left hand toward the puzzle to take hold of the first piece and at the same time turned to his right, as if inviting the woman to join the activity. As the woman positioned herself to face the exhibit, the man moved his right foot forward to lie between the woman and the table. During his turn, the man's upper body remained slightly bowed forward and his gaze directed toward the puzzle. By sliding his right foot forward he produced a physical "barrier" the woman would have to cross if she were to get her hands on the puzzle. It is as if the man encourages the woman to join him at the puzzle table while simultaneously

obstructing her from taking hold of the puzzle; he encouraged the woman to act as an audience for his play rather than as a player in the game itself. Through his behavior, the man continued to obstruct the woman's use of the puzzle. Even when he finished, he did not stand back to allow his companion access to the table but rather stepped forward, between her and the puzzle, once again limiting her access to the exhibit and discouraging her participation.

(ibid.: 202–3)

Were the participants aware of their behavior? How did each one feel? Was the man disrespecting the woman? Did his behavior suggest a well-developed defense? While an observer can only speculate, a social worker could help the pair to critique the communication norms brought to light in the museum. Like empathy, healthy communication norms can be fostered through couples therapy and relationship enhancement programs, especially in pairs facing increased risk (Corliss and Steptoe 2004; Meyerson 2008). The museum setting could be a powerful resource in any initiative aimed at fostering relationship-enhancing communication norms.

Role complementarity

Selves require roles, those recognizable parts we play in life that build and express identity, as discussed in Chapter 3. For close pairs, the "harmonious fit" (Greene 1994: 111) between partners' roles is essential to interdependence, especially the ability to take turns. Museums provide opportunities to exercise role complementarity and flexibility. As research demonstrates, close pairs use the museum environment to express and trade complementary roles like expert and novice, teacher and student, and storyteller and interested listener (Silverman 1990). Even the acts of initiating a museum visit and agreeing to go along affirm complementary roles of leader and follower (Debenedetti 2003). As the science center example above suggests, hands-on exhibits and other participatory experiences in museums can also provide close pairs with opportunities for various role turns, although it is up to each pair to take them.

As individuals and their partnerships develop, a once "harmonious fit" may become untenable. From aging to war, altered circumstances can necessitate unwelcome or difficult change in pair roles. Museums can help as couples adjust to new kinds of role complementarity, as when mutual responsibility morphs to more uneven loads because of illness or physical disability. Museums provide a flexible setting and a safe public place to practice new roles. For example, programs that encourage reminiscence may keep a physically dependent partner feeling valued for his or her role as a historian.

Couple language

Personal meaning-making in museums is an important vehicle for self-identity. When close pairs make meaning together, especially through conversation about objects they encounter, they express their couple language, an important mechanism of interdependence as well as pair identity. As studies demonstrate, pair conversations evoked by museum objects are often full of unique references and shorthand symbols of shared experiences, mutual friends and family members, possessions, favorite places, popular culture, and shared values (Silverman 1990). Through this unique couple language, close pairs bond and express their sense of "we" in the world (Backman 1990).

Close pairs who lack positive affect and a system of shared meaning are at risk for relationship dissolution (Gottman 1999). For example, spouses nearing divorce may find that blame and angry words have overtaken their couple language. With help from a social worker, couples at risk could use the museum and its contents to help restore their special language and the interdependence it represents. For example, they could be tasked with searching the museum for symbols of good times and shared values or guided to create their own symbolic objects like collages, memory boxes, or altars to visually represent their special language. Even on their own, outside of the counseling context, some close pairs may find museum activities like these enjoyable and relationship-enhancing.

Love stories

As soon as a relationship starts, partners begin to co-author love stories – purposeful narratives that they tell and retell to themselves and others. From tales of meeting to challenges endured, love stories are "vehicles through which individuals link themselves as relationship partners and characterize their joint relational identity" (Burleson et al. 2000: 253). As a key mechanism of interdependence, love stories "reflect and affirm the values, standards, norms, and rules" of the close pair (ibid.). While describing the past, they direct the future. For some close pairs, especially those who have been together for more than five years, paintings in an art museum and familiar household objects in a history museum act as symbols and trigger the retelling of such love stories together (Silverman 1990). For others, like spouses Jeffrey and Melinda Cornwell, the act of museum visiting itself figures prominently in their love stories, like this account of their first date at a John Cage exhibit opening at the Guggenheim Museum in New York as told to a news reporter:

> "Melinda was wearing this amazing absurd Dolce & Gabbana dress," Mr. Cornell recalled. "She looked like a couture trapeze artist." His wife added, "It started a great legacy of dating and life together at museums." Mr. Cornwell explained: "Mr. Cage's way of looking at the world fit in with our general philosophy that art and music are happening around us all the time, as much as what's performed and exhibited. It's like saying, 'Look at how great that is – open your eyes.' Melinda opened my eyes." The couple said that their son, Anderson, now 4, took his first steps in front of the Temple of Dendur at the Met.
>
> (Koppel 2008: B3)

When close pairs face challenges and difficult times, love stories can be helpful. As research suggests, "the ability to invoke the past through stories lends relationships continuity in the midst of change" (Burleson et al. 2000: 253). Some couples at risk, like trauma survivors or those coping with loss, may find the museum a soothing place to encounter familiar objects and pictures that bring to mind their beginnings, history, and shared values. Given their evocative nature, museums also seem extremely well suited as settings for solution-focused therapy and narrative therapy, social work techniques that use stories as vehicles for relationship growth and change. Further research and practice development is warranted in these very promising areas.

Museum contributions

Some museums provide close pairs with unique opportunities to contribute to collections and exhibits by sharing their love stories and symbolic possessions. For example, *Travelling for Love*, an exhibition of the Philip Bacon Heritage Gallery of the State Library of Queensland, Australia, gathered the moving tales and illustrative artifacts of "ten couples who have travelled to and from Queensland to be with the ones they love" (State of Queensland 2008). Among the contributors was a resident of Sydney born in Japan, and her husband, a native Australian, who found something meaningful to do with mounds of airline tickets, visa applications, and other legal evidence of the multiyear, ultimately successful battle with Immigration that preceded their marriage. Many other couples shared their love stories while visiting the exhibit or responded to an online invitation. Also recognizing the power of the Internet, the ambitious Global Love Museum, an initiative of the European Heritage Association, solicits "contributions of … living lovers" for a virtual museum to jumpstart an entire movement of love interpretation. As described on their Web site, the project aims to develop an international network of love museums and visitor centers, plaques marking places of love, and love tourist sites (European Heritage Association 2008). More research is needed to identify the precise benefits for close pairs who share their love stories and objects with museums. However, these initiatives appear at the least to offer an opportunity for couples to express and affirm their interdependence and experience a sense of shared achievement and relationship pride.

Not all close pairs find their love stories welcomed or included by society, let alone in museum collections and displays. Yet, museums have an ethical responsibility to interpret cultural experience in all its diversity and an obligation to engage people of all backgrounds in their right to culture making. In recent years, some museums have taken important steps to redress the historical exclusion of formerly ignored or stigmatized pairs, including gay, lesbian, bisexual, and transgendered couples and couples with disabilities (Sandell 2007). An impressive example is the *Wedding Album Project*, a collection and exhibition initiative of love stories and artifacts from same-sex couples who married during the fifty days in 2004 when such marriages were legal in Oregon. The invitation from county officials to share materials netted donations from 260 pairs – moving stories of their relationship histories, shared experiences, and importance of their marriages, permanently archived at the Oregon Historical Society. For some, the opportunity "provided validation of these couples' experience and guaranteed their place in Oregon history" as well as "hope that their visibility may lead to changes in attitudes and policies" (Clark and Wexler 2008: 121).

Museums, interdependence, and society

From love stories to division of labor, some interdependence patterns are unique to each close pair. At the same time, the experience of being "we" is, for better or worse, clearly shaped by social forces. Museums foster close pair interdependence through opportunities for communication norms, role complementarity, couple language, love stories, and museum contributions. They also support close pair interdependence at the societal level through gender equity advocacy and the commemoration of marriage laws.

Gender inequity

The unfair or disparate treatment of men and women based on gender is a global social problem that violates women's rights as it dictates harmful patterns of close pair interdependence. From oppressive customs to unequal vocational opportunities, gender inequity limits women's development as well as the potential and well-being of close pairs. As noted by Isabelle Vinson, editor-in-chief of *Museum International,* museums about women "are becoming the new battle-fields on which to fight for gender equality" (2007: 5). In growing numbers, gender museums with explicit social action missions are taking aim at gender inequity around the world through various forms of advocacy and activism. For example, the Vietnam Women's Museum in Hanoi is both a gender museum and a research center; its techniques include museum-produced documentary films and field trips to different communities to assess gender equity knowledge, identify gender obstacles, and raise public awareness on "women's roles, positions, rights and contributions to the construction of the country" (Tuyet 2007: 75). The museum has been deemed successful, particularly in informing the younger generation as well as policymakers (ibid.). In Buenos Aires, Argentina, the Museo de la Mujer interprets and encourages women's involvement in diverse kinds of work, including the tradition of social activism that has fostered more gender equitable laws. Modeling such activism, the museum helps link people and resources by spearheading key events such as the Second International Feminist Congress of Argentina and other collaborative initiatives (Tejero Coni 2007). Women's museums like these benefit women and close pairs alike by helping to help promote gender equity.

Commemorating marriage laws

Widely debated in a number of countries, marriage laws dictate a host of critical issues for close pairs, such as whether or not partners have access to each other's finances or hospital visiting rights, as well as determining their status as good citizens or punishable criminals. Laws can provide some leverage for fighting lingering discrimination against once illegal marriages, like partners of the same gender or different race. Increasingly, museums are playing small but valuable roles in fostering public discussion and commemoration of hard-won historic marriage laws. For example, in Johannesburg in 2008, the Apartheid Museum served as the venue for several exhibits and a community book launch of *To Have and To Hold: The Making of Same-Sex Marriage in South Africa*, a highly anticipated chronicle of the country's struggle to legalize gay marriage. Providing the event's address was the Honorable Chief Justice Pius Langa, "an embrace at the highest levels of the judiciary that would be unthinkable in other countries" (LaMarche 2008). In Los Angeles in 2008, the Japanese American National Museum hosted the *Mixed Roots Film and Literary Festival*, a celebration to commemorate Loving v. Virginia (1967), the U.S. Supreme Court case that legalized interracial relationships in America. As hosts of such events, museums remind the public of the diversity of legal marriages and the power of citizens to change laws.

Separation

Every close pair that joins together will one day have to part. With a dyad's end comes the need for separation, each partner's movement to independence though grief, integration, and growth. As essential to well-being as the need to bond is the need to survive its loss. For many people, separation has a silver lining – the possibility of pairing again.

Separation may be welcome at times, but it is often a hard process. Adjustment to life without a once-significant other can be painful even when it is desired and far worse when it is not. Many pairs face additional risk for healthy separation, as in circumstances of betrayal, violence, or sudden death. Social attitudes about "appropriate" grief can slow a natural process, especially for disenfranchised pairs who do not have much support. In many parts of the world, discriminatory norms and unequal opportunity make separation especially difficult for women.

Museums contribute to close pairs' separation needs in several ways. As the following projects suggest, museums help partners cope with loss and look toward the future. They do so by providing pair members with death education and bereavement support. At the societal level, they also support separation needs by promoting economic empowerment for women and by fostering hope.

Death education

Grasping the concept of death is one of life's greatest challenges. Therefore, society offers many educational resources about this definitive separation, and museums are among them. From Egyptian mummies to funerary art, death, like sex, seems to appear in nearly every museum. In growing numbers around the world, special exhibits like *Farewell – Death and Bereavement in Multi-Cultural Norway* at the International Cultural Centre and Museum in Oslo in 2000–1 and dedicated museums like the Funeral Museum in Vienna and the Museum of Piety in Hungary, educate people about death customs, rituals, and meanings. Visitor studies would help to explain their precise impact. Pair conversations would likely demonstrate increases in visitors' awareness, discussion, and understanding of death.

Death is a complex concept, one that is hard to fathom. For school-age friends or partners with cognitive disabilities, direct communication and discussion opportunities are very important. In an historic exhibit opened in 1984, staff at the Children's Museum of Boston, in consultation with psychologists, religious leaders, and other advisors applied these strategies to create *Endings: An Exhibit about Death and Loss*. Featuring familiar examples, relevant objects, and feedback forums, the exhibit promoted meaningful engagement for visitors of all ages (Kamien 1985). Many pairs, like those coping with terminal illness, have a pressing need to address the subject quite personally. Museums could be inspiring places to assist close pairs with funeral planning, will-writing, and other death preparation activities. If anyone could make death education more creative and engaging, it is museum staff, social workers, hospice staff, and pairs in need working together with museum resources. This is clearly an area ripe for further development.

Bereavement support

No matter how much we think about loss, we are rarely prepared for its impact. When a dyad ends, for whatever reason, partners move head-on into the necessary process of bereavement, a highly personal set of emotional, physical, social, and spiritual responses to a relationship loss (Harvey and Hansen 2000). The work of bereavement happens everywhere, especially in settings that evoke varied responses. As social, spiritual, restorative environments full of symbolic objects and stories, museums are well suited to provide bereavement support. No project embodies this potential more elegantly than the Museum of Broken Relationships (MBR), a traveling exhibition initiative created by artists Olinka Vištica and Dražen Grubišić of Croatia. In each stop on its ever-growing itinerary, including Berlin, Stockholm, and Sarajevo, MBR has solicited the leftover artifacts of ended marriages, partnerships, and flings, and offered healing in the process. With deceptively brief explanations from anonymous donors in each city, MBR displays a moving assortment of cathartic objects of lost love, including a wedding dress, an axe, and a wooden leg. In the words of its creators,

Figure 4.3 The Museum of Broken Relationships provides unique opportunities for making emotional history. Photo by Ana Opalić.

The Museum offers every individual the chance to overcome the emotional collapse though creation – by contributing to the Museum's collection. The individual gets rid of 'controversial objects,' triggers of momentarily 'undesirable' emotions, by turning them into museum exhibits, and thereby participating in the creation of a preserved collective emotional history.

(Museum of Broken Relationships 2007)

A 36-year-old woman who donated her wedding dress agreed: "I liked the idea that I could give something away that awakened painful memories for me" (in Connolly 2007). Besides the traveling exhibit, MBR maintains an on-line confessional and a virtual museum where users may store photographs and love messages.

Many circumstances can complicate the bereavement process, such as the horror of losing a partner to war or suicide. For some survivors, bereavement requires extra support from a specially trained counselor or a group facing similar loss. Museums are effective providers of these traditional bereavement services. For example, the Veterans Museum and Memorial Center of San Diego includes in its mission the intent to "serve as a host to programs that perpetuate the memories of deceased veterans or members of the United States Armed Forces and to comfort their survivors" (Veterans Museum and Memorial Center 2003). To this end, the museum has collaborated with the VITAS Innovative Hospice Care of San Diego to offer free bereavement support groups and grief education programs for the community. The Thackray Museum in Leeds, a museum devoted to advances in medicine, hosted an important conference entitled *Before and After Suicide* in 2008. The conference contributed to the professional development of the Leeds Bereavement Forum, a city-wide network of agencies and people who provide bereavement services. The museum setting and its resources offer a safe space for the social support of bereavement.

Museums, separation, and society

Movement from interdependence to independence is a highly personal journey. Still, the ease of each partner's transition is affected by many social factors, including religious attitudes, cultural stereotypes, and availability of financial opportunities. Museums foster separation through death education and bereavement support. At a macro level, they provide public healing resources as discussed in Chapter 3. They also promote the economic empowerment of women, and they foster hope.

Economic empowerment of women

Because of economic inequality, separation for women in many parts of the world can mean a harrowing decline in quality of life and an increase in risk of all kinds. Indeed, the most disadvantaged people in many countries are women who are widowed, divorced, or abandoned, prevented from an adequate living by limited financial access and opportunity. Museums serve the economic empowerment of women in two key ways. First, museums help raise public awareness of this pervasive problem and promote solutions to it. For example, the International Museum of Women, a unique on-line museum for social change that connects more than a million participants around the world, has helped publicize inspiring stories and images gathered by photographer Phil Borges. The collection *Women Empowered, Inspiring Change in the Energizing World*, part of an international campaign for women's economic development organized by CARE, clearly demonstrated the importance of microcredit loans to women in Ghana, Bangladesh, and other countries through stories of their success (International Museum of Women 2008). Second, some museums have harnessed their status as respected cultural institutions as well as their popular gift shops in service to economic empowerment initiatives. For example, at the Kurdish Textile Museum in Irbil, the *Women's Income Generation Project* created job opportunities for women while sustaining and promoting Kurdish weaving traditions (Presto 2008). Through the museum program, older tribal weavers share their skills with younger women, who work together to create blankets, clothes, and other products for sale in the museum shop. Across the globe in New Mexico, where half of all women struggle to live on incomes of less than $10,000 per year, the New Mexico Women's Foundation social service agency helped women launch home-based arts and crafts businesses and sell their wares through museum gift shops and festivals around the state, like the annual *Rag Rug Festival and Design Collective* at the Stewart Udall Center for Museum Resources. As noted by project coordinator Frieda Arth, each participating museum plays an essential role, by giving "women instant credibility that they have done something and been in a museum. … We want to give them every bit of leverage they can possibly get" (in Kamerick 2008).

Hope

Museums are memory banks that preserve and salute that which has passed. At the same time, museums celebrate the eternal prospect of new beginnings through stories and experiences of human resilience, improved quality of life, and new relationships. Effective separation requires hope – that phoenix-like belief that all will again be well someday beyond a dyad's end. From the friendship and economic empowerment fostered among Kurdish women weavers in Irbil to the meeting of future life partners at exhibit openings in New York, museums demonstrate good reasons for hope and the inevitability of growth through separation.

Museums serve close pairs as we quest for companionship, intimacy, interdependence, and separation. In other words, museums foster the human capacity to love another, what many believe is the single thing that best ensures our survival as a species. At a practical level, this is surely true, for only through the union of two, no matter how temporary, does the next generation come about. How *do* we arrange our selves and expand our love across the ages into our precious groups known as family? This is the remarkable relationship we consider next.

Figure 5.1 Peering into a Somali Aqal. OSCA and Ragged School Museum. Photography: Anna Robertson. Copyright: London Museums Hub.

Chapter 5

Treasures of home

The family is one of nature's masterpieces.

George Santayana

Of all our bonds, none reveals more innate artistry than family. Be they near or far, families shape us as we shape them, blending textures from the past, colors in the present, and visions for the future. Always works-in-progress, families are among the greatest treasures gathered in museums today.

How do museums inspire the eternal art of family? In nineteenth-century Chicago, social work pioneer Jane Addams believed her modest Hull-House Labor Museum helped foster "more meaning and a sense of relation" between European immigrant parents and their increasingly American children and so provided a bridge across the inevitable "chasm between fathers and sons, yawning at the feet of each generation" (Addams 1910: 236). These days, major institutions like the Canadian Museum of Civilization and the National Museum of Australia are helping families cast even further back and connect to distant ancestors. Some very eclectic museums, like the Spiny Babbler Museum in Kathmandu and the National Museums of Kenya, are assisting seriously challenged families with basics like shelter and support. Children's museums from California to Greece are linking diverse families with each other to face shared challenges and foster social change. As much research attests, museums of all kinds routinely provide parents and children with valued experiences (e.g., Falk and Dierking 1992; Falk and Dierking 2000; Kelly et al. 2004). In short, museums serve important needs of families, even in circumstances of risk, and help promote family-enhancing social conditions. To understand the place of museums in this critical arena of social work, let's begin with a look at the family.

Understanding the family

No definition adequately conveys the rich variety of families today, from the single mother raising adopted sons to the communal group of aging friends. While traditional definitions emphasize the presence of parent(s) and child(ren), social workers increasingly consider as family any primary group of people who call themselves one and share a home, resources, and/or the duty to care for and mentor each other (Barker 2003; Featherstone 2004). Families are both our "earliest and most enduring social relationships" (Basic Behavioral Science Research for Mental Health 1996: 622) and the "foundation of every civilization in human history" (Logan et al. 2008: 175). Recognized by the United Nations as the fundamental unit of society and a basic human right (General Assembly of the United Nations 1948), family relationships are understandably among social workers' most essential concerns.

As historian John Gillis has noted, two kinds of families matter to most of us: the families we live *in* and the families we live *by* (Gillis 1997). The first kind, our family environment or household, refers to the current constellation of close others with whom we share living space and responsibilities for daily life (Hartman and Laird 1983). Problems here may necessitate social work assistance. In their efforts to help, social workers also take interest in the highly influential family of the second kind: our family of origin, the complex network of "ties .... living or dead ... accessible or inaccessible, but always in some way psychologically relevant" (Hartman and Laird 1983: 29). As John Gillis puts it, the families we live by "not only occupy a much larger space than the household, but are extended over time, belonging to the past and the future as much as to the present" (Gillis 2001: 31). From genetics to values, the families we live by contribute much to the families we live in. With the arrival of the next generation, the latter becomes the former. Social workers help families make sense of these powerful interconnections and their impact upon our lives.

Like the self and the close pair, every family is fundamentally a system, enacting its own routine patterns of thought, interaction, and behavior (Goldenberg and Goldenberg 2002). While some of the "ways things are done" come from our families of origin, others are created anew in our current households. Ultimately, social work aims to help each family understand and improve its communication patterns and maintain a thriving family system. Together, family members must negotiate their inevitable differences and pursue goals that benefit the family and generally reflect family needs.

Families help their members meet many self needs, like competence and health. At the same time, social workers have long been concerned with the essential requirements of the family itself (Towle 1987; Logan et al. 2008). As family social work expert Allie Kilpatrick has explained, family problems signal family needs (Kilpatrick 2003: 2). For example, an intergenerational group in which one adolescent belongs to a gang and uses drugs may indicate a family need for greater cohesion. Many social workers categorize family needs by levels that range from basic survival to family enrichment, much like Maslow's hierarchy of needs (e.g., Kilpatrick and Holland 2003). Understanding both the general level and the specific need can help social workers identify the most appropriate interventions (Kilpatrick and Holland 2003; Logan et al. 2008).

A healthy society requires healthy families. Just as our families prepare us to be part of the citizenry, society at large greatly influences our family experience, whether for good or ill. Throughout history, for example, many government policies about indigenous people have torn families apart, both physically and emotionally.

Sometimes, the most critical family interventions are those pursued at the societal level, like adoption advocacy and family preservation laws. Meeting family needs is often a collective responsibility.

What needs do families share, despite their great variety? How do these needs change in situations of risk, and what social factors play a role? Among the family's numerous needs, four interest us here. Home, cohesion, continuity, and flexibility are needs of families that museums serve. How are museums currently contributing to families, our treasures of home? Let us examine each need in turn, beginning with an indispensible roof overhead.

Home

Every family needs a home – a regular living space to support family life, literally and symbolically. As a physical structure, home offers shelter from the elements and a location for family activity. As the place where most family members share resources and provide care for each other, home can signify stability and belonging. Home defines the families we live in, and reflects "the most basic level of family need" (Kilpatrick 2003: 2).

Having and keeping an adequate, comfortable home may be a universal right (General Assembly of the United Nations 1948), but it is far from a worldwide reality. Instead, family homelessness is a growing global problem, and families who are poor, chronically unemployed, or struggling with addiction and/or mental illness face particular risks (Polakow and Guillean 2001). Any family may find its home threatened by natural disaster, accident, or violence. Others may find their need for home affected by rising costs, failing economies, or substandard housing options. Home is indeed a social issue.

Museums contribute to the family's pursuit of home in five notable ways. First, museums serve as agents that promote safety. Second, museums offer temporary shelter, sometimes to those at great risk. Third, some museums provide stable housing. Museums also address broader social conditions related to home by advocating for acceptable public housing conditions and by championing sustainable living and design.

Safety promotion

From animal habitats to historic houses, family homes of all kinds regularly appear in museums, where they convey valuable lessons about home management and meaning. Essential to both is the subject of family safety. Increasingly, museums help equip families with knowledge, understanding, and actual practice in mitigating a range of dangers both inside and outside their homes. At the Fire Safety Museum of Taipei City, Taiwan, for example, families encounter simulated disasters like earthquakes and fire and practice effective responses including emergency calls, home evacuation, and cardiopulmonary resuscitation (CPR) (Chien and Wu 2008). The Habitot Children's Discovery Museum in Berkeley, California, in collaboration with local police departments, hospitals, and the State Farm Insurance Agency, mounts an annual early childhood safety campaign of special events and demonstrations on topics like baby proofing, poison control, and accident prevention. To date, "thousands of families have benefited directly" (Habitot Children's Discovery Museum 2008). The Capital Children's Museum in Washington DC and the Derry Children's Museum in New Hampshire have even offered workshops on thwarting child abduction, in which grateful families gained physical movement strategies and confidence in dealing with would-be assailants. As these examples suggest, engaging demonstrations and hands-on practice appear to be effective museum techniques for promoting family safety.

Not everyone equates home with safety, especially those at risk of child abuse or domestic violence. When the threat of danger comes from within one's family, the need for protection intensifies along with fear, confusion, and vulnerability, especially among younger victims. In Calgary, Canada, the Calgary Police Service Interpretive Centre offers an inspiring model of abuse education, recognition, and action. Through an interactive exhibition featuring a recreated kitchen and counseling center, outreach programs, a school curriculum, and a friendly, informative Web site, children learn about healthy family relationships, child abuse, and domestic violence as well as why and where to get help if they need it. For many visitors, the museum's efforts promote awareness and safe behavior. For some child victims, the museum has prompted disclosure about their own abusive situations and connected them to appropriate school, police, and/or social work personnel who can intervene on behalf of child and family safety (Pieschel 2005). In the best of circumstances, museums equip families with resources to keep their homes safe. When additional support and intervention is needed, museums can help secure it.

Temporary shelter

An ideal home serves many functions, like protection from the elements, a setting for nurturing activity, and a place to belong. For families with or without adequate homes, museums provide a kind of temporary shelter or haven that actually serves homelike functions for limited periods of time. As noted by museum leader Suzanne LeBlanc, when a wartime coal shortage closed local schools during the brutal winter of 1918, the Children's Museum of Boston kept kids off the freezing streets and engaged in activities (LeBlanc 1999). Today, the well-known travel guide *Frommer's* reminds families worldwide that museums offer welcome relief from extreme summer heat and humidity (Rubin 2008). The museum sleepover for families has recently exploded in popularity. From the American Museum of Natural History in New York, featured in the 2006 comedy film *Night at the Museum,* to the Auckland Museum of New Zealand, museums of all kinds offer families the chance to spend a night among dinosaurs and other displays. For parents or caregivers who work or can't be home with their kids, many museums offer the attractive and safe alternative of after-school programming for children, a long-time staple of museum family service. As museums strive to become more family friendly, offering new temporary shelter experiences that emphasize their homelike qualities appears to be a promising area for continued innovation.

For an alarming number of families around the world, the need for temporary shelter is far more severe than a day's refuge from bad weather or a few hours of after-school supervision. Remarkably, even some families who are homeless or living in transient housing are finding a bit of "home" through museums – among them single mothers and their children who are residents of New York's West End Intergenerational Residence and participants in the Children's Museum of Manhattan's *Shelter Program*. As detailed in the museum's *Replicable Curriculum Handbook*, the three-month-long weekly program begun in 1993 has regularly provided families in transition with lunch, social support, enjoyable activities, literacy education, and counseling from a dedicated museum staff that includes a social worker and writers-in-residence (BLiP Research 2007). To help break the cycle of abuse endured by more than 95 percent of the participating mothers, the program also models nonviolent techniques of child discipline and problem resolution (BLiP Research 2007). Formal evaluation through weekly post-session process meetings and participant progress charting have demonstrated the program's effectiveness, yet participants' own words speak volumes. During program sessions, one mother noted, "I feel like I have something to say and someone to listen when I come to the museum program," while another observed, "I see my son laughing and singing and being free at the Museum – he's not like that at the Shelter" (Bushara 2009).

Families who live in shelters and temporary residences may face increased risks of stress, illness, and demoralization (Levinson 2004; Kraybill and Olivet 2006). Some museums bring their resources directly to these settings to enhance the environments and energize and empower the residents. For example, a collaboration of the Rokpa Nepal Children's Residence and the Spiny Babbler Museum of Kathmandu enabled orphans, street children, and/or children from impoverished families living at the Rokpa Residence to create art, decorate the shelter, visit local museums, and develop their own traveling display. The program gave the six- to eleven-year-old residents a great psychological boost by reminding them of their capabilities (Spiny Babbler Museum 2007); such was the case with Pema, who announced that she was "thinking of becoming an artist when I grow up," and Santosh, one of the youngest participants, who said that he liked to "draw a football because I want to be the best foot ball player in Nepal" (in Yonzon 2007).

Across the world in Hollywood, Florida, a kindred program called *ArtREACH* has also thrived as a successful collaboration of the Young At Art Children's Museum, the Salvation Army's Plymouth Colony Shelter, and the School Board of Broward County. Together these agencies developed an arts center program that has beautified the homeless shelter while providing young residents with homework assistance, outdoor recreation, counseling, and art activities. According to project evaluations, "children feel safer, happier, and more self confident. They look forward to coming 'home'" (Institute of Museum and Library Services 2005). Through initiatives like these, museums help children and families in transition experience a taste of the protection, nurturing activity, and sense of belonging that families deserve from home.

Stable housing

For many families, home is ideally a long-term place – a structure to call their own emotionally, if not financially. Increasingly, museums provide stable housing for selected families through creative reuse efforts that benefit people as well as institutions. Sustaining the world's numerous historic houses has become a huge challenge as costs rise, visitation declines, and communities change (George 2002). Among the solutions explained by preservation expert Donna Ann Harris is the *Resident Curatorship* program, in which a family enters a long-term lease with state or private owners for a reduced sum in exchange for the often costly but unique experience of restoring and maintaining a historic house while living in it (Harris 2007). For the Endres family, resident curators of an 1860s farmhouse near Boston, more than $150,000 of their own money as well as $270,000 in sweat equity have been worthwhile investments. As Darrold Endres, a nursing home administrator, has said, "We could not afford to live in an incredible spot like this, in a town with wonderful public schools for the girls, if not for the curatorship program" (in Kahn 2007: F1). In many locations, similar programs save millions of taxpayer dollars and preserve significant properties (Chavers 2008). In most existing program models, the competitive application process favors middle- and upper-middle-class tenants who have funds to invest and existing skills in preservation and restoration. Ripe for development by house museums and government agencies, in collaboration with social workers and social service agencies, are new programs with components like skills training and loans that will help insure the equitable application of this broadly beneficial concept and match houses in need with families that most need them.

Families who are poor face the greatest risk in the search for stable long-term housing. Museums can help, even indirectly. For example, Art of Home, a nonprofit organization in Baltimore, Maryland, aims to "redevelop abandoned and rundown houses in partnership with local and international artists. These homes are then sold, below market price, to low income families in the community" (Art of Home 2008). Although not a museum itself, the project was inspired by a visit to the Peggy Guggenheim Museum, during which project creators marveled at the impact of living life amidst art and wanted to foster that experience for others. In Mexico City, a defunct sports museum donated by the mayor and city council has been transformed into a home for a remarkable family – a close-knit group of female sex workers over the age of sixty who live together. According to Carmen Muñoz, activist, founder, and director of Casa Xochiquetzal, "For us, this house is a place of peace, because it is ours" (in Johnson 2007: A5). Even a former museum can serve a family's need for home.

Museums, home, and society

Where and how families live may seem like a private matter; it is also a public issue. Many societal factors like poverty, unemployment laws, and the availability of suitable housing influence a family's search for home. In addition to serving as agents of safety promotion, temporary shelter, and stable housing, museums address social conditions relating to home in at least two ways. They advocate for acceptable public housing conditions, and they champion sustainable living and design.

Advocacy for public housing conditions

Many countries address families' need for homes with subsidized public housing. Throughout history, those who cannot afford a better option than this have often grappled with substandard or deplorable conditions. Since *The Tenement-House Exhibition of 1899* in New York and Otto Neurath's housing displays in Vienna in 1924, exhibits have served as effective tools for informing citizens about substandard housing conditions and motivating public advocacy for their reform. Today, history museums do this particularly well by using the past to inform the present. At the Lower Eastside Tenement Museum in New York, for example, the *Tenement Inspectors* program helps local children explore turn-of-the-century housing law violations "not only to teach this history but also to train a new generation of public advocates" (Abram 2002: 130), some of whom immediately apply what they've learned by recognizing and reporting violations in their own buildings. In Chicago, the National Public Housing Museum aims to interpret seventy years of American experience in public housing through exhibitions and public forums that link history to present urban challenges. Not all museums feature the distant past. In 2005, for example, the exhibit *Living It Up: The Tower Block Story* and related webcast discussions – a collaboration of National Museums Liverpool, the Liverpool Housing Action Trust, and Tenantspin, a community-led TV channel – reminded visitors and viewers of the power of activism to improve living conditions in England's controversial tower block high-rise buildings since 1993 (National Museums Liverpool 2008). In such ways as these, museums promote advocacy for acceptable conditions in public housing.

Championing sustainable living and design

According to the worldwide movement to reduce the use of natural resources, green or sustainable living is healthier, more economical, and simply better for us and the planet. Museums support families at every systems level by fostering sustainable living and green design. From the *Go Green at Gressenhall* hands-on fair at the Gressenhall Farm and Workhouse Museum of Norfolk Life in England to *Ecologic: Creating a Sustainable Future*, a permanent exhibition at Sydney's Powerhouse Museum, museum initiatives of all kinds are showing families how and why to green their homes and their lives. By practicing what they preach and going green themselves, many museums are serving as models. Partnering with international designers, architects, and innovators, museums like the National Building Museum in Washington DC and New York's Cooper-Hewitt Museum have mounted symposia, web blogs, and international competitions to raise awareness and help set new standards for sustainable, affordable home and building design. By championing sustainability, museums help support every family's need for home, now and in the future.

Cohesion

Every family needs cohesion, a healthy degree of emotional bonding, closeness, and mutual reliance among family members (Goldenberg and Goldenberg 2002). As the word *healthy* suggests, cohesion also involves "the degree of individual autonomy a person experiences in the family system" (Olson et al. 1979: 5). In short, cohesion is the ability of family members to be apart as well as together. Family cohesion prevents breakdown, increases satisfaction, mediates stress, and promotes well-being (Harris and Molock 2000; Lightsey and Sweeney 2008). Without it, a family household could not exist.

Family cohesion can be surprisingly challenging to maintain. Daily demands and varied schedules can make togetherness difficult. Cohesion needs may clash for family members of different ages or personalities. Cohesion may take a back seat to more pressing family concerns like employment or health. From prison visitation rules to adoption laws, an alarming host of social factors influence family cohesion.

Museums foster family togetherness and member autonomy in several key ways. Museums provide families with opportunities for quality time – simply to be together. They also promote positive communication, effective patterns of interacting absolutely necessary for family cohesion (Goldenberg and Goldenberg 2002). Museums foster family learning, drawing families close while strengthening individual autonomy. Museums also support family cohesion at the societal level by enhancing family service environments and by increasing public awareness of the families of missing persons.

Quality time

Museums provide families with the place and opportunity to be together and engage in shared activities, to enjoy what family participants in museum visitor studies around the world commonly call "quality time" (e.g., Dierking et al. 2001; Kelly et al. 2004; How 2007). As social workers and families agree, quality time is an essential vehicle of family cohesion. In addition to bringing members close, family quality time in museums can also promote experiences of interconnected autonomy, like toddlers' independent exploration in play spaces while caregivers watch nearby or programs for kids that leave parents free to wander on their own. For some families, exhibit content and knowledge gain are important aspects of museum visits. For many others, it is simply "enough to be together in the same place" (Kelly et al. 2004: 18).

For families separated by court or prison or involved in the child welfare system because of abuse or neglect, quality time may no longer be a free choice despite the dire need for parents and children to remain connected. Visitations, or scheduled family time supervised by a social worker, become a lifeline to family cohesion and an opportunity to help rebuild bonds, practice being a family, and lay the groundwork for family reunification, the most common goal of mandated separations. In the United States, children's museums are enhancing the quality of these visitations. *Families Together*, a remarkable partnership of the Providence Children's Museum and the Rhode Island Department of Children, Youth, and Families developed in 1991 by clinician and program director Heidi Brinig and museum director Janice O'Donnell continues to provide biweekly therapeutic visitation at the museum for children under twelve and parents separated by court order following abuse and neglect (Brinig and O'Donnell 1999). With gentle guidance from social service workers employed by the museum, families use the welcoming environment to be together, play, rebuild their relationships, and strengthen their bonds (Brinig and O'Donnell 1999). According to program evaluations, 98 percent of parent participants felt that they "learned better ways to be with their children" because of *Families Together* (Providence Children's Museum 2007: 5).

Museums are also enlivening the visitation experience in its more traditional settings. For example, the Please Touch Museum in collaboration with the Philadelphia Family Court and the Medical College of Pennsylvania/Hahnemann University developed activity carts with hands-on games, puppets, and books that families and therapists put to enthusiastic use in the Philadelphia Family Court visitation room. This program brought about an observable increase in families' relaxation and interaction during supervised visitations (Groce 1996). With careful planning and proper expertise, museums can foster beneficial quality time even in very delicate family circumstances. As these models suggest, close collaboration with experienced family social service professionals, like social workers, is "integral to the development of a workable, responsive program" (Providence Children's Museum 2007: 7).

Positive communication

Museums stimulate family interaction (Brinig and O'Donnell 1999; How 2007). In doing so, they routinely provide families with opportunities for relational awareness: "learning through experience about themselves, each other, and their functioning as a group" (Silverman 1989: 135). As research demonstrates, families deeply value the way that the museum setting alone enables them to "have family discussions" and "express their views, debate things and accept that they may have differences of opinion" (How 2007: 7). Parents also appreciate being able to "tune in to what fascinates their children" (Kelly et al. 2004: 26). In short, museums enable families to practice and refine positive communication, effective patterns of listening, speaking, respect, boundary setting, and discipline that are absolutely necessary for family cohesion (Goldenberg and Goldenberg 2002). Recognizing this potential, many museums aim to enhance positive communication by offering family programs and parenting workshops. In the work of encouraging healthy interaction between parents and children "there are few resources so purposefully and creatively designed ... as children's museums" (Providence Children's Museum 2007: 2).

Many families face risks for positive communication, from a lack of role models to insufficient skills. Museums like the Habitot Children's Discovery Museum in Berkeley, California, offer parenting classes and take-home activities to families of all kinds, including teenage parents who may lack effective communication abilities. For some, like the court-separated participants in the *Families Together* program, new problem-solving and negotiation skills are requirements for reunification (Brinig and O'Donnell 1999). From the staff perspective, work with families like 22-year-old "Maria," a drug user, and her four children under the age of six, can be stark, frustrating, and ultimately, remarkable, as museum veterans Heidi Brinig and Janice O'Donnell recall:

> It was our responsibility to help this mother learn how to play and talk with her children without losing her patience, raising her voice, or ignoring their need for comfort and reassurance. Although it has not been an easy task, Families Together staff has supported Maria when she did not consistently come for visits, lost her temper with the Museum staff, or was reluctant to try a different approach when setting limits with her children. Over a ten-month period, we could see that she had developed the patience and understanding we tried to guide her toward ... Due to her determination, willingness to learn, and control of her drug use, Maria and her children are now closer to being a family again. They will begin seeing each other more often without supervision from the social work professionals.
>
> (Brinig and O'Donnell 1999: 2)

Museums can be used in several other ways in clinical work with families whose interaction patterns need attention. They make excellent settings and partners for the practice of art therapy and music therapy with families, especially in museums that house objects needed for these interventions (Silverman 1989). For example, in the innovative *Toddler Rock* program at Cleveland's Rock and Roll Hall of Fame, music therapists make use of the exciting Hall environment and instruments from the collection to engage preschoolers at risk and their parents in therapeutic music making. The experience promotes positive family interaction and children's pre-academic skills.

In the office of a social worker or family therapist, the mere idea of a museum becomes a powerful metaphor to foster expression and insight among family members. In a technique called the Family Museum, family members draw and compare their respective ideal museums and the most important things in their lives that they contain (Cadena 2007). When clients have trouble remembering difficult family feelings, giving tours of their personally imagined "anger museums," "hurt museums," and "loss museums" helps inspire recall and sharing (Crosby 1989). Real, virtual, or made-up museums may also be used for therapeutic exercises that bring family members together between sessions with the therapist (Silverman 1989). The use of museums in clinical work with families is an exciting area full of promise for further research and development.

Family learning

Few subjects in museology regularly garner more attention than family learning in museums. As scholar Lynda Kelly and her colleagues concluded from reviewing the extensive literature, "family visitors go to museums in order to *learn together*" (Kelly et al. 2004: 15). They do so through play, conversation, and other forms of interaction with museum resources, each other, and the larger social world (e.g., Hilke 1989; Falk and Dierking 1992; Morrissey 2002; Ellenbogen et al. 2004). From a social work perspective, family learning not only draws family members close through shared experience and mutual growth, it strengthens their capacities as autonomous individuals. In short, family learning in museums is a vehicle of family cohesion.

For many families, learning together provides not only a pleasurable experience but the gateway to a better future. For parents who are illiterate, for example, learning to read, write, and do math can make the difference between employability and poverty. As demonstrated by *Reading the Museum*, the national program of the Canadian

Figure 5.2 In the Transport exhibit at the Powerhouse Museum in Sydney, a family shares a thrilling sound and light experience. Photo by Jean-François Lanzarone. Reproduced courtesy of the Powerhouse Museum, Sydney.

Museums Association that supported the development of thirty-four model projects from 1993 to 2001, museum resources and environments are particularly well suited for literacy initiatives for families at risk, especially through partnerships with community organizations (Dubinsky 2006). For example, working with the London and Middlesex Literacy Network and the Limberlost Chaplaincy, the historic Eldon House, the oldest surviving home in London, Ontario, became the site of *Inside and Out*, a family literacy program for low-income mothers and their children, who learned together through activities, games, and journaling (Mercer 1998).

Preschool age children in low-income families face increased risks for inadequate growth and development (Fraser 2004). The *Head Start* program that began in the United States in 1965 and similar government-funded social service programs for families at risk such as *Sure Start* in the United Kingdom have fostered family learning as a key strategy to nurture healthy, school-ready children. Museums are now among their most valuable partners. From the Florida Museum of Natural History in Gainesville to the National Football Museum in Preston, England, many museums work with their local early start agencies to engage caregivers in children's learning, from science to health to the value of cultural institutions. As museum educator and former Head Start Fellow Natalie Collins has observed, museums and early start programs complement each other well:

> Museums can provide early childhood programs with opportunities for object-based learning experiences that may not be otherwise available. In addition, museums have the capacity to disseminate public awareness information in ways that are engaging and easily accessible. Head Start programs have expertise engaging ethnic, language and racial groups that have traditionally underutilized the services of museums.
>
> (Collins 2006: 9)

Together, they foster family cohesion for preschooler families at risk through family learning.

Museums, cohesion, and society

Societies need families to function effectively as groups and as autonomous individuals. Yet, family cohesion is influenced by society in many ways, from service availability to family policies. At the micro level, museums aid cohesion by fostering quality time, positive communication, and family learning. At the macro level, museums enhance family preservation service environments and increase public awareness about the families of missing persons.

Enhancement of family service environments

Cohesion needs often require special institutions, such as adoption agencies, family courts, and visitation rooms. These environments can be frightening or boring, especially to children. As in health care, museum professionals are helping make these settings more engaging and family friendly. For example, the Please Touch Museum's activity carts described earlier have clearly enhanced the Philadelphia Family Court experience for families. In New York, the Long Island Children's Museum has helped enliven the nearby Health and Human Services Welcoming Center, a busy social service hub for families. With input from caseworkers, administrators, and families, museum staff designed colorful, interactive spaces for the Center and planned weekly activities for waiting families (LeBlanc 2008).

Although children's museums have been leaders in making family service environments more enjoyable, nearly any museum could use its resources and expertise to this end. In so doing, museums facilitate positive change in the nature and culture of family service itself and its ability to promote family cohesion.

Public awareness about families of missing persons

Around the world, families endure separation for horrific reasons beyond their control, from abduction to terrorism. Families of disappeared or missing persons are tortured by their loved one's absence as well as the lack of definitive knowledge about their fate. Museums worldwide are among the many organizations actively involved in increasing public awareness, supporting affected families, and pressuring governments to address this human rights abuse. To help create *Voices of the Missing,* a traveling exhibition developed by the International Commission on Missing Persons (ICMP) in 2002, Bosnian photographer Haris Memija spent months with the families of ten missing persons in order to "portray them and their stories the way the media never does" (ICMP 2004). The powerful exhibition provoked conversation and concern in a number of venues, including the National Gallery of Bosnia and Herzegovina and the Memling Museum in Bruges, Belgium (ICMP 2004). In Tbilisi, Georgia, *Expectation,* a three-room, makeshift museum filled with black and white photographs and personal belongings of soldiers missing from armed conflict, served as the site of the 2005 International Day of Missing Persons, which brought affected families and government officials together (Helsinki Citizens' Assembly Georgian National Committee 2005). Museums and their resources are helping to foster cohesion even for families at extreme risk.

Continuity

As historian John Gillis has noted, families "are extended over time, belonging to the past and the future as much as to the present" (2001: 31). While we need cohesion to maintain our households, we also need a sense of meaningful connection to family members who have come before as well as those who may come after. From discovering ancestors to making a will, family continuity involves consistency as well as change. Through continuity, families evolve their unique culture and special identity as they come to terms with who they were, are, and hope to be from generation to generation.

Many families experience continuity risks. For example, children who are adopted may feel an intensified need for family history that is legally inaccessible. Without adequate health care, some families watch helplessly as their elders fade and, with them, precious heritage. For others, continuity means a biological predisposition to addiction or other illness that links generations in unfortunate ways until genetic research advances. Family continuity is a social issue.

Museums contribute to the need for continuity in several ways. They foster intergenerational history sharing and they also preserve and disseminate critical primary resources for family history research. Museums provide opportunities for many kinds of meaningful family rituals, some that continue the old and others that begin the new. They also give families the means of leaving a legacy for the future through museum donations. At the societal level, museums support family continuity through adoption advocacy and the promotion of national apology for historical trauma.

Intergenerational history sharing

Nothing connects family members to their common past like engaging with those who recall it. Asking mother about her great-great grandparents or hearing uncle's stories about the farm brings family history into the present for discussion, questioning, and reinterpretation. Through their evocative objects and displays, museums stimulate reminiscence. From Australia to the United Kingdom, research demonstrates that families view and value museums as good places to share family history across generations (Kelly et al. 2002; Kelly et al. 2004; How 2007). Recognizing this, many museums, sometimes in partnership with schools, use creative techniques to promote such sharing, especially between parents and children. For example, in 1990, the Canadian Museum of Civilization pioneered *Family Treasures*, now in CD-ROM format, a versatile program that taught scores of children how to conduct oral history interviews with family members and gather stories of deeply valued family possessions to display in museum and classroom exhibits (Bruce and Tilney 1991). Occasionally, such projects have dramatic benefits. Thanks to the *Cultural History Program* at the Judaica Museum of Bronx, New York, and its history-sharing exercises, one fifth-grade boy learned who his father was and "met him for the first time" (in Franklin 2000: 47).

In families where parents are absent, working, or imprisoned, grandparents are often significant caregivers of grandchildren, despite the age difference and possible generation gap. As many grandparents grow older, their desire to connect and contribute to later generations intensifies (King and Wynne 2004). Museums are helpful resources to these precious relationships. As intriguing research reveals, grandparents use museums to share their lives with their grandchildren, including the kind of work they did (Beaumont and Sterry 2005), and to talk about their shared histories (Kelly et al. 2002). As scholars Ela Beaumont and Pat Sterry have observed, "Grandparents and grandchildren often act independently of parents in developing meaningful relationships with each other in the context of the art gallery visit" (2005: 175). Museums play a role in family continuity and cohesion across two generations.

Family history resources

When relatives have passed away, families often rely on photographs, government records, and other primary documents to identify and learn about their ancestors. Many genealogists, family historians, and other interested people find significant family history resources as well as research assistance in museums. For example, local history museums and historical societies often preserve birth, death, and adoption records, maintain dedicated resource rooms, and host family history events. Immigration museums, like Pier 21 Canada's Immigration Museum and the U.S. Ellis Island Immigration Museum, often contain searchable databases of passenger ship records and other invaluable documentation. Some museums, like the Imperial War Museum in England and the Garda Siochana Museum and Archives in Ireland, help families trace ancestors who served in the military and police. Museums help enhance family continuity by offering resources and assistance for family history research.

World history is marred by many tragic events that have damaged families and left little accessible trace. Travesties like the Stolen Generations phenomenon in Australia and the Holocaust of World War II in Europe left countless family members searching for information as a matter of life and death. Over time, museums have taken on a critical role in restoring these painful chapters of family history. By preserving and sharing material evidence, from touching photographs to deportation records, museums help foster family continuity across some of the world's darkest times. For example, in 2000, the Berndt Museum of Anthropology at the University of Western Australia began *Bringing the Photographs Home*, a digitization and repatriation project involving nearly 15,000 photos taken from 1920 to 1970 that document government and mission settlements and other settings relevant to the Stolen Generations. As the museum's Web site states, "Not only is it important for the older generations to identify their family history ... it is also crucial that this information is passed to younger generations, which is imperative for reclaiming and forming identity" (Berndt Museum of Anthropology 1998).

Since 1953, Yad Vashem, Israel's Holocaust Memorial, has actively collected pages of detailed testimony about victims. The now online *Central Database of Shoah Victims' Names* contains 3.6 million names of individuals (Wroclawski 2009) and has been used by 10 million people (Berman 2006). Among them were the adult grandchildren of Hilda Shlick of Israel, Benny and David Shlick, whose research in 2006 dramatically demonstrated the database's utility. The grandsons located Hilda's brother, Simon Glasberg of Canada, and reunited two siblings who had presumed each other dead since 1941 when the Glasberg family of Chernowitz, Romania, were separated by the Nazi invasion (Berman 2006). Among the first places they visited after their reunion was Yad Vashem, where they toured the exhibits and shared their story with the world in an emotional press conference (Berman 2006). As project manager Cynthia Wroclawski reports, the database "has led to hundreds of family

Figure 5.3 At Yad Vashem, Israel, David Shlick (grandson of Hilda) tells how the siblings came to be reunited. Sitting to his left – Zali Shlick, Hilda's son; Hilda; Simon Glasberg; and Irwin Glasberg (son of Mark Glasberg – the other brother who lives in Canada). Credit: Yossi Ben-David, Yad Vashem.

reunions and discoveries of information on family connections that were lost more than six decades ago" (2009).

Family rituals

Generations are linked through family rituals – symbolic acts and customs repeated over time that express a family's values, goals, and identity (Wolin and Bennett 1984). Whether drawn from past tradition or created anew with an eye toward the future, rituals help families embrace transitions and change by fostering continuity (Imber-Black 2005). Since rituals often involve symbolic objects and special settings, museums support family rituals in a number of ways. For some families, museum visiting is itself an important ritual that affirms bonds and the value of culture and is often lovingly repeated across generations (Beaumont and Sterry 2005). Many museums of history, culture, or religion teach about rituals through exhibits and programs, and even sell ritual objects in their gift shops and online. Countless museums offer seasonal activities, workshops, and even party packages to enhance important family celebrations like birthdays and holidays. Museums have even become active host sites for family reunion, an increasingly popular family ritual. For the occasion, some museums like the Yarmouth County Museum of Nova Scotia will even "arrange displays of artifacts, documents, and photographs pertaining to your family" (Yarmouth County Historical Society 2007).

Families who lack positive traditions may find it challenging to start some. For example, museum visiting can be especially intimidating for those who have never done it. At the New Jersey Historical Society, a model program entitled *Partners in Learning: Teen Parents and Their Children* has helped some often-overlooked families make museum visits a regular part of their lives. Through interactive sessions in Newark's cultural institutions, teenage parents and their children have become familiar with the benefits of museum going. To assist those struggling with difficult transitions, social workers sometimes help families create their own healing rituals, like ceremonies to mark important changes or launch new identities (Imber-Black 2005). With input from social workers and creative arts therapists, the use of museums for family rituals is indeed a ripe area for further development.

Museum donations

Like selves and pairs, families contribute stories, possessions, photographs, historical documents, or money to museums. While doing so may affirm family bonds and pride, museum donations also appear to be a powerful vehicle of family continuity and a means of legacy to future generations. In a unique visitor survey at the Hood River County Historical Museum in Oregon described by consultant Sherene Suchy, visitors were inspired to donate money or precious family heirlooms like clothing and quilts when exhibits triggered their personal memories of family and home. Through their contributions, visitors felt they were "keeping family memories alive" (Suchy 2006: 5). Miles away in Wisconsin, this was surely true for Steve Taylor, a businessman, family historian, and grandson of Pullman car porter Emmanual Hurst. Upon learning that the National Railroad Museum of Green Bay, Wisconsin, was developing an exhibit about African-American Pullman car porters and their importance to the U.S. civil rights movement, Taylor "felt compelled" to share his late grandfather's uniform, manual, union pin, and oral history for the exhibit "to help educate kids on the importance of the civil rights movement and the stepping stones laid by my grandfather and his peers" (in Sampson 2008). Through the use of video monitors, a computer-generated avatar based on Hurst's image and speaking Hurst's words as shared by Taylor guides visitors through an original Pullman sleeper (ibid.). Growing numbers of museums around the world support family continuity by actively collecting and interpreting family stories and photos, like the Museum of Chinese in America in New York and the Llangellen Museum of Wales. Many other museums have discovered that their biggest financial supporters are people with family-based emotional connections to their mission, exhibits, and themes.

In families without children or obvious heirs, the need for a trusted beneficiary for valued family possessions, money, or even history may become a pressing issue. As present generations age, those who have cared for their relatives' gifts may feel a deep responsibility to ensure their continued preservation and/or good use. Museums provide a comforting option. For Janice Laster, a Georgia native who moved to Maryland in 1993, it was a "dream come true" to find a black history museum in the planning stages by the local African American Resources Cultural and Heritage

Committee (*Frederick News-Post* 2008). Her decision to donate the 100-year-old collection of family artifacts belonging to her Maryland great-grandparents and willed to her by her grandmother felt "as though the ancestors [were] guiding me" (*Frederick News-Post* 2008).

Museums, continuity, and society

From treasured heirlooms to holiday celebrations, families reveal their artistry as they express continuity. Yet, patterns of connection across generations are influenced by society at large, which shapes continuity possibilities. Museums foster intergenerational history sharing, family history resources, family rituals, and museum donations. They also support family continuity at the societal level through adoption advocacy and the promotion of national apology for historical trauma.

Adoption advocacy

Adoption, the legal sanction of a formal family bond between a child and at least one nonbiological parent, is a powerful societal mechanism for family and child welfare. For many people at risk, like potential parents with fertility problems or children of terminally ill parents, adoption literally enables family continuity. In notable ways, museum resources are effective tools in adoption advocacy. From the Austin Children's Museum to the Smithsonian Institution, museums are frequent venues for the remarkable work of *Heart Gallery America*, a traveling exhibit program featuring art-quality portraits by volunteer professional photographers of children awaiting adoption. Begun in 2001 by the New Mexico Children, Youth, and Families Department, the widely replicated program has fostered adoptions of 60 to 75 percent of participating children in some states, occasionally by the photographers themselves (Austin Children's Museum 2007; Neil 2007; Granito 2008). Inspired by the *Heart Gallery* program, London photographer Cambridge Jones created *Home Time,* an exhibition at the Getty Images Gallery in 2008. For the project, Jones partnered children awaiting adoption through Barnardo's, a fostering and adoption agency, with popular celebrities like actor Colin Salmon and singer Heather Small. Photos taken of each other by the children and their celebrity partners formed a compelling display that prompted "visiting the gallery and … inquires about adoption" (Mower 2008). From *National Adoption Day* at the Miami Children's Museum in 2008, an event that finalized 98 adoptions at one time, to *Celebrate Adoption Night* at Stepping Stones Museum in Connecticut, many other museums collaborate with social service agencies on model events, ceremonies, and programs that celebrate and commemorate adoption.

Promoting national apology for historical trauma

When families endure massive group trauma, like slavery or genocide, their descendents suffer increased risks of suicide, physical illness, substance abuse, and domestic violence (e.g., Ledesma 2007). Such historical trauma, aptly named and defined by social work scholar Maria Yellow Horse Brave Heart as the "cumulative emotional and psychological wounding across generations, including one's own lifespan" (2005: 4), has all too often resulted from governmental policies and actions that interfere in family continuity. One widespread, heinous practice in Australia, Canada, the United States, and other countries was the attempted acculturation of indigenous children through forced attendance at special boarding schools, where many experienced abuse and trauma. Since 2008, some offending governments have offered national apologies for these actions, and museums have played a part. At the request of the Stolen Generations Alliance, for example, the National Museum of Australia in Canberra offered a live broadcast of Prime Minister Kevin Rudd's apology speech on 13 February 2008 in the museum hall and so provided "a comfortable venue for Aboriginal visitors to view the apology, specifically elderly people and those with mobility difficulties" (National Museum of Australia 2008). Museum staff also gathered extensive documentation of the apology as well as people's reactions to it, including members of the Stolen Generations. Later that same year, the National Museum of the American Indian in Washington DC mounted *Harvest of Hope,* a summit of international leaders who gathered to examine conditions and strategies for governmental apologies to Native peoples. During the program, the museum projected a huge column of light from its roof into the night sky and a slide show on its exterior wall featuring photos of Indian delegations to Washington throughout history to help "highlight national apologies made to Native peoples and educate society more deeply about the American Indian experience" (Johnson in Capriccioso 2008: 1). In such ways as these, museums are helping to promote national apology for state-induced historical trauma, a critical step toward intergenerational healing and reconciliation.

Flexibility

From life cycle transitions to unexpected crises, families face all sorts of challenges. To survive and thrive, families need flexibility, the capacity to change and grow as individuals and as a system (Goldenberg and Goldenberg 2002). Of special interest to social workers is the family's ability to change its leadership, roles, and rules (Olson 2000). Through flexibility, families transform themselves, others, and the world around them as they balance needed change with cohesion and continuity.

For many families, flexibility itself is the biggest challenge. For a rigidly controlling parent, an adolescent's choice of friends can become a family crisis. For a family that values privacy, seeking help from a social worker may be uncomfortable but necessary. From natural disasters to changing workplace laws, many external factors force families into new routines that test their flexibility. The burdensome conditions that strain family flexibility sometimes require social activism.

How do museums contribute to the family's need for flexibility? By promoting play, museums help foster imagination, problem solving, role switching and adaptability in children and families. Museums also provide opportunities for family-to-family connections that enable friendship and social support. At a societal level, museums support flexibility by promoting respect for family diversity. They also help cultivate norms of social responsibility in families and society at large.

Play

Families play in museums, from spontaneous hide-and-seek in the galleries to dress-up in a fantasy exhibit. For many children's museums, promoting play is a basic mission while countless museums of science, history, art, and culture routinely use play to engage children and families. As research demonstrates, play builds children's individual adaptability and resilience (Lester and Russell 2008) as well as imagination, creativity, and problem-solving capacity among family participants of all ages (Patton 1998; Davis et al. 2002). By providing opportunities for play, museums foster skills and interaction essential to family flexibility.

Not every family knows the importance of play or healthy ways to encourage it. In hands-on museum exhibits, for example, some parents play along with or alongside their children while others disrupt or stifle their children's efforts (Wigington 1995). Many museums, like the Strong National Museum of Play in Rochester, New York, offer workshops, lectures, or other experiences to guide families toward healthy play; one such example is *Puppet Play in Child Development*, a public program by art and play therapist Matthew Bernier. In serving families at risk, social agencies sometimes use trips to museums to teach and model play. For example, the Center for Childhood, a family service organization in Los Angeles, features trips to local museums as a key component of enrichment programs that foster flexibility for teen parents and recently immigrated families. The center's advisory board includes play scholars, social workers, and museum professionals.

No one understands the power of play for family transformation better than practitioners of play therapy, a therapeutic modality that uses play as a medium for self-expression, communication, and growth. From modifying family behavior to processing trauma, family flexibility is effectively nurtured through play therapy techniques like role play and toy play. Given rich resources like interesting objects, make-believe areas, and other play environments, museums make valuable partners for play therapy (Silverman 1989). To this end, professor Stephen Demanchick, program director of the Advanced Certificate in Play Therapy, a professional training program offered by Nazareth College in Rochester, New York, collaborates with the nearby Strong National Museum of Play to provide students with relevant experience in the galleries. In his *Foundations of Play Therapy* course, which meets regularly at the Museum, students play in the exhibits themselves and conduct observations of children and parents that are critical to developing their skills as play therapists (Demanchick 2009). In the concluding class, students share their own research with museum staff and visitors in a poster session that is educational for all involved. Although this collaboration is young, Demanchick sees "many exciting possibilities for our work" (ibid.). While children's museums may be the most obvious choice, museums of all kinds could benefit greatly from collaboration with play therapy practitioners and students.

Family-to-family connections

From the local play group to the family next door, families stay flexible with a little help from friends and neighbors: connection to other families provides information, perspective, and social support. Even brief exchanges may yield solutions, encouragement, and inspiration for transformation great or small. As research demonstrates, families value museums as places to meet and connect with other families for interaction, information, and friendship (Ellenbogen et al. 2004; Lamb et al. 2008). Through events and programs that attract families, museums facilitate connections that contribute to flexibility. For example, a *Toddlers and Carers* group meets every Wednesday at the Museum of London for art activities and information sharing. To serve families with homeschooled children, Plimoth Plantation history museum in Massachusetts turned an unused classroom into a homeschool lounge where visiting families meet and network (Richter 2007). Even one-time lectures and special events can yield meaningful exchanges that offer ideas and advice.

When crisis hits, like job loss or an episode of domestic violence, friendly connections can quickly become sustaining lifelines. While professional help may be useful or necessary, there is no substitute for the social support of families facing similar challenges together. In 2002, the Virginia Commonwealth University Health System, the Virginia Commonwealth University Psychology Department, the Association for the Support of Children with Cancer (ASK), and the Children's Museum of Richmond created *Living Well*, a support group for families coping with chronic illness (Mehalick 2009). Each weekly two-hour session at the museum included dinner, a family art project, group problem solving, informal counseling, and play in the exhibits, facilitated by trained volunteers and counselors. Evaluation demonstrated that participants experienced greater feelings of social support, less family conflict, and fewer mental health symptoms following the program (Brodeur 2005). In Aviemore and Nairn, Scotland, the Community Domestic Abuse Programme (CoDAP) also used museums to inspire the Highland Support Group for families affected by violence against women. To jump-start family creativity and connection, the group visited the Highland Folk Museum in Newtonmore and later crafted an exhibit for the Community Gallery of Inverness Museum and Art Gallery featuring their original photography and writings (Highland Council 2006). Museums offer resources that help families to help each other in difficult times.

Museums, flexibility, and society

Every family has inherent strengths that enable growth and change. Family flexibility is also affected by social norms, cultural beliefs, and other social factors. Museums bolster family flexibility through opportunities for play and family-to-family connection. They also support family change capacity at the societal level by promoting respect for family diversity and cultivating social responsibility.

Promoting respect for family diversity

Families need to feel valued and accepted by society. Instead, families who live "differently" or look "different" often experience discrimination that limits opportunities, demoralizes members, and stifles flexibility. Often in collaboration with family advocacy organizations, museums are responding by showcasing the rich spectrum of families today and their varied paths to resilience. They have, for example, hosted exhibits designed by Family Diversity Projects, a nonprofit organization in Massachusetts. Displays like *Love Makes a Family: Portraits of Lesbian, Gay, Bisexual, and Transgender Families* feature families' candid accounts of how they cope with prejudice and intolerance daily. Based in California, the Respect for All National Coalition provides workshops, films, and professional training on family diversity in a number of locations, including museums. Among its six collaborative members are the Association of Children's Museums and the Child Welfare League of America. In concert with others, museums model respect for family diversity that supports family flexibility.

Cultivating social responsibility

From improving health care to ending poverty, many changes that matter most for families must happen in society rather than at home. Yet, home is where we discover our abilities to influence others and alter our environment, essential components of family flexibility, social activism, and civic engagement. With increasing urgency, museums are working specifically within families to cultivate social consciousness, an awareness of the world's suffering and how to help. By engaging young children and older generations in service experiences such as volunteering together, donating to charity, and taking action against injustice, museums help promote lifelong habits as well as societal norms of social responsibility. At the Children's Museum of Indianapolis, *The Power of Children: Making a Difference* exhibit has helped families develop and commit to their own social action plan, including a Web site to report their progress. Through their *Power of Children Awards,* the museum also rewards and creates role models of secondary school students who demonstrate outstanding service. At the Creative Discovery Museum in Tennessee, the *Helping Hands* exhibit teaches children and their families about philanthropy, volunteerism, and other forms of giving through hands-on participation in letter writing, art making, donating pennies, and other social action campaign activities. Through initiatives like these, museums help foster a society of empowered families who routinely act to ensure the ability to grow and change for all.

Museums help families create the treasures of home, cohesion, continuity, and flexibility together. In so doing, they showcase families themselves, the true masterpieces of nature that in fact provide the preparation, models, and inspiration for nearly all subsequent works of important human connection. What happens when we share our artistry in other purposeful collectives? The amazing beauty of groups is our next concern.

Figure 6.1 Museum Steps. Photo by Ed B. Flowers.

Chapter 6

Birds in flight

> In dreams we are able to fly, and … it is a remembering of how we are
> meant to be.
>
> Madeleine L'Engle

Like birds in a "V", we humans demonstrate our greatest strength and grace as
we move in groups. What heights we reach when we fly in close formation! In the
updraft of others nearby, we flex our wings, gain efficiency, and rise more easily
to a common cause. From the steps of the world's museums, birds of a feather are
taking off together.

How do museums propel groups? When the Smithsonian Institution sought
to reach inner-city residents during the civil rights unrest of 1960s America, they
chose the Washington DC area of Anacostia to start a neighborhood museum
because "of the enthusiastic interest of the Greater Anacostia Peoples, Inc. (GAP),
an aggressive broad-base community group" (Kinard 1985: 220) willing and
interested in partnering to improve peoples' lives (Marsh 1968). Together with
director John Kinard, the revolutionary Anacostia Neighborhood Museum went
on to serve a range of groups, from a performance troupe of former prisoners
to an anti-methadone organization (Kernan 1996). Decades later, groups of all
kinds are still finding essential support in and through museums. A youth theater
group in Liverpool and a smoking cessation class in California are being inspired to
pursue their goals because of encounters with museum artifacts. Volunteer groups
in Australia and teenage care groups in Scotland are among those building their
teamwork skills through museum programs. International advocacy groups and
national public health organizations are using museums as tools to fight stigma.
Cultural arts groups in Malawi and landmine-amputee orphans in Cambodia are
receiving care and guidance from museum-based group service. In other words,
museums serve key needs of groups, even in situations of risk, and help foster
group-enhancing social conditions. To understand the role of museums in this last
specific area of social work, let's examine the group.

Understanding the group

Since Aristotle, many scholars have noted that humans are social animals. In his important theory of mutual aid, late-nineteenth-century Russian anarchist Peter Kropotkin noted that, like birds, we possess the particular instinct to aid each other and form countless associations to do so (Kropotkin 1902). From cliques to clubs, corporations to communities, groups gather people "who need each other in order to work on certain common tasks" (Schwartz 1971: 7). In daily life, even the largest collectives rely on the efforts of small groups, units with members who come to know each other as they interact for a shared purpose, often face to face, and with frequent success. From overcoming addiction to enacting a community law, groups can foster change in their members and their immediate environment. Witnessing the power of groups in settlement houses and community centers at the century's turn, social work pioneer Mary Parker Follett declared group process to be no less than "the key to democracy" and "our chief hope for the political, the social, the international life of the future" (1918: 22–3). Many decades later, the health of group relationships continues to be a foundational concern in social work.

Small groups figure prominently in nearly every aspect of social work practice, from psychotherapy to global activism. As mezzo- or middle-sized social systems, groups link individuals and society at large. Be they naturally occurring or formed, brief or enduring, formal or informal, voluntary or involuntary, self-directed or led by a social worker, groups hold great potential as systems of mutual aid, cooperation, and synergy (Schwartz 1976; Gitterman 2004). Groups are therefore "the major vehicle for service and ... the setting in which service takes place" (Garvin and Galinsky 2008: 290).

While groups form for many reasons, some social workers distinguish two types: clinical or treatment groups and community or task groups. In groups of the first type, formed for therapy, support, or education, members focus on growth and change in themselves and each other. In the broadest sense, even a third grade class and a hobbyist group can be included here. On the other hand, neighborhood committees and social action groups focus on growth and change in organizations, communities, and/or society at large. Regardless of their primary focus, many groups benefit both members and the broader social environment. Like other important relationships, all clinical and community groups are communication systems in which members interact in patterned ways. Ultimately, social workers strive to help each group interact effectively and achieve its potential as a unit of mutual aid, synergy, and change (Middleman and Wood 1990). Central to the task is an understanding of group needs.

Groups help their members meet many shared needs, from social support to self-actualization; they can also create change in society. To do either, groups must meet needs as entities in their own right that enable their existence (Schriver 2004) and their curative nature (Yalom 2005). While we tend to think of groups as collectives of similarity, members are still human beings. Therefore, most groups must negotiate complex differences among their members on a regular basis. As groups form and develop, their needs become apparent. For example, members who are confused and hesitant about participating may signal a need within the group for clearer purpose. To intervene effectively, social workers must address and blend the needs of individuals in service to the whole (Schriver 2004).

Groups help build society as well as shape it. At the same time, every group is a microcosm of society at large, subject to countless social forces. For example, support groups and interested members multiply when health care reform deinstitutionalizes patients, stresses family caregivers, and limits the options of people who are poor. Community groups working to reduce hate crimes and promote tolerance may struggle to achieve cohesiveness among their own diverse members because of entrenched racism, sexism, and homophobia. For groups to survive and thrive, interventions may be necessary at the broadest levels of society, and not just within groups themselves.

From citizens to social workers, our futures depend on groups. What needs do all groups share, even in circumstances of risk? What societal issues are particularly relevant and where do museums fit in? Groups have many needs. However, purpose, cohesiveness, empowerment, and linkage are needs of groups that museums serve. We will now consider each need in turn, and the contributions of museums. To appreciate museums and groups, those birds in flight, we begin with the reasons they flock.

Purpose

Every group needs a purpose, a shared reason or goal that unites members and defines their collective pursuits. From motivating participation to guiding content and action, purpose shapes every aspect of group life and provides its "single most important therapeutic force" (Jacobs et al. 2002: 39). More than a starting point, purpose is an ongoing need that may grow and change as a group does, fostering common ground and collective identity. A fundamental requirement of every group, purpose follows from important need(s) shared by each of its members (Northen and Kurland 2001).

Group purposes are as plentiful and varied as society's strengths and ills. From bereavement support to neighborhood action, some group purposes arise from grassroots efforts to share resources and expertise. Others, like anger management education or sex offender therapy may be created by social service agencies or mandated by legal or penal institutions. Some groups form to oppose other groups, promoting purposes that harm, rather than heal, society. In these and many other instances, purpose is a societal matter as well as a group concern.

Museums foster a group's purpose in several important ways. First, museums provide many groups with a gathering place and sometimes the reason to meet. Second, museums provide groups with collections-based activities relevant to their purposes. Third, museums offer inspiration. Last but not least, museums address broader social conditions supporting group purpose by enhancing group care and providing resources for public communication.

Gathering place

From the quilting club to the neighborhood association, groups need places to gather in order to do their work. Notwithstanding the growing role of the Internet for linking people in virtual space, most clinical and community groups still seek physical settings for regular or periodic face-to-face interaction. From hosting the monthly meeting of a local cancer support group to convening a one-time symposium on the use of art in health care, museums serve group purpose in a most foundational way. They provide a gathering place for actual and potential members to come together that is desirable for a number of reasons. As Elaine Heumann Gurian has described, museums offer "safe, neutral congregant spaces" (1995a: 15) that promote interaction among people and are often used by informal groups to their own ends (2001). Museums are widely considered trustworthy information sources and often viewed as places where groups can learn. From the society of volunteer docents to the advisory committee, many groups convene around museum purposes. In these ways, among others, museums provide a gathering place where groups can form or meet.

Not every group has a gathering place, let alone a clear purpose. As Andrew Newman has noted, some individuals in extreme hardship may not belong to any group at all (2005b). Others, like young people at risk for antisocial behavior, may join groups or gangs for support and wind up pursuing crime. According to the Group for Large Local Authority Museums (GLLAM 2000), several museums in the United Kingdom have indeed become youth gathering places ... as targets of group vandalism. Some museums have invited these groups inside to engage in more positive purposes. For example, recognizing at a local park some pre-adolescents who had recently damaged a museum building, a staff member of the Wolverhampton Museum Service asked them to come and examine their impact as well as the museum's contents. Before long, the group had reassembled around a new location and purpose, first as gallery visitors and then as workshop participants (ibid.). At the Discovery Museum in Newcastle Upon Tyne, a spray-can art workshop led by a respected expert convened a new group of fifteen teens at risk who had each "'made pieces' around the city" (ibid.: 43). Together, the members learned to produce work on commission, and many returned to the museum with friends to seek out other opportunities when the project ended (ibid.). As these examples suggest, the relationship-building efforts of a museum representative or teacher can help museums provide a gathering place and beneficial purpose for a variety of groups.

Purposeful collections-based activity

Groups fulfill their purpose by doing relevant things together. Purposeful activities and "action-oriented experiences," both a hallmark of social work practice with groups, can keep a group together and moving toward its goals (Garvin and Galinsky 2008: 291). Museum collections provide groups with raw materials and opportunities for such purposeful activity. Sometimes, museum resources offer an obvious, fundamental fit, like educational tours and classroom kits for school groups or archives for research groups. In other cases, museums may offer new opportunities, like a relaxing outing for a stressed caregiver support group or an exhibit about the environment that informs an advocacy group.

One particularly popular activity embraced by museums, social agencies, and citizens alike is the use of collections to foster reminiscence for recreational, social support, and health care purposes among groups of older adults and those with dementia. Since the 1980s, when "therapists began to ask museums for artifacts and archival images to be used in reminiscence sessions" (Chapman 1998: 41), countless museums have used their resources to develop reminiscence kits, exhibits, and programs, from the Edinburgh City Museums and London's Reminiscence Centre Museum, to the Glenbow Museum in Alberta and the Osaka Museum of Housing and Living in Japan. In addition to history, archaeology, and world culture collections, art collections are also being used effectively today to foster group reminiscence. At the Museum of Modern Art in New York, the Museum of Fine Arts in Boston, and the Bruce Museum of Arts and Science in Greenwich, Connecticut, among others, programs such as *Meet Me at MoMa* and other guide-led group tours harness the apparent ability of art to provoke long-term and/or emotional memory for people with Alzheimer's disease and other forms of dementia (Shaw 2006; Museum of Modern Art 2007). As research and observation indicate, museum reminiscence can promote group interaction and foster beneficial changes in brain activity and blood flow for some people (Sone et al. 2007). With further research, museums can identify other collections-based activities that are well suited for other specific group purposes.

Whether uncomfortable or unaware, many groups avoid museums, missing interesting experiences that could serve their purposes if barriers were removed. In its pilot phase in 1990, the Open Museum initiative of Glasgow Museums offered artifact loans, guidance, and exhibit-making opportunities to community groups at risk and demonstrated how outreach to and partnership with diverse groups could expand the purposeful uses of museum collections. Its first collaborative partner was the Wellhouse Women's Group, a member-organized arts and crafts group of about twelve women that "had exhibitions from the very beginning … but … wanted to go further" (in Dodd et al. 2002). Working with the Open Museum and a local college, The Wellhouse women created *Wear It Well*, a touring exhibition about women's roles and fashion that they took turns accompanying at each venue as costumed interpreters. In a project evaluation, one of the group members was asked to consider the impact of the experience on her life. As her words suggest, the project served the group's explicit purposes and also afforded some unexpected opportunities:

> The Open Museum heard of the group and someone came out from Kelvingrove and did a few classes with us. They invited us to become involved. … We tried new mediums, printing and everything on the arts side. We visited different

museums. We went to libraries and researched through books. ... We were a bit dumb in the beginning. It took us a while to learn and get into the history and I would say that's because history wasn't out there for us in the first place. ... We really got into this and began to know what we were talking about. ... We experienced it together, shared it. Three of us got divorced over that period. We were more independent. Local people were really amazed. A lot had never ever been to museums ... they just wouldn't have thought of it.

(ibid.: 19–20)

Inspiration

As they pursue their purpose, groups need inspiration – those motivational nudges toward insight and action that often arise suddenly. Since their earliest iterations, museums and their collections have inspired many groups toward their purposes, from Alexandrian scholars to nineteenth-century social reformers to contemporary school children. As information sources, models for art and design, symbols of the creativity of humankind, and in other ways, artifacts and exhibits can be inspiring. Groups with creative aims may be particularly well served, especially through unexpected connections. For example, World Museum Liverpool launched a youth theatre program in 2006 in which teens used the museum collections to "help inspire and create its productions," presented at the Museum's Treasure House Theatre and including new short plays as well as longer works (Spicer 2006). For support groups pursuing behavioral change, compelling objects have proved powerful. For example, when cleaning crews at the *Body Worlds* exhibitions kept finding discarded packs of cigarettes atop the display case of a former smoker's blackened lungs, the lung disease prevention agency Breathe California took note. During the run of *Body Worlds 2* at the Tech Museum of Innovation in San Jose, California, the agency offered a free six-session smoking cessation class that utilized group support and the *Body Worlds* display. As agency president Margo Sidener explained, "By bringing our stop-smoking class to the Tech, we will be able to offer assistance to those visitors who are inspired to quit" (in Body Worlds 2007).

For groups with members who have been mandated or pressured to join, like some in addictions treatment, offender rehabilitation, and youth programs, the group facilitator or sponsoring agency may well view the purpose quite differently from its members, who may be resentful, uncooperative, or simply deny its relevance to them (Northen and Kurland 2001). In these delicate situations, inspiration can take on a critical role, and museums have been able to help. For example, members of a treatment group for co-occurring substance abuse and mental illness in Indiana became more positive and engaged during time with staff from a local botanic garden where they saw plants and learned about plant care and its relevance to them (Silverman and McCormick 2001). In the case of a ten-month partnership of National Museums Scotland (NMS) and the Rural and Urban Training Scheme (RUTS) called *Wheels of Time*, a group of ten teenage boys disengaged from mainstream education and referred through support workers restored a 1920s motorcycle from the museum's collection. Inspired by the activity, as well as the guidance of museum staff and a RUTS project worker, the group demonstrated a significant shift in attitude and commitment as they worked on the bike (NMS and RUTS 2007). As one sixteen-year-old member recalled, "Maybe in the beginning, it was about getting out of school but once we got into it, it wasn't about skiving, because most of us left school during RUTS and we still went every week [to the project], even in our holidays" (NMS and RUTS 2007: 13).

Museums, purpose, and society

Groups activate the collective effort of members to serve shared need. During this process, groups are helped as well as hindered by the broader social environment. Museums foster the purpose of many groups by offering a gathering place, purposeful collections-based activity, and inspiration. They also support groups at the societal level by enhancing group care and providing resources for public communication.

Enhancement of group care

Much of the world's health and human services are provided in the context of groups, from nursing home units to group therapy. For some people, the routine formats of social group care are uncomfortable, unpleasant, or stigmatizing. Some who need it may avoid it, while others simply have no choice. Around the world, museums are quietly enhancing and invigorating group care. For some groups, museums offer a neutral, nonclinical setting for care, which may feel affirming, special, or prestigious. For others, collections-based activities may provide fresh, engaging alternatives to boring talk about problems or simplistic arts and crafts. In collaboration with creative arts therapists, museums and their collections are being used to enliven dance, art, drama, music, and poetry therapy groups. As the *Wheels of Time* program and other examples suggest, museum opportunities can motivate some groups when other experiences do not. In these ways, museums are fostering positive change in the nature and culture of social group care and providing new approaches and resources to better serve their purposes.

Public communication resources

From recruiting members to advocating their cause, groups rely on communication with the public. Community groups in particular often pursue their purposes on the public stage and use the media, government, the Internet, and other social institutions to good advantage whenever possible. As illustrated throughout this book, many groups use museums and their resources to create or host advocacy exhibits and events to spread their messages, draw media attention, and help set public agendas. As respected cultural authorities that generally garner public trust (e.g., Kelly 2006), museums can lend credibility to such groups and bolster their public communication. For example, by collaborating with the Open Museum, the Faslane Peace Camp in Britain shared their messages of concern about nuclear issues and peace widely through a compelling exhibition (Dodd et al. 2002). As John Fraser points out, however, museums are not always willing partners in public communication: they are also used by groups as sites of public protest, petitioning, and harassment, as when some groups with creationist missions have responded negatively to exhibits about evolution (Fraser 2006). These uses raise complex ethical and practical issues that museums must address regarding the protection of visitors' rights and civil liberties (ibid.). Groups themselves, citizen activists, and social workers are perfect partners for tackling these issues and further expanding museums' potential for social service as public communication resources for groups.

Cohesiveness

The difference between a group and "a collection of people who happen to occupy the same time and space" is the necessary element of cohesiveness (White 2000: 32). Like cohesion in families, group cohesiveness involves an emotional dimension: the positive feelings and attitudes of members toward each other and toward the group as a whole. When applied to groups, cohesiveness also involves a practical dimension: members' cooperation skills. In short, group cohesiveness is the amalgam of bonds and abilities that keeps a group working together. With cohesiveness, groups endure conflict and challenge, increase their performance and productivity, and activate their curative capacities (Dyaram and Kamalanabhan 2005; Yalom 2005).

Group cohesiveness is a volatile need, subject to internal and external social forces. Cohesiveness may be slow to form when members differ greatly in experience, ability, or cultural background or when leadership or facilitation is weak. On the other hand, some of the most diverse or untrusting groups may become highly cohesive when faced with a shared social danger like violence or natural disaster. As some scholars point out, cohesiveness can have negative social effects, like the phenomena of groupthink and its impaired decision making and dangerous conformity (Janis 1972; Dyaram and Kamalanabhan 2005). Group cohesiveness can influence and be influenced by the broader social environment.

Museums foster group cohesiveness in at least five important ways. Museums promote group disclosure. They also help model and promote respectful interaction within groups. Museums foster teamwork experiences in which groups build cooperation and skill. At the societal level, they promote civic engagement and raise awareness of the dangers of groupthink.

Group disclosure

Just as disclosure creates intimacy in pairs, it is essential to the cohesiveness of groups (Yalom 2005). By exchanging personal information within a group, members get to know each other, find common ground, build trust and confidence, create bonds, and gradually increase their sense of involvement with and responsibility to one another (ibid; Dyaram and Kamalanabhan 2005). With their evocative objects, exhibits, and activities, museums foster group disclosure. Older adult care groups, women's support groups, social action groups, and college classes are among those who have benefited (Carnegie 1992; Hemming 1992; Williams 1994; Dodd et al. 2002). For example, when the Geffrye Museum of London invited a group of Chinese elders from the local community to view exhibits on British life and home, members

> talked to each other about their experiences, something many of them had not done before. Some of them even found out that they came from the same town or had other experiences that were common but hadn't come to light before.
> (Hemming 1992: 33)

In an exploratory study conducted in a university gallery, Ray Williams found that small groups of graduate students readily shared personal responses, including "talk about family relationships, self-perceptions, and professional turning points," when a group facilitator asked them to engage emotionally with artwork and ponder evocative personal questions (Williams 1994: 4). This guided group sharing was enjoyable and meaningful for new groups as well as established ones, and several participants noted increases in feelings of trust and/or intimacy as a result of the experience (ibid.).

For groups coping with memory loss, communication difficulty, or social phobia, disclosure among members may be challenging. Even in such cases, art and artifacts often promote some degree of verbal sharing, and sometimes from the quietest members. For example, in a project of the Eastvale Resource Centre for older people involving artifact kits from Glasgow's Open Museum, "even the shyest woman ... participated" (Dodd et al. 2002: 30). Similar responses have occurred in museum projects with care groups for people with chronic mental illness and older adults with dementia (Silverman 1998). Clearly, the discussion facilitator must help create a safe space for sharing (Williams 1994). Approaches to this responsibility can be greatly informed by the skills and experience of social workers and other group therapists.

Respectful interaction

According to group psychotherapy expert Irvin Yalom, cohesiveness is not synonymous with comfort: it includes a group's ability to effectively handle the sometimes challenging differences and disagreements that inevitability arise in all relationships (2005: 70). Cohesiveness is thus served when groups learn and practice forms of respectful interaction like active listening, informed debate, and civil dialogue that can help prepare them to navigate conflict without coming apart. As Elaine Heumann Gurian has noted, "organized consensual rules of interaction help us humans ... live relatively peaceably" (1995b: 37). With growing intention, museums are using their stimulating collections and the museum environment to model "consensual rules." For example, the museum visit or guided tour regularly affords countless groups of school children with opportunities to practice turn-taking, self-expression, and respect for others' unique responses to objects and exhibits. In community advisory groups and focus groups convened to foster exchange between museum staff and visitors, norms of nonjudgmental listening and honest communication are advocated. Some museums, like the Museum of Tolerance in Los Angeles use their collections to teach debate, conflict resolution, and tolerance of multiple viewpoints. In these and other ways, museums help equip groups with skills and experiences of respectful interaction.

Many groups face intensified need for the skills to navigate group conflict. Groups with members who don't know each other well and those concerned with controversial social problems are especially vulnerable to breakdown when views or emotions clash. One worldwide trend addresses both situations. From Sydney to New York, museums are hosting facilitated civic dialogue programs and events that convene temporary small groups to discuss and debate challenging social issues using exhibits, art, and other museum resources for stimuli, information, and/or context (Casey 2001; Bacon et al. 2002; Schwarzer and Koke 2007). For example, in a remarkable research-based model program of the Science Museum's Dana Centre, London, a team is working to identify approaches to dialogue events that can truly promote "equitable interaction" among experts, social scientists, policymakers, and citizens about contemporary science issues (McCallie et al. 2007). Beyond ephemeral groups of current museum users, civic dialogue events may also serve the cohesiveness needs of long-term groups, groups at risk of social exclusion, and groups that link people of radically different background, perspective, and power. Social workers are the perfect partners to help museums develop broader applications of these extremely promising group cohesiveness tools.

Teamwork

Groups build their cooperation capacity and their bonds through action as well as talk. From attending meetings to achieving goals, members' interdependent efforts can hone skills, strengthen group efficacy, and yield achievements that foster group pride, all contributions to cohesiveness. Increasingly, museums provide groups of all kinds with meaningful teamwork experiences. As scholars Christine Burton and Janette Griffin discovered through intensive study of three small museums in Australia, volunteers and repeat class participants are among the groups that naturally build cohesiveness through teamwork (Burton and Griffin 2008). Recognizing this potential, many museums regularly use their resources to offer customized team-building programs to corporate management groups, agency boards, and other work groups. At the Maritime Museum of San Diego, for example, groups can take their teamwork to new heights by sailing a 140-foot schooner for hours or even days. For those who prefer a land-based adventure, museum scavenger hunts and collaborative art-making activities are also popular team-building opportunities at a host of institutions, from the Ulster Folk and Transport Museum to the Cincinnati Art Museum. Through memorable activity in a new environment, groups can hone skills like problem solving, communication, and collaboration as they strengthen group trust (Maritime Museum of San Diego 2006).

For some people with behavioral health challenges, learning to work effectively with others is best achieved in a therapeutic group setting. In such groups, teamwork becomes not only a means to group cohesiveness but a major group purpose. As social agencies, museums, and groups alike have discovered, creating a group artwork or exhibit can be an effective way to promote interaction, cooperation, teamwork skills, and cohesiveness for some client groups with behavioral health issues and/or severe mental illness (Hannah 1992; Dick 2001; Dodd et al. 2002). For example, at a hospital in Florida, a three-session project facilitated by an art therapist helped a psychiatric inpatient group create and display an original collaborative "under-the-sea"–themed mural, during and after which members demonstrated increased interaction with each other and with hospital staff (Dick 2001). With help from staff and volunteers from Glasgow's Open Museum, a group of teen boys with behavioral problems from Castlemilk Electronic Village "learned to work collaboratively, to develop specific skills and a sense of empathy and tolerance" (Dodd et al. 2002: 32) by creating their own exhibit about football – a passionate and hotly debated subject for them. As the project evaluators eloquently concluded, "In a world in which the wrong colour strip or an outdated logo can trigger exclusion, tolerance of each other's interests and affiliations was the only way to agree together on display; objects represented their interests but also symbolized their compromises" (ibid.). Clearly the use of collaborative artwork and exhibit making as a therapeutic tool holds great promise and broad applicability for learning teamwork and thereby fostering group cohesiveness.

Museums, cohesiveness, and society

For groups to develop and thrive, they must nurture their internal strengths. Encounters with society at large can encourage as well as thwart group cohesiveness. Museums foster cohesiveness through group disclosure, respectful interaction, and teamwork. To facilitate social conditions that support group cohesiveness, museums promote civic engagement and raise awareness of the dangers of groupthink.

Promoting civic engagement

A healthy democracy needs its citizens to take part in civic action activities like voting, volunteering, and community service that tend to occur in groups. As Robert Putnam has implied, such participation is volatile and cannot be taken for granted (2000). As much or more than individual initiative or group ability, civic engagement depends on how a society supports and responds to citizen participation and the opportunities it affords for it. In growing numbers around the world, museums have joined the ranks of social institutions committed to facilitating civic engagement (American Association of Museums 2002; Bacon et al. 2002; International Coalition of Sites of Conscience 2009). From convening action groups to modeling dialogue skills, museum efforts help build a social climate in which group cohesiveness is not optional but essential for the well-being of society.

Awareness of groupthink

Although group cohesiveness is generally a positive force, it can sometimes foster negative consequences. When cohesiveness is high and leadership is directive, there may be pressure for group members to avoid conflict, yielding to the problematic conformity, failure to evaluate ideas critically, negative stereotyping of outsiders, and poor decision making known as groupthink (Janis 1972; Dyaram and Kamalanabhan 2005). From peer pressure to terrorism, groupthink can have disastrous results for members, others, and society. Museums help raise public awareness of this social phenomenon, especially through compelling history. For example, the museums that make up the International Coalition of Sites of Conscience have urgent stories to tell of egregious human rights abuses and struggles for justice. Many, like the Terezin Memorial in the Czech Republic and the Constitution Hill Prison in South Africa, offer historical case studies of groupthink with important lessons for the present. These lessons are relevant to contemporary visitor groups, especially young people. As the United States Holocaust Memorial Museum (USHMM) staff have observed, "Most students demonstrate a high level of interest in studying the Holocaust precisely because the subject raises questions of fairness, justice, individual identity, peer pressure, conformity, indifference and obedience – issues which adolescents confront in their daily lives" (USHMM 2001: 2). By tackling issues of group cohesiveness abuses, museums help prepare citizens for more responsible and informed group participation.

Empowerment

Whatever its purpose or goals, every group needs to chart its own course and wield influence on obstacles encountered along the way. From support circles to social action committees, groups must come to recognize, understand, and use various strengths and resources to effect the changes they seek. As social workers know, the process of group empowerment involves a decidedly macro perspective. Through empowerment, groups become aware of the impact of social factors on their experience, confident in their ability to foster change in the social environment and not just in themselves, and effective through action in doing so (Robbins et al. 2006). While often discussed in relation to communities, populations at risk, and other large collectives, empowerment is essential even in small groups and those with seemingly sufficient influence. All groups must learn to navigate the society within which they function.

The need for group empowerment emerges from a stratified society in which people possess different and unequal levels of control over resources, from knowledge to money to culture (ibid.). Empowerment is therefore a societal issue that involves redistributing power and access (Gutierrez et al. 1995). In any community, temporary or long-standing prejudices may keep barriers in place that prevent groups from achieving their goals. Groups whose members are poor, of a racial or ethnic minority, female, or have otherwise endured a history of oppression face particularly intensified needs for increased power and control.

Museums foster group empowerment in several notable ways. First, museums serve as tools of consciousness-raising for groups. Second, museums offer experiences of group exhibit making. Third, they provide groups with opportunities to engage as museum advisors and consultants. Fourth, they are institutions that groups can start and operate themselves. At the societal level, museums support group empowerment by fighting stigma and improving their own practices regarding group representation.

Consciousness-raising

Empowerment often begins with the processes of sharing, reflection, and critical thinking by which a group considers its relationship to society and gains "a heightened awareness and knowledge base about situations of oppression" (Lee 2001: 86). Consciousness-raising also involves a group's increased understanding of its strengths and capacities to respond to such situations. From historical artifacts to interpretive exhibits to participatory experiences, museums offer many resources for group consciousness-raising. As scholar Elizabeth Crooke has noted, because history has long fueled social movements and social action, history museums and heritage projects are understandably effective consciousness-raising tools (2007). For example, Boston's Project HIP-HOP (Highways into the Past: History, Organizing & Power), a project of the American Civil Liberties Union (ACLU) of Massachusetts, takes care to include stops at sites like Harper's Ferry and the National Civil Rights Museum on its yearly "rolling classroom" trip for high school students of color studying the civil rights movement. To share their learning with others, trip alumni groups have created project newspapers, presentations to area schools, and other forms of advocacy (Murray 1999). Museums that address contemporary concerns, like some science museums and centers, can also fuel group consciousness-raising. As Erminia Pedretti (2004) concluded from a decade of research, the growing trend of critical, issues-based exhibitions that address the interrelationships of science, society, and politics appear to owe their success in enhancing group learning to four factors: they personalize the subject matter, evoke emotion, stimulate dialogue and debate, and promote reflexivity. While more research is needed, this may be a replicable formula for consciousness-raising exhibits, at least for certain groups and issues.

Consciousness-raising as a group empowerment technique is widely associated with the radical feminist movement of 1960s and 1970s America when women began meeting in informal discussion groups to share experiences of gender discrimination and oppression. At the same time, groups of women artists gave rise to a remarkable period of art, from anti-establishment installations to performance art and satire. In 2007, two major touring exhibitions of art by women opened: *Wack! Art and the Feminist Revolution*, the first comprehensive exhibit of feminist art from 1965 to 1980, at the Museum of Contemporary Art (MOCA) in Los Angeles, and *Global Feminisms*, the first international exhibit of feminist art from 1990 forward, at the Brooklyn Museum in New York. As demonstrated by recent works in the exhibitions and reactions in the visitor comment books, women are still at risk for discrimination and oppression, especially in some countries and contexts, like the workplace. In a salute to the artistry and continued importance of women's consciousness-raising groups, artist Suzanne Lacy and a team of female students, activists, and MOCA staff created *Stories of Work and Survival*, a unique installation in MOCA's Geffen Contemporary Museum Reading Room to complement *Wack!* Over six days, fifteen small groups of Los Angeles women from a range of work environments and neighborhoods came together to share their insights and struggles. While seated comfortably in a beautiful room with white couches, they were visible but not audible to visitors who could watch them from outside two glass doors. Many of the teachers, nurses, clerical temps, bike messengers, and other workers had never visited MOCA before but freely shared moving stories within their groups (Daleiden 2007). Their conversations were recorded and made publicly available in a subsequent sound installation.

Group exhibit making

From a student group learning collaboration skills to a peace camp spreading its message, many different groups have become more confident in their ability to foster change and effective in doing so by making their own exhibits in museums, community centers, schools, hospitals, and other public settings. As we saw in Chapter 3, a growing body of research indicates that the processes and products of exhibit making can develop skills, competencies, confidence, self-esteem, and a sense of achievement and pride among participants, with lasting effect (e.g., Dodd and Sandell 2001; Dodd et al. 2002; Davison and Orchard 2008). Collectively accrued, such benefits fuel empowerment as groups build strengths, capacity, and a shared sense of accomplishment through exhibit making (Dick 2001; Dodd et al. 2002). Fundamentally, exhibit making affords a critical opportunity for a group to represent itself to others and "The freedom to speak for oneself, in a place where one will be heard" (Crooke 2007: 134). Exhibits have indeed become a medium of the people, as countless heritage projects, impromptu street displays, and web exhibits attest. Whether influencing popular exhibit forms from afar or showcasing the creation of local groups, museums foster group exhibit making and subsequent group empowerment.

Groups who most need empowerment may be among those least likely to visit museums. Yet, these groups, who often deal regularly with unfair judgments and misperceptions, are also among those most likely to benefit from the opportunity to represent themselves in respected public venues. In growing numbers, museums around the world offer outreach programs, dedicated community galleries, and other means of exhibit making for groups at risk of discrimination and social exclusion. At the Art Gallery of Ontario in 1996, for example, a teenage graffiti artist group and an English as a second language class were among the groups that enriched the innovative *OH! Canada Project* with "installation[s] reflecting their unique response to the themes of identity, nationhood and the environment" (Worts 1997: 21). At the Migration Museum in Adelaide, South Australia, a community access gallery called *The Forum* has for many years been a place where a variety of groups, like former refugees, can present their own exhibits, "telling their history from their own perspective" (Szekeres 2002: 147). Through such means, groups whose voices are not always heard, let alone in museums, find a platform and "a feeling of belonging" (ibid.: 150).

Museum advising

Over many decades, the museum profession has come to realize the critical importance of engaging actual and potential users and other stakeholders as evaluators, advisors, consultants, and direct participants to inform the design and implementation of effective museum fare. While techniques like focus groups, evaluation panels, and advisory boards have become standard tools used by museums to enhance and expand their services, they also serve a valuable purpose for participating groups. As opportunities to share opinions and ideas with professionals, feel listened to and valued by an important institution, influence people, and help shape museum policy and projects, museum advising experiences can promote group empowerment. For example, to gain feedback to improve *The Human Factor*, a permanent exhibition on sustainability at the Royal Saskatchewan Museum, and its related *Youth Forum on Sustainability* program, staff utilized an evaluative exercise in which teams of students and teachers visited the galleries and reflected on researchers' questions (Sutter 2008). With students making most of the decisions and providing feedback while teachers took notes, the technique gave students a chance to take charge, which fueled their own action-oriented sustainability projects (Barrett and Sutter 2006; Sutter 2008). To reach more visitors, the Japanese American National Museum in Los Angeles involved a range of groups, like Self Help Graphics and local high school students, in community forums and interviews to help guide the development of *The Power of Place: The Boyle Heights Project* exhibition and related programming. As a result of their involvement, participating groups displayed a "great sense of ownership and pride" in the products (Conwill and Roosa 2003).

To some groups facing challenges, museums may not seem like places of opportunity. Some museums remove perceived or actual barriers by involving groups directly on museum teams where their contributions help improve services for themselves as well as others. In England, for example, a project of the

Nottingham Castle Museum and Art Gallery, the Nottingham Health Action Zone, and artists recruited fourteen- and fifteen-year-old teens to help tackle the topics of teenage pregnancy, contraception, and parenting in an exhibit called *Sexwise* and related programming (Dodd 2002). The teen group created a video component entitled *A Teenage Guide to Being Sexwise* and helped insure the exhibit's use of peer-appropriate communication. In a program of therapeutic museum visits to the Wylie House Historic Museum in Indiana, people with HIV/AIDS serving as voluntary team members helped museum staff and social workers understand the importance of program privacy to insure the anonymity of participants (Silverman 1998). While many museums today engage groups in advisory, evaluative, and team roles, few are regularly evaluating the impact of such participation on the groups themselves. Further formal research could be very helpful to museums and groups alike. As scholar Theano Moussouri has pointed out (2007), museums have much to gain by applying the emancipatory research framework utilized by many disability researchers that requires any research process or product to be one of control, choice, and empowerment for participants. Further development and widespread application of this approach is essential to the social work of museums.

Museum creation and operation

In 1997, museum scholar Stephen Weil noted the proliferation of "identity and interest groups of every kind ... creating their own museums from which to speak in their own voices and address what they consider to be their own issues" (Weil 1997: 262). Today's community-run museums provide those who start and operate them with deep experiences of empowerment. As many scholars agree, empowerment is a defining feature of an ecomuseum, which locates responsibility, control of, and decision-making about their own resources and representations in the hands of the community (e.g., Boylan 1992; Davis 1999; Sandell 2002). More often than not, the work is done by one or more small groups who reap their own empowerment benefits as they strengthen a larger collective (Davis 2004; Layne 2006). As Peter Davis has noted, "local specialist interest groups or community associations manage many of them, taking decisions about what aspects of heritage are conserved, exhibited and interpreted to local people and visitors" (2004: 94). In some cases, like the Hirano-cho Ecomuseum in Osaka Prefecture in Japan, the museum is run by a "loose confederation of local people who share the vision of preserving local heritage and encouraging dialogue between local people, young and old" (ibid.: 99). In others, like the Aboriginal keeping places and culture centers of New South Wales that are served by the Aboriginal Heritage Unit at the Australian Museum in Sydney, community groups may train, receive support from, or even collaborate with an established museum or cultural agency (Gordon 1998). Through such collaborations, these participant groups increase their professional skills, resources, and capacities. Groups that create and operate museums gain opportunities to preserve their culture, control how their history and identity is presented, and contribute to society. It is no wonder that ecomuseums and other community-run museums are increasingly popular around the world.

When groups have been oppressed, traumatized, and/or chronically depicted in a negative light, their need for empowerment can intensify. Starting a dedicated museum can be a beneficial experience (Layne 2006). For example, the District Six Museum of Cape Town, South Africa, founded in 1994, helps keep alive the memories of District Six and the more than 60,000 residents who were forcibly removed in 1965 by the apartheid government. Begun and maintained by groups of ex-residents, artists, activists, and others, the museum provides a place for community members to reclaim the past by sharing the memories, stories, and artifacts that lie "at the heart of the process of reconstruction of District Six and Cape Town" (District Six Museum 2005). As noted by Valmont Layne, former director, telling their own stories "was particularly important for a community that had been misrepresented over such a long period of time … District Six would make the news [only] in stories about poverty and alcoholism" (Layne 2006: 7). Thanks to the groups involved in the museum, District Six, its former residents, and the museum staff and volunteers are now often associated with dignity, effective activism, and social justice (ibid.; Crooke 2007).

From Brazil to New York, some unique art museums have become impressive empowerment tools for groups dealing with mental illness. While frequently launched and mentored by psychiatrists, psychologists, or social workers on behalf of their client groups, members of these client groups become active collaborators, most often as artists. For example, in the 1940s, psychiatrist Nise da Silveira transformed the treatment of schizophrenia by offering painting and clay modeling classes and devoted studios for patient groups at the National Psychiatric Centre, Rio de Janeiro (Amendoeira and Cavalcanti 2006). By 1952, their remarkable art became the collection of Museu de Imagens do Inconsciente (Museum of Images of the Unconscious), a museum within the hospital facility for which client groups still regularly produce original artwork of great interest to staff, visitors, mental health professionals, and the art world (Camargo-Moro 1981; Holston 2004). Through the museum, a "group marginalized by society as well as by psychiatric institutions prior to the museum's founding were finally able to find space and affection to express their deep emotions" (Amendoeira and Cavalcanti 2006: 1348). Supported by encouraging instructors and each other, studio participants today continue to benefit from this empowering creative community (Holston 2004).

In a similar vein, the Living Museum, founded in 1983 by artist Bolek Gryczenski and psychologist Janos Martin, is a lively art studio and museum on the grounds of the Creedmoor Psychiatric Center in Queens, New York, where people with mental illness in outpatient or inpatient treatment at the Center create, display, and talk to visitors about their art. In recent years, the Living Museum artists have been the subject of a critically acclaimed television documentary and have had group exhibitions in a number of prestigious venues, including the Queens Museum of Art and the Dabora Gallery. Through museums like Museu de Imagens

Figure 6.2 A group of artists work with clay in the modeling atelier of the Museu de Imagens do Inconsciente, Brazil. Photo courtesy of Museu de Imagens do Inconsciente (www.museumimagensdoinconsciente.org.br).

do Inconsciente and the Living Museum, groups of people with mental illness have been empowered with enhanced abilities and identities as artist collectives.

Museums, empowerment, and society

As a group becomes empowered, members come to understand how society has influenced their circumstances. Social workers and other activists have long known that group empowerment often requires intervention at the macro level to right power imbalances, eradicate discrimination, and address other social factors that escalate the need for empowerment. Museums aid groups through consciousness-raising, museum advising, group exhibit making, and museum creation and operation. Supporting group empowerment at the macro level, museums fight stigma and improve their own practices of representation.

Stigma

In social work practice, empowerment involves efforts with clients "to reduce the powerlessness that has been created by negative valuations based on membership in a stigmatized group" (Solomon 1976: 29). In other words, the need for empowerment is intensified by stigma, the "cluster of negative attitudes and beliefs that motivate the general public to fear, reject, avoid, and discriminate against" certain groups (New Freedom Commission on Mental Health 2003). In growing numbers, museums are recognizing their ability to contribute to increased awareness of the damaging effects of stigma. For example, many health promotion exhibits aim to influence people's attitudes toward those who live with illness or disability (Bender 2003). The Culion Museum of the Philippines, which is devoted to the history of leprosy, or Hansen's disease, addresses the subject of stigma directly by interpreting the discriminatory legislation against people with the disease that forced their placement in the Culion Leper Colony, and their treatment there (Cunanan 2001).

Acknowledging the challenges of fighting stigma in society, some museums are joining forces with other museums, stigmatized groups, specialists, and activist organizations in promising multi-partner initiatives. In the United States, for example, more than two dozen significant public health organizations and museums have allied to form the National Public Health Partnership, an education and advocacy coalition devoted to the health needs of American society, including the reduction of stigma (Late 2002). As part of a global initiative in 2005, the Robben Island Museum of South Africa, in association with the International Association of Integration, Dignity and Economic Advancement and the International Leprosy Association Global Project on the History of Leprosy, hosted a conference entitled *Stigma, Identity, and Human Rights: The Experience of Leprosy in the Era of HIV/AIDS*. At the landmark event that drew participants from sixteen countries, individuals impacted by stigma associated with leprosy or HIV/AIDS met with historians, museum professionals, and activists for debate and discussion, interviews, and social action planning aimed at "eliminating the power of stigma to destroy people's lives" (Robertson and Law 2005: 283). Inspired by the Robben Island Museum and its history of empowerment, the conference yielded many benefits, including the recording of participants' experiences with and strategies for fighting stigma, research dissemination, and the creation of international advocacy networks (ibid.). By joining such coalitions, museums widen their scope of influence.

Representation

Closely related to the issue of stigma is representation, the portrayal of groups in society. From advertisements to art to museum displays, all media have the potential to reflect as well as influence societal attitudes toward groups. Unfortunately, some portrayals contribute to stereotypes, fixed simplifications of groups that often fuel prejudice, stigma, and oppression. Barriers to empowerment may also result when groups are not represented at all, raising questions about their worth. With growing conviction, the museum field is engaging in serious self-reflection and redress of some of its own inappropriate representation practices (Hein 2005). As many scholars have pointed out, actually including oppressed groups like people with disabilities and gay, lesbian, bisexual, and transgendered people and their "hidden histories" in the collections, exhibitions, and fare of museums is a fundamental first step (Delin 2002; Vanegas 2002). Even one staff member can be an activist. In a effort to dispel a stereotype of subservient women, a new curator at the Ethnographic Museum of Tetouan, Morocco, "replaced the old 'typical' display of a woman seated on the floor doing domestic work with one of a well-dressed woman in her home, seated at a table, and taking refreshment" (Malt 2005). Working together on *Rethinking Disability Representation*, nine museums and galleries across the United Kingdom, the Research Centre for Museums and Galleries in the University of Leicester's Department of Museum Studies, and a think tank of experts in the disability field applied a social model of disability to develop nine experimental museum projects meant "to counter negative stereotypical representations and to engender support for the rights of disabled people" (Dodd et al. 2008: 140). Evaluation of this innovative collaboration "powerfully revealed the museums' capacity to offer ways of seeing which have considerable influence on visitors' thinking. Many left the museum[s] talking about disability differently in ways that reflected the projects' overarching aim" (ibid.: 163). This project offers a highly replicable model for developing new representation practices with a variety of groups. By improving their own representation practices, museums support group empowerment at the societal level.

Linkage

As examples throughout this chapter demonstrate, groups cannot live by their members alone. Even the most self-sufficient group needs linkage, connections with other groups for resources, support, and the exchange of energy (Anderson and Carter 1990). From the bonds between an inpatient care group and a hospital nursing team to the coalition of agencies joined by complementary goals, groups need links with other groups to realize their full potential. Through linkage, groups develop and share their strengths as they weave the fabric of society.

The linkage concept is by definition a social issue, a clear illustration of a group's interrelationship to its social environment. Yet, linkage may not come easily. As the need for empowerment reveals, some groups face severe societal barriers to equitable connection with other groups. When resources are scarce, potentially collaborative groups can become competitive instead. Some groups have difficulty transcending differences and injustices even though their connection could yield mutual benefit. To foster group linkage, social workers must promote social conditions of peace, respect, and collaboration.

Museums contribute to group's need for linkage in several ways. Museums foster intergroup contact. They also promote multigroup collaboration, linkages among several groups. Museums facilitate direct relationships of service from one group to another. At the societal level, they foster positive conditions for group linkage by advocating peace and advancing museum–social service collaboration.

Intergroup contact

From intergenerational programs to religious coexistence initiatives, museums can foster beneficial contact between two groups. For example, through the Romanian Peasant Museum's *Creativity Workshop* begun in Bucharest in 2002, urban school groups and practicing Romanian village artisans have come together to preserve the "knowledge and traditions of the Romanian Village and its main actor, the peasant" (Tilinca 2007: 6). On the grounds of this open-air museum with its recreated village environment and handmade artifacts, children learn the skills of traditional arts and occupations from experienced craftspeople who share their knowledge with younger generations (ibid.). In care settings like nursing homes and hospitals, research demonstrates that staff and patient groups experience increased interaction through exhibit-making activities. Outcomes include more frequent communication and greater respect between groups (David et al. 2001; Dick 2001). Distant groups as well as those who routinely interact may both benefit from such programs. The possibilities for effective pairings are endless.

As we saw in our discussion of close pairs in Chapter 4, groups that view each other as enemies are not likely to pursue friendly contact even though it might well benefit everyone involved. While programs such as *The Image of Abraham* for Palestinian and Jewish families and the Ulster Folk and Transport Museum programs for Catholic and Protestant children use team activities to spark friendship among pairs, they also foster contact between groups. According to scholars, such contact may reduce intergroup prejudice. In 1954, Gordon Allport described four requirements for a prejudice-reducing contact setting: equal status of participants in the situation, common goals, intergroup cooperation, and the support of authorities (Allport 1954) – four elements present in both the Israel and Northern Ireland museum programs. Analyzing a wealth of research from around the world, scholars Thomas Pettigrew and Linda Tropp have concluded that intergroup contact typically reduces intergroup prejudice across a range of groups and contact settings (Pettigrew and Tropp 2006). They also found that while Allport's four conditions are not necessary to reduce prejudice, their presence does enhance desired outcomes, especially the factor of authority or institutional support that museums can naturally provide. Perhaps most intriguing is their finding that contact has a strong ripple effect and tends to generalize beyond the immediate situation: "Not only do attitudes toward the immediate participants usually become more favorable, but so do attitudes toward the entire outgroup, outgroup members in other situations, and even outgroups not involved in the contact" (ibid.: 766). Clearly, further study in museums is needed. Yet, as intergroup contact research suggests, museum initiatives may indeed help combat prejudice and improve social relations between groups.

Multigroup collaboration

Museums can foster linkages across multiple groups. For example, the Computer Clubhouse, a technology skills development program for underserved youth created in 1993 by the Museum of Science in Boston and the MIT Media Laboratory, has since been replicated in twenty-one countries. The Museum of Science now maintains *The Intel Computer Clubhouse Network* to provide guidance and support for more than one hundred clubhouses and helps facilitate an online community and a biannual Teen Summit where clubs convene, share resources, and work together (Michalchik et al. 2008). Museums can also link different kinds of groups around common concerns through symposia and other dedicated programs. For example, the Calvert Marine Museum in Solomon, Maryland, regularly hosts *Patuxent River Appreciation Days* and *State of the River Summits* that gather volunteer groups, scientists, politicians, and fishermen for debate and action planning about river clean-up. Collectively, participants have helped shape new public policy and recruited additional volunteers to help protect the river.

From women's rights to cultural repatriation, many issues of social justice are routinely ignored until victim groups link with advocacy groups, lobbyists, and others to form coalitions of sufficient political power to foster change. For groups pursuing controversial issues, multigroup collaboration can be an especially welcome means of empowerment. As hosts of galvanizing events and as participating institutions, museums help foster multigroup collaboration that can yield support, understanding, and strength, especially for victim groups that have endured social injustice. As we have seen, the *Stigma, Identity, and Human Rights* conference hosted by the Robben Island Museum in South Africa and the *International Day of Missing Persons* program at Expectation, the makeshift museum in Tbilsi, Georgia, are but two examples of museums' coalition-building capacity that can even extend across nations.

Intergroup service

When museums link groups together, all parties often benefit. In growing numbers, however, museums are fostering direct relationships of service from one group to another. Mentorship is one popular mechanism, especially in youth programming. For example, through the Miami Museum of Science and Planetarium *Mentoring Programs*, groups of college students majoring in science, engineering, and computer science mentor teams of Florida high school students, including girls of color and others underrepresented in those professional fields. In addition to demonstrating increases in learning, graduation rates, and college-level science study, many of the youth participants return to serve as program mentors themselves (Asia-Pacific Economic Cooperation 2007). Across the globe in a small country in southeastern Africa, the *Saturday Morning Children's Club* at the Museums of Malawi has regularly taught cultural and craft skills to children aged six to thirteen who have grown up to become some of the country's self-employed artists (Maluwa 2006). "Graduates" have formed cultural groups like the Visual Arts Association of Malawi and the Cultural Heritage Arts Association, which help promote and employ other artists (ibid.). Within and beyond their walls, museums foster group linkage through intergroup relationships of service.

While some groups face dire needs for care, others feel compelled to serve. Sometimes, a hybrid museum–social service agency facility can link a group in need with a service group, and both with curious visitors. For example, the Cambodia Landmine Museum and Relief Facility, begun by Aki Ra, a former child soldier and

Figure 6.3 The Cambodia Landmine Museum and Relief Facility provides public education as well as care and support for children affected by landmines. Photo by Tamara Bournival 2007.

landmine activist and his family, pursues two goals: to provide landmine accident prevention awareness and public education to locals and tourists alike, and to provide education and rehabilitation for survivors of landmine injury (Nicholls 2009: 2). In addition to a museum full of rockets, bombs, and defused landmines, the facility also includes a residential care center for more than twenty landmine-amputee children from impoverished communities, and plans for a school, clinic, and dormitories are under way (Graceffo 2009). The "incredible group of people who provide education and support" for the children as well as the museum include locals, teachers, and ex-soldiers and their families who are themselves supported through employment at the facility (Nicholls 2009: 3). Grateful for medical care, a place to live, education, and prosthetic limbs, teenage residents work as museum guides and explain in detail the devastating impacts of the exhibited weapons (Graceffo 2009). This creative and frequented tourist site is clearly raising international awareness of the continued need for de-mining in Cambodia and elsewhere, as it is the subject of many news articles, interviews, and documentary films. For museums and social workers, the Cambodia Landmine Museum and Relief Facility offers a remarkable model for linking collections and direct care.

Museums, linkage, and society

From reducing prejudice to fostering aid, the outcomes of group linkage shape society while benefiting the groups involved. At the same time, many social factors influence which groups connect, how, and under what circumstances. Museums foster intergroup contact, multigroup collaboration, and intergroup service. At the societal level, they support group linkage by promoting peace and fostering museum–social service collaboration.

Peace promotion

According to Ikuro Anzai, Director of the Kyoto Museum for World Peace, peace can be understood

> not only as 'absence of war' in its narrow sense of the word but also as 'absence of structural violence' in its wider sense, including those issues of starvation, poverty, social discrimination, environmental destruction, retarded quality of education and hygiene that are the fundamental social factors preventing full-scale development of human ability.
>
> (Anzai 1999)

Although war and structural violence often prompt outpourings of mutual aid, peace is more supportive of healthy group linkages. Working individually and collectively, peace museums and sites have become active agents of peace promotion around the world. For example, more than ninety-five institutions have joined forces as the International Network of Museums for Peace to foster international conferences, peace literacy education, and the promotion of values that can help "build a global culture of peace" (International Network of Museums for Peace 2005). From the Nobel Peace Center in Oslo, Norway, to the Children's Museum for Peace and Human Rights in Pakistan, peace museums stand up for respect, tolerance, and other social conditions that best support positive linkage.

Museum–social service collaboration

As this book demonstrates, museums and social service agencies are working together in new ways on behalf of the people they both seek to serve. Because of this interdisciplinary collaboration, many different groups are having new experiences and new kinds of linkages. Some groups who have never viewed museums favorably before are developing meaningful connections and positive perceptions. Other groups are seeing social service agencies and the helping professions in a different light because of their new approaches. Among those more inclined to link together are museum and social work professionals. By working together, museums and social work agencies are indeed experiencing what Elaine Heumann Gurian has called "a blurring of the boundaries" (1995b) as they enhance and expand their capabilities and collective potential. Modeling the group linkage they seek to foster for others, museum–social service collaborations are enriching both professions as they evolve a truly remarkable interdisciplinary practice.

Museums help groups flock and fly by fostering purpose, cohesiveness, empowerment, and linkage. In short, they help people to care together, that boundless human power that daily changes our lives, our relationships, and our world. What can happen as more people care together about the social work of museums? We turn now to the requirements and promise of that near future.

Figure 7.1 Louvre Old & New. Photo by MacTabbie.

Chapter 7

Toward the next age

From caring comes courage.
                    Lao Tzu

From shamans to scientists, many predict that the twenty-first century will soon bring the human community to an inevitable and irrevocable turning point. As we enter what scientist Edward O. Wilson has called "humanity's bottleneck" (2002), a time of peak strain and an unprecedented challenge to our natural, economic, and intellectual resources, humankind will either meet its dire need to transform on a global scale or collapse (Musser 2005). Already, the century's escalating epidemics, extreme natural disasters, and ruthless international violence seem like glaring symptoms of a world at risk. We are quite capable of destroying each other and the planet. To survive and thrive in the next age, we must evolve new strategies for beneficial coexistence, using every suitable means to do so. In this light, the social work of museums no longer seems optional, or a clever way to keep collections-based institutions relevant, but an essential responsibility to humankind. The world's museums have always been committed to caring for culture. To insure the next age, museums must help foster cultures of caring.

Not long into the twentieth century, John Cotton Dana, the visionary director of the Newark Museum in New Jersey, advocated a deceptively simple strategy for a "new" and useful service-oriented museum: "learn what aid the community needs: fit the museum to those needs" (1917: 38). Nearly 100 years later, with thanks to the social work profession, a theoretically grounded needs-based approach to museum practice is taking shape that promises to strengthen caring relationships throughout the worldwide human community. Just how far have museums come in terms of applying social work perspectives, and what further development is necessary to achieve this potential? What conclusions can we draw from our four-chapter survey about the social work of museums today, and the requirements for the future? These are the questions we will now examine as we move toward the next age.

Elements of change

With relevant research, practice trends, and compelling examples scattered around the globe and no appropriate framework for their synthesis, museums have lacked an understanding of the collective significance of their evolving social service efforts. As our integrative survey demonstrates, museums of the world are indeed engaging in social work, at least in terms of five key perspectives: people-in-environments and close relationship systems, relationship needs, people at risk and altered needs, client-centered empowering relationships, and interventions. Museums are serving close human relationships by addressing relationship needs for a variety of people, including those in circumstances of risk, through key interventions at multiple systems levels. In other words, museums are intentionally and/or unintentionally pursuing social work goals and applying social work methods. Exactly what are museums doing, for whom, and how? Viewed collectively through the lenses of social work, our survey brings focus to these elements of change and their broader significance.

Service to relationships

Museums are clearly serving selves, close pairs, families, and groups, four fundamental human relationships that constitute the building blocks of society. While the existence of museum service to close relationships may not be surprising, its breadth, depth, and geographic diversity is remarkably rich, and so is the creativity and compassion demonstrated across initiatives. From sex workers and their clients in India to ex-soldiers and landmine victims in Cambodia, a variety of relationships are benefiting from museum visits, resources, and experiences. For growing numbers of museums today, service to close relationships indeed seems to be their most important purpose, as the social work perspective of people-in-environments and close relationship systems would suggest.

At the same time, there are even broader implications to this social work of museums. As they foster close relationships, museums bolster the social functioning of society, including our capacity to build new relationships across diverse circumstances. For every relationship we sustain, we practice and hopefully evolve social skills to apply to our bonds with others. To begin a relationship, for example, one must first be willing and able to interact effectively with a relative stranger, while to survive and thrive, every self, close pair, family, and group must participate effectively in their broader social environment. Museums help foster new relationships through a range of means, including singles events, family support groups, civic dialogue initiatives, and religious diversity encounter programs. They also strengthen our collective caring capacity as they serve our closest relationships.

Table 7.1 Relationship needs served by museums

Needs	Relationship			
	Self	*Pair*	*Family*	*Group*
Transformation	transcendence	separation	flexibility	linkage
Evolution	identity	interdependence	continuity	empowerment
Development	competence	intimacy	cohesion	cohesiveness
Foundation	health	companionship	home	purpose

Common human ground

As demonstrated in Chapters 3 through 6, museum service to relationships centers on the common human ground of relationship needs. Across selves, pairs, families, and groups alike, four needs emerged as major themes to organize definite clusters of museum activity. When viewed as a whole, an intriguing four-fold framework takes shape, summarized in Table 7.1. Museums appear to serve four essential categories of relationship needs, reminiscent of Maslow's Hierarchy of Needs (1943) and similar models (e.g., Kilpatrick 2003).

First, museums serve what may best be described as foundation needs: those that help define the relationship and are basic to its existence. These were the first needs addressed in each chapter: health for the self; companionship for the pair; home for the family; and purpose for the group. Second, museums serve what we will call development needs, those that build or deepen the relationship: competence for the self; intimacy for the pair; cohesion for the family; and cohesiveness for the group. Next, museums address needs that reflect the evolution of a relationship's potential: identity for the self; interdependence for the pair; continuity for the family; and empowerment for the group. Last but not least, museums foster transformation needs, or different forms of required change for relationships: transcendence for the self; separation for the pair; flexibility for the family; and linkage for the group. Two important caveats must be noted. First, these needs are not necessarily hierarchical; they may occur or be fulfilled in a different order from that implied in Table 1. Second, there may be other important relationship needs that museums can serve. However, this analysis suggests that museums can serve human relationships as they begin, develop, move toward their potential, and transform. This clearly bodes well for the use of museums in social work across the lifespan of each relationship.

Many museum scholars have noted the relevance of human needs to museum practice (e.g., Annis 1974; Graburn 1977; Knudson et al. 1995; Silverman 1995; Gurian 2006a). The term continues to be used in museum literature with remarkable frequency and little explanation. As our integrative survey reveals, a needs-based approach is not only feasible for museums, it evolves naturally from applying the fundamental perspectives of social work. When museums engage in social work, they implement a theoretically grounded needs-based approach to practice – an essential step for making Dana's vision a reality.

Service across circumstances

Museums have long been associated with serving the more privileged segments of society. Yet, for each of the sixteen relationship needs discussed in this book, there are compelling examples of service to people in recognizable circumstances of risk as well as those who are not. On nearly every continent, museums are fostering more caring cultures by providing direct social service and addressing relevant societal conditions. Like social work, museums are also serving the needs of all people and paying special attention to those facing risk.

From individuals with dementia to victims of violence and persecution, many of society's most vulnerable people are finding support in and through museums. As illustrated in our survey, museums are providing service to relationships complicated by such difficult circumstances as stress, addiction, cognitive or physical disability, depression, grief, life-threatening illness, and mental illness. They are aiding people as they cope with unemployment, displacement, imprisonment, trauma, terrorism, war, prejudice, discrimination, stereotyping, and stigma. Museums are tackling issues like sexual violence, domestic violence, inequity, poverty, homelessness, substandard living conditions, illiteracy, and historical trauma. Museums also provide service to relationships that do not appear to be facing particularly difficult circumstances, but appearances can be deceiving. Any relationship may be involved in circumstances of risk, now or in the near future.

While museums have traditionally viewed their work with people at risk as outreach, "special" programming, or otherwise nonessential, it is clear that such work is fundamental to museums' social service. By meeting relationship needs across varied circumstances, museums in fact demonstrate their inherent capacity to provide *universal* social service. Understanding the best methods and approaches for doing so is critical work for the future. However, a respectable foundation is emerging on which to build.

Client-centered museum relationships for change

In addition to illustrating the goals of museum social work, our survey also reveals details about its strategies and methods. While museum staff and visitors do not generally meet to devise an explicit planned change process as social workers and clients often do, much museum social work is implemented through empowering relationships that aim to bring about desired change. These relationships closely connect museums and their clients, and sometimes involve one or more museum representatives, social workers, creative arts therapists, social service agencies, and/or other institutions. The most effective of these relationships nurture the contributions, self-determination, and strengths of museum clients to foster change for themselves – in their relationships and in the broader social environment.

Some museums achieve a close relationship with clients without any explicit personal involvement by a staff member, social worker, or other representative. As our survey has shown, plenty of people use the museum and its contents on

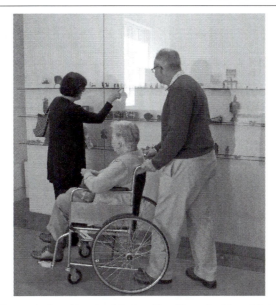

Figure 7.2 The Museo de Arte Popular, Mexico City. Photo by Fiona M. Barnett.

their own terms – for example, to relax, meet potential friends, or spend quality time as a family – and some maintain relationships with particular museums over many years and multiple generations. These are empowering relationships because the openness of the museum experience allows people to decide for themselves when, where, how, why, and with whom they will engage. Many museums forge relationships with the help of a museum representative like a tour guide, workshop educator, or project leader who facilitates beneficial experiences and changes. From the opportunity to restore a historic motorcycle with a museum expert to employment training for the cultural sector, longer-term project experiences with repeated client-representative contact, like the *Wheels of Time* program of NMS and RUTS or the *East Sussex Archaeology and Museums Project*, often build relationships of depth and intimacy. In these projects, participants set goals and are supported in their pursuits by museum and agency representatives. Projects that encourage people's contributions of personal possessions, stories, opinions, or even money are also empowering because people often feel valued and affirmed by being included in these ways.

Growing numbers of museums are building relationships with clients with help from professional social workers, creative arts therapists, and/or social service agencies as collaborative partners. Not only are they generally more experienced and knowledgeable in building new relationships with people at risk, they can act as intermediaries with their own clients and help foster therapeutic experiences for them. Their involvement typically insures emphases on planned change and client empowerment. When museums seek to serve people who may be at risk for abuse, self-harm, or harming others, or when other legal issues are at stake, professional social workers and agencies are essential partners. In still other cases, museum–client relationships may involve one or many other institutions, from hospitals to advocacy groups to workplaces. Often used as a vehicle for societal level interventions, multi-partner collaborations and coalitions can be especially empowering since they multiply participants' strengths and resources and wield collective power for fostering change.

In sum, museums are engaging in social work through client-centered empowering relationships that may involve clients, museum representatives, social workers, creative arts therapists, and others. All of these partner configurations have been used effectively to serve selves, close pairs, families, and groups. Museums have good reason to learn much more about how best to foster empowering relationships with clients and with collaborative partners. These relationships are the essential agents of change of the social work of museums.

Social work interventions using museum resources

Museums achieve their social work through a variety of interventions. For each of the sixteen needs discussed in this book, our survey revealed two to five micro or relationship interventions and two macro or societal interventions. All told, we examined a total of eighty-three different interventions. Every one of them features one or more standard museum resources: 1) the museum environment or setting; 2) objects; 3) exhibits; 4) collections-based activities and programs; 5) creative arts activities; 6) exhibit making and/or contributions; 7) museum making and/or museum work; and 8) special events and initiatives.

As we learned in Chapter 3, for example, museums serve the self's need for health through relaxation, introspection, and health education at the micro level, and through public health mobilization and the enhancement of health care environments at the macro level. The museum environment itself figures prominently in fostering relaxation; objects and creative arts activities can provoke introspection; exhibits are useful for health education and public health mobilization; and collections-based activities and programs help enliven hospitals and other health care settings. For many interventions, multiple museum resources are suitable and useful. In fact, every museum resource has been applied in service to selves, close pairs, families, and groups across a variety of circumstances.

Upon further analysis, there is a significant pattern to the eighty-three different museum resource-based interventions described in this book. This seemingly disparate assortment of planned change activities in fact reflect ten of the most fundamental categories or functions of professional social work intervention: 1) education, or fostering knowledge, understanding, and skills; 2) facilitation, or catalyzing beneficial experience; 3) networking, or linking people for interaction; 4) brokerage, or linking clients to essential resources and organizations; 5) psychotherapy, or assisting clients in problem solving and planned change; 6) values demonstration, or exemplifying particular norms and standards; 7) mobilization, or motivating people toward a cause or activity; 8) advocacy, or speaking out on behalf of people and their rights; 9) social action, or coordinated effort to foster change in social institutions; and 10) activism, or planned behavior to foster social or political objectives toward social change (Barker 2003; Kirst-Ashman 2003). Interventions one through five are perhaps the most common categories of micro level intervention in professional social work, while six through ten reflect major macro interventions. Many of the eighty-three museum interventions clearly fit one or more of these ten categories. Viewed collectively, museums are obviously applying the fundamental interventions of social work.

Museums implement these key interventions in particular ways. Consider *education,* the intervention that all museums readily understand and most offer. To serve relationship needs, however, museums provide education on subjects that are essential to social functioning and relationship well-being, like health education for selves, sex education for close pairs, safety promotion for families, and consciousness-raising for groups. Objects, exhibits, and collections-based activities and programs are especially useful for these education interventions. Museums are also increasingly familiar with the notion that they facilitate different kinds of beneficial experiences for people. To serve relationship needs, museums facilitate many important experiences, including spiritual encounters for selves, shared activity for close pairs, rituals for families, and inspiration for groups. Objects appear frequently in museums' *facilitation* interventions because they stimulate many kinds of responses and experiences. Museums are also expanding their ability to link people together and foster interaction through *networking* interventions. They do so through interventions like affiliation and membership for selves, social connection for pairs, family-to-family connections, and intergroup service. The museum environment is frequently key to such interventions because it is for many people a relatively safe, trustworthy, respected, and even esteemed environment in which people come together and engage with objects that stimulate social interaction. Museum making and museum work are also important activities in many networking interventions. They appear to empower people and relationships.

Museums may be less familiar with *brokerage* interventions. However, museums connect people with essential resources and organizations when they foster work for selves, bereavement support for close pairs, temporary shelter and stable housing for families, and multigroup collaboration for groups. Collections-based activities and programs, the museum environment, and special events and initiatives are frequently used in brokerage interventions. In the latter, partnering organizations help expand museums' reach. Presently, many museums may not be prepared for offering *psychotherapy* interventions. However, they lay the groundwork for doing so when they foster introspection for selves, communication norms within close pairs, positive communication for families, and respectful interaction for groups. Creative arts activities and exhibit making are useful tools to these ends, as they can engage people, promote communication, and foster reflection. Appropriately, true psychotherapy interventions in museums today involve the presence of a social worker or creative arts therapist to guide the work.

Museums also engage in fundamental macro or societal level interventions. To help foster societal conditions that support relationship needs, museums promote and model particular positive values, like stability as well as change for selves, hope for pairs, respect for diversity in families, and peace among groups. While *values demonstration* can occur through all museum fare, exhibits are often intentionally crafted for this purpose through particular content and presentation. Many museums aim to mobilize people to engage in specific activity or behavior in support of a cause or goal. Examples include public health mobilization for selves, fighting prejudice and discrimination for close pairs, cultivating social responsibility among families, and promoting civic engagement for groups. Frequently, museum-based *mobilization* interventions take the form of programs and activities guided by a museum representative.

In growing numbers, museums are speaking out on behalf of particular groups of people and human rights. Such *advocacy* interventions at the societal level can influence relationship needs, for example, addressing the issue of unemployment to support selves, economic empowerment of women in relation to close pairs, families of missing persons, and stigma against groups. Museum advocacy interventions often involve special initiatives and events that link people and agencies to increase collective impact. Sometimes these initiatives use creative activities and exhibit making to attract attention to their cause.

Museums demonstrate strength in *social action* – fostering change in various social institutions, including their own. Interventions of this type include the enhancement of public service that can impact selves, the commemoration of marriage laws that can support close pairs, the enhancement of family service environments, and the improvement of museums' own practices in terms of representing groups. These interventions frequently use collections-based activities and programming, exhibits, and special events, sometimes in museums and frequently in other institutions where change is sought such as hospitals, family service centers, court visitation rooms, and prisons. The portability and flexibility of museum fare is especially suited to such interventions. Last but not least, many museums are engaging in *activism* – the pursuit of specific social and political objectives for social change. This includes activism on behalf of religious and spiritual tolerance for selves, building common ground among pairs, promoting national apology for historical trauma to benefit families, and promoting awareness of the dangers of groupthink to help foster healthy groups. As our survey suggests, activism interventions often involve collections-based activities and programs and special events and initiatives that bring people together and disseminate information widely.

While they have yet to become a consistent practice, the evaluation studies reported in our survey have documented the positive impact of these various museum interventions. Overall, museum interventions appear to be engaging and enjoyable for participants, and they benefit people and relationships in a variety of circumstances. For clients, museum representatives, and social workers alike, museum interventions appear to represent refreshing, desirable, positive vehicles for the often difficult endeavors of social work. Clearly, the further development of an empirical body of knowledge and evidence is one of the most critical requirements for the future. It will be especially important to determine whether some museum resources are consistently more effective for particular interventions than others. At least now there is a useful framework on which to build.

In sum

Museums may not presently see themselves or be seen by others as institutions engaged in social work. Yet, when relevant visitor studies, practice trends, and compelling examples are assembled into a framework of key social work perspectives, a clear new vision emerges: museums around the world are pursuing social work goals and applying social work methods, and finding their unique resources quite appropriate and useful for doing so. They are laying a foundation of service to the relationship needs of all people, including those in circumstances of risk, through client-centered empowering relationships and museum resource-based interventions that foster planned change. Museums are at last evolving a needs-based approach to practice that promises universal social service. What further development is necessary to reach this potential? In other words, what are the requirements for the next age of the social work of museums? Let us now consider what must be done.

Care for the future

While some social work perspectives are evident in museum social service to date, others are comparatively weak or scant. Museums may be pursuing social work goals and applying fundamental social work methods, but they are generally not abiding by a formal and sustained commitment to human rights, social justice, or other key social work ethics and values; they are not engaging regularly in social work evaluation and theory-building efforts nor drawing upon them to inform interventions; and they are not consistently approaching relationships as essential parts of culture. In other words, museums are not collectively practicing *professional* social work. Museums and social work remain two distinct professions, each guided by its own ethics and values, body of knowledge, and competencies.

Yet, as history shows, museums and social work have long been laying the groundwork for a significantly deeper interprofessional relationship and a more informed interdisciplinary practice. Since the earliest days of public museums and settlement houses, they have shared goals, beliefs, and the fundamental desire to benefit society. While visionary leaders and foundational social work organizations used objects, exhibits, and museum environments as resources in their work, early museums drew inspiration from social work pioneers as they aimed to enrich their communities. Over time, these exchanges have become more personal and intentional. As our survey demonstrates, many of the most effective projects to date involve social workers, museum staff, and clients participating together. Given this foundation and the demands of the future, museums and social work are facing an unprecedented opportunity: to commit to building an interprofessional relationship in order to realize the full potential of the social work of museums. Not only will both fields benefit, but more importantly, so will their clients.

As in all relationships, new horizons and potential change may activate fears and concerns. Professions and their members may be content to maintain firm boundaries and undisturbed domains of expertise. Yet, through relationship and interaction, even professions can further define, develop, evolve, and transform. In growing their interprofessional practice, museums and social work can model the very capacities they seek to foster for all people. Many needs must be met in order for this endeavor to survive and thrive. Four needs in particular are illuminated by the strengths and gaps of current practice: collaboration; ethics and values; body of knowledge; and innovation. Let us now consider each need and how we can meet it.

Collaboration

Growing numbers of museum staff, social workers, and their institutions are engaging in what social worker Colin Whittington describes as the "process of partnership in action" (2003a: 16). From new pilot projects to theory development, progress in building a truly interdisciplinary practice will require a firm foundation of museum personnel and social workers acting together. Both fields have long borrowed from and dabbled in each others' arenas. It is well past time for museums and social work to participate regularly in explicit, sustained collaboration so that they may make more significant advances.

Another group of primary participants is also fundamental: those who use the resources and services of museums and/or social work. This would seem a given, since social work and, more recently, museums, view their clients and users at the center of their work and therefore essential to service planning, decision making, implementation, and evaluation, at least in theory. Yet, in both fields, involving clients and users in practice, planning and development can be challenging for countless reasons, from inadequate inclusion mechanisms to logistical issues. As growing evidence demonstrates, service initiatives that involve clients as collaborative partners can be particularly empowering for them, informative for practitioners, and key to effective service delivery (Leiba and Weinstein 2003; Whittington 2003b). Those who care about museums, social work, and relationship needs must together chart the course of this evolving practice. Their varied perspectives are needed.

As our survey demonstrates, professions like medicine, law, and the arts can serve as important collaborators to museums and social work. The creative arts therapies – including art therapy, music therapy, and play therapy – have particularly invaluable light to shed on ways to use museum resources, especially in psychotherapy and clinical work. Museums are obviously providing resources, settings, and opportunities that are useful and beneficial to various fields. In return, these collaborative partners add rich new dimensions to the social work of museums.

Many interventions can help to foster collaboration among museums, social work, clients, and others. Potential partners can contact existing or former groups to learn their strategies and gather advice. Some of the projects described in our survey have been profiled in detail elsewhere or have created resource materials. Information-sharing and mentorship are vital forms of collaboration.

New initiatives can begin through exploratory conversation. According to Whittington (2003b), effective interprofessional collaboration requires practitioners to identify and use their commonalities, distinctive contributions, complementary areas, and potential conflicts as they work together (2003b: 49). Convening a small group of museum staff, social agency workers, and clients to discuss these topics – perhaps after visiting a museum together – would be good groundwork for allaying fears and beginning to establish trust. Conversation and exploration is also critical at the macro level. For example, inter-professional discussion groups, publications, and conferences could bring museum workers, social workers, clients, and others together to discuss and chart a course for dedicated collaboration. Through interventions like these, the social work of museums can meet its need for a strong foundation of "partnership in action" (Whittington 2003a: 16).

Ethics and values

Museums and social work each abide by their own codes of ethics and values to guide professional behavior and social responsibility. To advance a truly interdisciplinary practice, both fields urgently need to review, identify, and adopt a shared set of ethics and values that will provide appropriate ground rules for their joint professional interaction, action, and obligation. As social workers use museum resources, and museum staff apply social work goals and methods, many are facing new situations and ethical questions for which existing professional codes provide insufficient or even conflicting guidance. This may be especially true in terms of the rights and proper treatment of people and material culture. Museums, social work, and the public are in dire need of a clear statement of the values and ethics that will insure ethical practice and healthy relationships among all those involved.

Many social work ethics as reflected in the internationally adopted *Ethics in Social Work, Statement of Principles* (IFSW and IASSW 2004) seem increasingly relevant and important to the changing focus of museum work, although these principles are not currently reflected in the International Council of Museums' *Code of Ethics for Museums* (2006). Principles across all three content areas of the IFSW and IASSW statement – human rights and human dignity (4.1), social justice (4.2), and professional conduct (5) – apply to museums' evolving social work practice and indicate areas of unresolved questions and important implications. For example, principle 4.1.2 guides social workers to promote peoples' right to participation and/or full involvement in the use of social services in empowering ways, while principle 4.1.1 emphasizes the importance of upholding all peoples' right to self-determination. In light of museum social work, these principles would suggest that museums have an ethical responsibility to foster "equal opportunity" across all kinds of museum experiences, self-guided as well as staff or social-worker led, and to respect peoples' right to choose how they wish to use museum resources and experiences. For museums to live up to these principles, they'd have a great deal of new work to do. However, it is precisely such ground rules that will insure ethical practice, and their implications must be faced.

In the area of social justice, principle 4.2.1 declares that workers "have a responsibility to challenge discrimination on the basis of characteristics such as ability, age, culture, gender or sex, marital status, socio-economic status, political opinions, skin colour, racial and other physical characteristics, sexual orientation, or spiritual beliefs" (IFSW and IASSW 2004). Some museums are voluntarily enacting this responsibility. Are all museums ready and willing to accept such an ethical principle as a professional requirement? In the arena of professional conduct, principle 5.1 states that "workers are expected to develop and maintain the required skills and competence to do their job." What new skills and competencies will museum staff and social workers need in order to provide ethical service in professional museum social work? The subject of relevant ethics and values raises many complex questions. In order for the relationship of museums and social work to develop further, professionals in both fields and service users must address the pressing need for a shared values and ethics base.

Interventions toward this end can occur at micro and macro levels simultaneously. Museum staff, social workers, service users, and interested others can together address the challenging work of appropriate interdisciplinary ethics through many forums, from individual project teams and student groups, to local interprofessional salons and international meetings. Several activities are essential. Detailed comparison of existing social work and museum ethics statements at agency, national, and global levels will help illuminate each professional culture. Identifying clear areas of common value as well as differences should help dispel some fear and begin to build the trust needed to wade into deeper waters. Joint study of ethical dilemmas in museum social work projects and their resolution, with input from all relevant perspectives, would be an invaluable exercise for identifying shared values already evident in actual practice. Examining colleagues' decisions and actions in recent situations can help clarify emergent ethics.

Crafting the best solutions to the need for interdisciplinary ethics and values will be a time-consuming and difficult process. It may entail revising or amending current codes of ethics, developing a joint statement, doing both, or, something different. Solutions must of course evolve with the input of all stakeholders. However, like the relationships they seek to serve, museums and social work don't have to "go it alone" and will benefit from the support of relevant organizations. Within the museum field, for example, the Institute of Museum Ethics (IME) at Seton Hall University in the United States holds conferences and provides resources on all aspects of "accountability, transparency, and social responsibility in the museum" (IME 2008). Within social work, successful linkages with other fields, like the nursing profession, may provide some worthwhile models. It is urgent that the social work of museums be grounded in an appropriate and explicit ethical base.

Body of knowledge

Every professional practice needs a foundational body of knowledge to inform its collective work. From guiding theories to empirical evidence to best practices, a knowledge base is like a profession's identity, shaping what is as well as what could be. Useable knowledge affects the health of continued practice in many fundamental ways, from advocacy efforts with policymakers and the public, to the training of new practitioners. Most importantly for the social work of museums, the body of knowledge ultimately influences clients' experiences. Our survey has revealed a preliminary foundation of practice trends, theory, and empirical evidence on which to build. As expectations of accountability and evidence-based practice continue to grow for all social institutions (Sheppard 2000), museums and social work face a pressing need for significant expansion in knowledge and in regular practices to generate and disseminate it.

Chapters 3 to 6 suggest several kinds of knowledge currently available to inform the social work of museums, as well as some gaps and opportunities. First and most obviously, practice examples abound. Each could be approached as an in-depth case study and mined for more detailed information about procedures, logistics, challenges, and lessons learned. Collectively, these cases begin to suggest the core competencies of interdisciplinary practice that must be identified to inform effective professional training. Second, as we have seen in Chapter 2 and throughout this survey, key theoretical perspectives from both fields complement each other well and apply readily to practice. This bodes well for the development of new interdisciplinary theories that further blend the knowledge of both fields, like an empowerment theory of museums or an objects-based approach to relationship enhancement. There is exciting work ahead in terms of interprofessional theory building for scholars and practitioners alike.

Third, there is scattered but growing evidence of the positive impacts and influences of museum social work based on both quantitative studies and qualitative evaluation using in-depth interviews, moving anecdotes, and/or professional reflections. While evaluation of any kind is not currently practiced as consistently and rigorously as it needs to be, model projects are emerging that incorporate theory building, research, and evaluation. They can help set new standards for the future regarding these fundamental knowledge-building practices.

Fourth, important research questions begin to come clear when we examine current practice trends and studies as a meaningful, integrated whole. For example, which museum resources are most effective for particular interventions? How can museums be used in clinical applications? What collaborative configurations are best in which particular circumstances? Developing a firmer knowledge base through practice examples, core competencies, theory building, evaluation, and a full research agenda will be essential for the future.

How to go about this work is an important consideration. Within the social work field, there is a growing desire to conduct evaluation, research, and all knowledge development in ways that clearly reflect the fundamental values of the profession, like quality of life, client empowerment, and social justice (Cheetham 1992; Plath 2006; Jordan 2007). While outcomes and evidence-based perspectives are highly valued and currently expected by many accreditation agencies, governments, and funders, some social workers are involved in pioneering alternatives. For example, empowerment evaluation (e.g., Fetterman 2003), inclusive evaluation, emancipatory research, and transformative theory (e.g., Mertens 2003) are all evaluation models that approach knowledge building as an opportunity to influence power imbalances, empower participants, and foster social change. Scholar Theano Moussouri has advocated the value and relevance of such models within the museum field (2007), although they have not yet been widely applied. It seems obvious that even the knowledge-building practices of the social work of museums should benefit people and relationships, serve society, and help to build cultures of caring. Understanding how best to insure this must be a high priority.

Building the body of knowledge for the social work of museums will both require and activate many relationship systems. Practitioners will need to master knowledge not only to deliver effective service, but to educate colleagues, board members, and potential collaborators and to advocate for the support of funders, governmental agencies, and the public. From informal discussions about this book to public campaigns that emphasize museums' service to human relationships, knowledge-building interventions can take many forms. With resourcefulness as a shared trait, museum and social work professionals will undoubtedly find creative ways to evolve a robust body of knowledge.

Innovation

Like all human relationships, professions grow and develop not just by generating new ideas but by using them to create change. To meet the challenges of the next age, the social work of museums will require innovation, what management scholars Richard Luecke and Ralph Katz define as the "embodiment, combination, or synthesis of knowledge in original, relevant, valued new products, processes, or services" (2003: 2). As currently practiced, this interprofessional, interdisciplinary endeavor already represents innovation for both fields. Yet, as the body of knowledge about the social work of museums grows, so too will the potential for innovative practice that "changes the prevailing paradigm" (Osbourne and Brown 2005: 121). Social work and museums both aim to foster positive transformations in their clients and in society. It is not only fitting but necessary that the social work and museum professions transform themselves.

As our survey suggests, the social work of museums is already pushing on paradigms, or collective views, in four key realms. Within the museum profession, which has begun to embrace social service in general, social work perspectives and methods open a fresh door to a potentially universal needs-based museum service to human relationships and society, perhaps what museums have always been meant to do. Within the social work field, often hindered by negative stereotypes, traditional approaches, and stigmatizing situations, museums and their resources are enlivening and empowering social work and its transformative capabilities through attractive opportunities and engaging experiences that involve people with culture.

For clients and their relationships, there is scattered but compelling evidence that culture is changing and people are caring together, one relationship at a time, in part because of museums. Among the public, frequent museum-goers and non-users alike, the prevailing view of museums may even be shifting from one of elite institutions relevant to a select few to places where everyone can care for themselves, each other, and the world at large. Through continued innovation, the social work of museums may well move mountains.

Doing so professionally will require careful attention to collaboration, values and ethics, and knowledge building. Through collaboration, museum workers, social workers, clients, creative arts therapists, and others will think and achieve things they could not alone. By identifying and committing to a shared set of ethics and values, collaborators will be able to work together responsibly with rules to ground and guide them. In building a body of knowledge, this interdisciplinary

Figure 7.3 In Our Hands. Photo by Emily Radecki.

field will amass a wealth of ideas and information to apply. By meeting these needs, the interdisciplinary and interprofessional practice of the social work of museums will be able to transform in ways we cannot yet know. However, we are more than ready to imagine the very near future, and the care that is within reach.

Visions of change

From homes and service facilities around the globe, groups of people and caregivers are using handheld devices to link once again to the famous *International Museum Tour Program*. Within moments, participants are viewing precious treasures in the world's museums on a large portable screen before them. Today's live tour, with optional guide, features paintings in a New Delhi museum that recent studies conclude are remarkably effective in stimulating memory and conversation among people with dementia. Before long, a petite woman with long, grey hair and a tall, slender man, friends who live in a nursing home in Virginia, are swapping long-lost memories unlocked by the powerful art in a museum half a world away. Later, participants log off from the tour refreshed, having tended to their needs for health, identity, companionship, and intimacy. Next week, participants will meet again and "visit" some of the world's most compelling spiritual sites. While they do, the creators of the *International Museum Tour Program* – a diverse team of people with dementia, their companions, museum workers, social workers, creative artists, and technology experts – will be hard at work developing new ways to enhance health and well-being for elders and others using museum resources and cutting-edge technology (Atkins 2001).

The Family Cultural Care Center (FCCC) embraces an intriguing mission: to serve and strengthen family relationships through empowering cultural activity. It is a vibrant, safe place in an urban environment where families of all kinds freely come and go. In one room, a ten-year-old boy and his father, a former prisoner, are setting up an exhibit about family separation based on their own difficult experience. The exhibit features drawings and graphics they designed using skills they learned at FCCC workshops. With help from a social worker, they lead a group discussion with other families facing separation about effective strategies for coping and staying connected. In another room, kids and parents participate in a music-making session. With much laughter and little talk, families practice turn-taking, cooperation, patience, and having fun. A music therapist demonstrates new ways to play. In another area, a young woman is interviewing her mother, grandmother, and three great-aunts about their life experiences. They are also creating holograms of each other to archive in the center's repository. At the FCCC, families make culture every day and preserve it for the future.

In a troubled part of the world, the leaders of two warring factions have reached a historic decision. Responding to unprecedented levels of citizen protest and pressure, they have consented to try and work out differences through a radically different intervention: joint care of their common cultural heritage. With some skepticism, the factions have agreed to create a museum together that aims to interpret their past, make sense of their present, and plan a mutually beneficial future. This delicate process will be facilitated by specially trained museum social workers. Understandably, early interactions are fraught with hostility about conflicting perspectives, multiple interpretations, and the meaning of things. As a glimmer of common ground grows, the group tries out some new ideas; some work and others clearly don't. Compromise is difficult and teamwork is tenuous. Yet, slowly it dawns on participants that caring together for culture means caring for each other and ourselves. It is hard work, but just may provide a promising path to a more peaceful coexistence.

The greatest treasures of culture are not sculptures or specimens, but rather, human relationships. Magnificent and precious, our selves, close pairs, families, and groups belong in the world's museums although *living* culture has quite different needs than rocks or bones. The next age is demanding change of global proportions and a nearly infinite human capacity for caring. Let us meet these needs with courage and creativity, one relationship at a time, through the social work of museums.

Bibliography

Abram, R. (2002) "Harnessing the Power of History," in R. Sandell (ed.) *Museums, Society, Inequality*, London and New York: Routledge.

—— (2005) "History is as History Does: The Evolution of a Mission-Driven Museum," in R.R. Janes and G.T. Conaty (eds) *Looking Reality in the Eye: Museums and Social Responsibility*, Calgary: University of Calgary Press.

Adams, G. and Plaut, V. (2003) "The Cultural Grounding of Personal Relationship: Friendship in North American and West African Worlds," *Personal Relationships*, vol. 10, no. 3: 333–47.

Addams, J. (1910) *Twenty Years at Hull-House with Autobiographical Notes*, New York: The Macmillan Company.

Advocates for Human Rights (2006) "Prevalence of Domestic Violence," *Stop Violence Against Women*. Online. Available HTTP: <http://www.stopvaw.org/Effects_of_Domestic_Violence.html> (accessed 11 September 2008).

Alexander, E. and Alexander, M. (2008) *Museums in Motion: An Introduction to the History and Functions of Museums*, 2nd edn, Lanham, MD: AltaMira Press.

Allport, G. (1954) *The Nature of Prejudice*. Reading, MA: Addison Wesley.

Ambrose, T. and Paine, C. (1993) *Museum Basics*, London: ICOM and Routledge.

Amendoeira, M. and Cavalcanti, M. (2006) "Nise Magalhaes da Silveira (1905–1999)," *American Journal of Psychiatry*, vol. 163, no. 8: 1348.

American Association of Museums (AAM) (2002) *Mastering Civic Engagement: A Challenge to Museums*, Washington, DC: American Association of Museums.

Amora (2007) "London Tourist Attractions, Museum, Attraction, Night Sights, Exhibition: Amora Homepage." Online. Available HTTP: <http:www.amoralondon.com> (accessed 30 August 2008).

Anderson, D. (1994) "Museum Education in Europe: Societies in Transition," *Journal of Museum Education*, vol. 19, no.1: 3–6.

Anderson, G. (ed.) (2004) *Reinventing the Museum: Historical and Contemporary Perspectives on the Paradigm Shift*, Lanham, MD: AltaMira Press.

Anderson, R. and Carter, I. (1990) *Human Behavior in the Social Environment: A Social Systems Approach*, 4th edn, New York: Aldine de Gruyter.

Angera, J. and Long, E. (2006) "Qualitative and Quantitative Evaluations of an Empathy Training Program for Couples in Marriage and Romantic Relationships," *Journal of Couple and Relationship Therapy*, vol. 5, no.1: 1–26.

Annis, S. (1974) "The Museum as a Staging Ground for Symbolic Action," *Museum*, vol. 38, no. 3: 168–71.

Anzai, I. (1999) "Museums for Peace in Japan and Other Asian Countries," in P. van den Dungen and T. Duffy (eds) *Exhibiting Peace: The Proceedings of the Third International Conference of Peace Museums*, Kyoto: Museum for World Peace. Online. Available HTTP:

<http://r-cube.ritsumei.ac.jp/bitstream/10367/185/1/Museums%20for%20Peace%20 in%20Japan%20and%20Other%20Asian%20Countries.pdf> (accessed 20 January 2009).

Aoki, P., Grinter, R., Hurst, A., Szymanski, M., Thorton, J. and Woodruff, A. (2002) "Sotto Voce: Exploring the Interplay of Conversation and Mobile Audio Spaces," Proc. CHI 2002. Online. Available HTTP: <http://citeseerx.ist.psu.edu/viewdoc/ summary?doi=10.1.1.16.8673> (accessed 11 September 2008).

Appelbaum, M. (2009) Personal communication (17 March 2009).

Appleton, J. (2001) "Museums for the People," *Spiked*, London: Signet House. Online. Available HTTP: <http://www.spiked-online.com/Articles/00000002D2BA.htm> (accessed 4 March 2007).

Argyle, M., Henderson, M., Bond, M., Iizuka, Y. and Contarello, A. (1986) "Cross-Cultural Variations in Relationship Rules," *International Journal of Psychology*, vol. 21, no. 2: 287– 315.

Art of Home (2008) "About Us." Online. Available HTTP: <http://www.artofhome.org/ about.html> (accessed 1 December 2008).

Asia-Pacific Economic Cooperation (2007) "Miami Museum of Science & Planetarium Mentoring Programs for Underserved Youth." Online. Available HTTP: <http://www. aspacnet.org/apec/case_studies/_pdfs/miami_mentoring.pdf> (accessed 19 December 2009).

Atkins, K. (2001) Personal communication (14 August 2001).

Austin Children's Museum (2007) "The Heart Gallery of Central Texas." Online. Available HTTP: <http://www.austinkids.org/Exhibits/Community-Gallery/The-Heart-Gallery- of-Central-Texas.aspx> (accessed 7 December 2008).

Backman, C. (1990) "Attraction in Interpersonal Relationships," in M. Rosenberg and R. Turner (eds) *Social Psychology: Sociological Perspectives*, Edison, NJ: Transaction Publishers.

Bacon, B., Korza, P. and Williams, P. (2002) "Giving Voice: A Role for Museums in Civic Dialogue," in American Association of Museums *A Museums and Community Toolkit*, Washington, DC: American Association of Museums.

Bardes, C., Gillers, D. and Herman, A. (2001) "Learning to Look: Developing Clinical Observational Skills at an Art Museum," *Medical Education*, vol. 35, no. 12: 1157–61.

Barker, R. L. (2003) *The Social Work Dictionary*, 5th edn, Washington, DC: National Association of Social Workers Press.

Barrett, M. and Sutter, G. (2006) "A Youth Forum on Sustainability Meets *The Human Factor*: Challenging Cultural Narratives in Schools and Museums," *Canadian Journal of Science, Mathematics and Technology Education*, vol. 6, no. 1: 9–23.

Basic Behavioral Science Research for Mental Health (1996) "Family Processes and Social Networks," *American Psychologist*, vol. 51: 622–30.

BBC News (2006) "Oslo Gay Animal Show Draws Crowds," *BBC News*, 10 October 2006. Online. Available HTTP: <http://news.bbc.co.uk/2/hi/europe/6066606.stm> (accessed 16 July 2008).

Beane, B. and Pope, M. (2002) "Leveling the Playing Field Through Object-Based Service Learning," in S. Paris (ed.) *Perspectives on Object-Centered Learning in Museums*, Mahwah, NJ: Lawrence Erlbaum.

Beaumont, E. and Sterry, P. (2005) "A Study of Grandparents and Grandchildren as Visitors to Museums and Art Galleries in the UK," *museum and society*, vol. 3, no. 3: 167–80.

Bedford, L. (2001) "Storytelling: The Real Work of Museums," *Curator*, vol. 44, no. 1: 27–34.

—— (2004) "Working in the Subjunctive Mood: Imagination and Museums," *Curator*, vol. 47, no. 1: 5–10.

Bender, E. (2003) "Depression Gets Own Exhibit at Innovative Museum," *Psychiatric News*, vol. 38, no. 2: 10.

Bennett, S. and Bareham, T. (2005) "Unearthing the Hidden Potential of Learners," *Talisman: The Newspaper for Adult Learning*, no. 44: 12–13.

Bennett, T. (1995) *The Birth of the Museum: History, Theory, Politics*, London and New York: Routledge.

Berman, D. (2006) "The Names Database," *Yad Vashem Jerusalem Quarterly Magazine*, vol. 43. Online. Available HTTP: <http://www1.yadvashem.org/about_yad/magazine/magazine_43/data_43/names.html> (accessed 9 November 2008).

Berndt Museum of Anthropology (1998) "Bringing the Photographs Home." Online. Available HTTP: <http://www.berndt.uwa.edu.au/Berndt/action.lasso?-database=Information.FP3&-layout=Show&-token=P> (accessed 9 November 2008).

Berns, M. (2006) "A Case for Being Awake: Buddhism, Collaboration, and Museum Practice," *Curator*, vol. 49, no. 3: 301–11.

Berscheid, E. and Reis, H. (1998) "Attraction and Close Relationships," in D. Gilbert, S. Fiske, and G. Lindzey (eds) *The Handbook of Social Psychology* 4th edn, New York: McGraw-Hill.

Bertman, S. (1991) *Facing Death: Images, Insights, and Interventions*, New York: Taylor & Francis.

Bitgood, S. (1993) "Social Influences on the Visitor Museum Experience," *Visitor Behavior*, vol. 8, no. 3: 4–5.

BLiP Research (2007) *Children's Museum of Manhattan (CMOM) Shelter Program Replicable Curriculum Handbook*. Online. Available HTTP: <http://www.childrensmuseums.org/docs/cmom%20Shelter20Program%20.pdf> (accessed 4 July 2008).

Body Worlds (2007) "Body Worlds 2 & Breathe California Pair Up for Some 'Ash Kicking,'" *Bio-Medicine*. Online. Available HTTP: <http://www.bio-medicine.org/medicine-news-1/BODY-WORLDS-2--26-Breathe-California-Pair-Up-for-Some-Ash-Kicking-5645-1/> (accessed 27 January 2009).

Bose, A. (1983) *Mobile Science Exhibition*, New Delhi: United Nations Educational, Scientific and Cultural Organization.

Boswell, G. and Wedge, P. (2002) *Imprisoned Fathers and their Children*, London: Jessica Kingsley.

Bowen, G. (1991) *Navigating the Marital Journey. MAP: A Corporate Support Program for Couples*, New York: Praeger.

Bowen, G. and Kilpatrick, A. (1995) "Marriage/Partners," in R. Edwards (ed.) *Encyclopedia of Social Work* 19th edn, Washington, DC: National Association of Social Workers.

Boylan, P. (1992) "Ecomuseums and the New Museology," *Museums Journal*, vol. 92, no. 4: 29–30.

Brinig, H. and O'Donnell, J. (1999) "The Children's Museum: An Oasis for Troubled Families," *Hand to Hand*, vol. 13, no. 1: 1–2, 7.

Brodeur, S. (2005) "Treating Families Coping with Chronic Illness: An Evaluation of the 'Living Well' Program," unpublished doctoral dissertation, Virginia Commonwealth University.

Bruce, J. and Tilney, P. (1991) *Family Treasures: Project Guidelines for Teachers, Students, and Quebec*, Hull, Quebec: Canadian Museum of Civilization.

Bruner, J. (1990) *Acts of Meaning*, Cambridge, MA: Harvard University Press.

Buchholz, E.S. (2000) "Echoes of Quietude: Alonetimes in Museums," *Journal of Museum Education*, vol. 25, no. 1–2: 3–8.

Burleson, B. (2003) "The Experience and Effects of Emotional Support: What the Study of Cultural and Gender Differences Can Tell Us About Close Relationships, Emotion, and Interpersonal Communication," *Personal Relationships*, vol. 10, no. 1: 1–23.

Burleson, B., Metts, S. and Kirch, M. (2000) "Communication in Close Relationships," in C. Hendrick and S. Hendrick (eds) *Close Relationships: A Sourcebook*, Thousand Oaks, CA: Sage Publications, Inc.

Burns Owens Partnership (2005) *New Directions in Social Policy: Developing the Evidence Base for Museums, Libraries and Archives in England*, London: Museums, Libraries and Archives Council.

Burton, C. and Griffin, J. (2008) "More Than a Museum? Understanding How Small Museums Contribute to Social Capital in Regional Communities," *Asia Pacific Journal of Arts and Cultural Management*, vol. 5, no. 1: 314–32.

Bushara, L. (2009) Personal communication (21 May 2009).

Cadena, C. (2007) "Therapeutic Benefits of Art Therapy in Children." Online. Available HTTP: <http://www.associatedcontent.com/article/310550/therapeutic_benefits_of_art_therapy.html?singlepage=true&cat=25> (accessed 13 October 2008).

Camargo-Moro, F. (1981) "Riches of the Psyche," *Museum*, vol. 33, no. 3: 166–8.

Cameron, D.F. (1972) "The Museum: A Temple or the Forum," *Journal of World History*, vol. 14, no. 1: 189–202.

Capriccioso, R. (2008) "Leaders Meet to Discuss Reconciliation," *Indian Country Today*. Online. Available HTTP: <http://www.indiancountrytoday.com/home/content/35159224.html> (accessed 11 December 2008).

Carles, M. (2002) "Universum: Non-Formal Sexual and HIV/AIDS Education," International Conference on AIDS, 7–12 July 2002. Abstract number G12641. Online. Available HTTP: <http://gateway.nlm.nih.gov/MeetingAbstracts/ma?f=102255186.html> (accessed 17 July 2008).

Carnegie, E. (1992) "Women's Pictures," *Scottish Museum News*, vol. 8, no. 1: 8–9.

Carr, D. (2006) *A Place Not a Place: Reflection and Possibility in Museums and Libraries*, Lanham, MD: AltaMira Press.

Cartmill, R. and Day, L. (1997) "Prevention of Substance Abuse: Can Museums Make a Difference?" *Curator*, vol. 40, no. 3: 197–210.

Casey, D. (2001) "Museums as Agents for Social and Political Change," *Curator*, vol. 44, no. 3: 230–6.

Chapman, S. (1998) "The Power of Reminiscence," *Alberta Museums Review*, vol. 24, no. 2: 40–3.

Chavers, M. (2008) "Saving States' Historic Jewels," *State News*, vol. 51, no. 3: 19–21.

Cheetham, J. (1992) "Evaluating Social Work Effectiveness," *Research on Social Work Practice*, vol. 2, no. 3: 265–87.

Chien, S. and Wu, G. (2008) "The Strategies of Fire Prevention on Residential Fire in Taipei," *Fire Safety Journal*, vol. 43, no. 1: 71–6.

Chinkin, C. (2001) "Women's International Tribunal on Japanese Military Sexual Slavery," *The American Journal of International Law*, vol. 95, no. 2: 335–41.

Choate, J.H. (1917) "Address of Joseph H. Choate: At the Opening of the Museum Building March 30, 1880," *The Metropolitan Museum of Art Bulletin*, vol. 12, no. 6: 126–9.

Clark, A. and Wexler, G. (2008) "Queer Collections Appear: Oregon's Wedding Album," *Museums & Social Issues*, vol. 3, no. 1: 115–24.

Clifford, J. (1988) "Objects and Selves: An Afterward," in G.W. Stocking, Jr. (ed.) *Objects and Others: Essays on Museums and Material Culture*, Madison, WI: University of Wisconsin Press.

Clow, A. and Fredhoi, C. (2006) "Normalisation of Salivary Cortisol Levels and Self-Report Stress by a Brief Lunchtime Visit to an Art Gallery by London City Workers," *Journal of Holistic Healthcare*, vol. 3, no. 2: 29–32.

Coelho, A. (2008) "Shut in Mumbai, Sex Museum Heads to Goa," *Mid-Day*. Online. Available HTTP: <http://www.mid-day.com/news/2008/jul/300708SexMuseum.htm> (accessed 14 September 2008).

Cole, H., Cole, A.S. and Cole, H. (1884) *Fifty Years of Public Work of Sir Henry Cole, K.C.B., Accounted for in his Deeds, Speeches and Writings, Volume 2*, London: George Bell and Sons.

Collins, N. (2006) "Playmates: Learning Through Play. A New Look at Museums as Head Start Partners." Washington DC: Unpublished report presented to the Office of Head Start/Institute of Museum and Library Services, Washington, DC.

Cone, C. and Kendall, K. (1978) "Space, Time and Family Interaction: Visitor Behavior at the Science Museum of Minnesota," *Curator,* vol. 21, no. 3: 245–58.

Connolly, K. (2007) "Museum of Broken Relationships Opens," *The Guardian,* 29 October 2007. Online. Available HTTP: <http://www.guardian.co.uk/world/2007/oct/29/artnews.germany> (accessed 3 August 2008).

Conwill, K. and Roosa, A. (2003) "Cultivating Community Connections," *Museum News,* vol. 82, no. 3: 41–7.

Corlis, R. and Steptoe, S. (2004) "The Marriage Savers," *Time Magazine,* January 19, 2004. Online. Available HTTP: <http://www.time.com/time/subscriber/covers/1101040119/the_marriage_savers_doe01a.html> (accessed 15 September 2008).

Correctional Association of New York (2007) *Women in Prison Project: Imprisonment and Families Fact Sheet,* New York: Correctional Association of New York.

Crooke, E. (2007) *Museums and Community: Ideas, Issues and Challenges,* London and New York: Routledge.

Crosby, J. (1989) "Museum Tours in Genogram Construction: A Technique for Facilitating Recall of Negative Affect," *Contemporary Family Therapy,* vol. 11, no. 4: 247–58.

Crow, K. (2001) "On a Site of Terror and Death, Survivors Find a Role," *The New York Times,* 2 May 2001: H6.

Csikszentmihalyi, M. (1993) "Why We Need Things," in S. Lubar and W.D. Kingery (eds) *History From Things: Essays on Material Culture,* Washington, DC: Smithsonian Institution Press.

Csikszentmihalyi, M. and Rochberg-Halton, E. (1981*) The Meaning of Things: Domestic Symbols and the Self,* Cambridge: Cambridge University Press.

Cunanan, A. (2001) *Leprosy History.* Online. Available HTTP: <http://www.leprosyhistory.org/cgi-bin/showdetails.pl?ID=47&type=Archive> (accessed 1 June 2008).

Cuno, J. (1997) "Whose money? Whose power? Whose art history?" *The Art Bulletin,* vol. 79, no. 1: 6–9.

Dadian, M. (2005) *Exhibition on HIV and AIDS Opens at Kenya's National Museum.* Online. Available HTTP: <http://www.fhi.org/en/CountryProfiles/Kenya/res_kenyamuseum.htm> (accessed 13 March 2007).

Daifuku, H. (1965) "An Experimental Mobile Museum for Tropical Africa," *Museum,* vol. 18, no.3: 126–9.

Daleiden, S. (2007) "Suzanne Lacy's Stories of Work & Survival: Behind Glass Doors," *WACK! Art and the Feminist Revolution.* Online. Available HTTP: <http://www.moca.org/wack/?p=246> (accessed 28 February 2009).

Daly, S. (2005) *Social Capital and the Cultural Sector: Literature Review Prepared for the Department of Culture, Media and Sport,* London: Centre for Civil Society.

Dana, J. (1917) *The New Museum,* Woodstock, VT: The Elm Tree Press.

David, P., Bourret, E., Dickinson, P., Goldhar, J., Sanders, A. and Vandelman, A. (2001) "Therapeutic Use of a Museum: A Holocaust Exhibit," *If Not Now E-Journal,* vol. 2, no. 1. Online. Available HTTP: <http://www.baycrest.org/If_Not_Now/Volume_2_Winter_2001> (accessed 5 June 2008).

Davis, L., Larkin, L. and Graves, S. (2002) "Intergenerational Learning Through Play," *International Journal of Early Childhood,* vol. 34, no. 2: 42–9.

Davis, O. Jr., (2001) "In Pursuit of Historical Empathy," in O. Davis, E.Yaeger, and S. Foster (eds) *Historical Empathy and Perspective Taking in the Social Studies,* Lanham, MD: Rowman & Littlefield Publishers, Inc.

Davis, P. (1999) *Ecomuseums: A Sense of Place,* London and New York: Leicester University Press/Continuum.

—— (2004) "Ecomuseums and the Democratization of Japanese Museology," *International Journal of Heritage Studies*, vol. 10, no.1: 93–110.

—— (2005) "Places, 'Cultural Touchstones' and the Ecomuseum," in G. Corsane (ed.) *Heritage, Museums and Galleries: An Introductory Reader*, London and New York: Routledge.

Davison, F. and Orchard, K. (2008) *Renaissance London: Keeping Cultures. Report on the London Museums Hub Refugee Heritage Project 2004–2008*, London: London Museums Hub.

Daykin, N., Byrne, R., Soteriou, T. and O'Connor, S. (2008) "Review: The Impact of Art, Design, and Environment in Mental Healthcare: A Systematic Review of the Literature," *The Journal of the Royal Society for the Promotion of Health*, vol. 128, no. 2: 85–94.

Deane, K., Fitch, M. and Carman, M. (2000) "An Innovative Art Therapy Program for Cancer Patients," *Canadian Oncology Nursing Journal*, vol. 10, no. 4: 147–57.

Debenedetti, S. (2003) "Investigating the Role of Companions in the Art Museum Experience," *International Journal of Arts Management*, vol. 5, no 3: 52–63.

Deci, E.L. and Ryan, R.M. (2000) "The 'What' and 'Why' of Goal Pursuits: Human Needs and the Self-Determination of Behavior," *Psychological Inquiry*, vol. 11, no. 4: 227–68.

DeLauro, R. (2005) "The Good, the Bad, and the Ugly – Social Work's Image on Screen," *Social Work Today*, vol. 5, no. 2: 18.

Delin, A. (2002) "Buried in the Footnotes: The Absence of Disabled People in the Collective Imagery of our Past," in R. Sandell (ed.) *Museums, Society, Inequity*, London and New York: Routledge.

Demanchick, S. (2009) Personal communication (7 June 2009).

Department for Culture, Media and Sport (2000) *Centres for Social Change: Museums, Galleries, and Archives for All*, London: Department for Culture, Media, and Sport.

de Varine, H. (2005) "Decolonising Museology," *ICOM NEWS*, vol. 58, no. 3: 3.

Dick, L. (2001) "Brief Group Art Therapy for Acute Psychiatric Inpatients," *American Journal of Art Therapy*, vol. 39, no. 4: 108–12.

Dierking, L., Luke, J., Foat, K. and Adelman, L. (2001) "The Family and Free-Choice Learning," *Museum News*, vol. 80, no. 6: 38–43, 67.

Dilevko, J. and Gottlieb, L. (2004) *The Evolution of Library and Museum Partnerships*. Westport, CT: Libraries Unlimited.

District Six Museum (2005) "About the Museum." Online. Available HTTP: <http://www.districtsix.co.za/frames.htm> (accessed 28 February 2009).

Dodd, J. (2002) "Museums and the Health of the Community," in R. Sandell (ed.) *Museums, Society, Inequality*, London and New York: Routledge.

Dodd, J. and Sandell, R. (eds) (2001) *Including Museums: Perspectives on Museums, Galleries, and Social Inclusion*, Leicester: Research Centre for Museums and Galleries, Department of Museum Studies.

Dodd, J., O'Riain, H., Hooper-Greenhill, E. and Sandell, R. (2002) *A Catalyst for Change: The Social Impact of the Open Museum*, Leicester: Research Centre for Museums and Galleries and Heritage Lottery Fund.

Dodd, J., Sandell, R., Jolly, D. and Jones, C. (2008) *Rethinking Disability Representation in Museums and Galleries*, Leicester: Research Centre for Museums and Galleries.

Doering, Z. and Pekarik, A. (1997) "Questioning the Entrance Narrative," *Journal of Museum Education*, vol. 21, no. 3: 20–2.

Dolev, J., Friedlaender, L. and Braverman, I. (2001) "Use of Fine Art to Enhance Visual Diagnostic Skills," *Journal of the American Medical Association*, vol. 286, no. 9: 1020.

Draper, L. (1984) "Friendship and the Museum Experience: The Interrelationship of Social Ties and Learning," Ph.D. Dissertation, University of California.

Dubinsky, L. (2006) "In Praise of Small Cities: Cultural Life in Kamloops, BC," *Canadian Journal of Communication*, vol. 31, no. 1: 85–106.

Duncan, C. (1995) *Civilizing Rituals: Inside Public Art Museums*, London and New York: Routledge.

Dyaram, L. and Kamalanabhan, T. (2005) "Unearthed: The Other Side of Group Cohesiveness," *Journal of Social Sciences*, vol. 10, no. 3: 185–90.

East Sussex County Council (2004) "East Sussex Scheme Tackles Unemployment the Bronze Age Way," East Sussex County Council. Online. Available HTTP: <http://www.eastsussex.gov.uk/yourcouncil/pressoffice/pressreleases/2004/05/04167th.htm> (accessed 28 February 2008).

Elder, N., Tobias, B., Luceo-Criswell, A. and Goldenhar, L. (2006) "The Art of Observation: Impact of a Family Medicine and Art Museum Partnership on Student Education," *Medical Student Education*, vol. 38, no. 6: 393–8.

Elkins, J. (2001) *Pictures and Tears: A History of People Who Have Cried in Front of Paintings*, London and New York: Routledge.

Eliot, G. (1977) *Middlemarch: An Authoritative Text, Backgrounds, Reviews and Criticism*, edited by B Hornback. New York and London: W.W. Norton & Company, Inc.

Ellenbogen, K., Luke, J. and Dierking, L. (2004) "Family Learning Research in Museums: An Emerging Disciplinary Matrix?" *Science Education*, vol. 88, no. S1: S48–58.

European Committee for Children of Imprisoned Parents (2007) *Who Are We?* Online. Available HTTP: <http://www.eurochips.org/uk_presentation.html> (accessed 10 April 2007).

European Heritage Association (2008) *The Global Love Museum*. Online. Available HTTP: <http://www.globallovemuseum.com> (accessed 30 September 2008).

Fackelmann, K. (2007) "Alzheimer's Program is One from the Art," *USA Today*, 16 October. Online. Available HTTP: <http://www.usatoday.com/news/health/2007-10-16-alzheimers-art_N.htm> (accessed 23 October 2007).

Falk, J. (2006) "An Identity-Centered Approach to Understanding Museum Learning," *Curator*, vol. 49, no. 2: 151–66.

Falk, J.H. and Dierking, L.D. (1992) *The Museum Experience*, Washington, DC: Whalesback Books.

—— (2000) *Learning From Museums: Visitor Experiences and the Making of Meaning*, Walnut Creek, CA: AltaMira Press.

Falk, J., Heimlich, J. and Bronnenkant, K. (2008) "Using Identity-Related Visit Motivations as a Tool for Understanding Adult Zoo and Aquarium Visitor's Meaning Making," *Curator*, vol. 51, no.1: 55–79.

Featherstone, B. (2004) *Family Life and Family Support: A Feminist Analysis*, Basingstoke: Palgrave Macmillan.

Fehr, B. (2000) "The Life Cycle of Friendship," in C. Hendrick and S. Hendrick (eds) *Close Relationships: A Sourcebook*, Thousand Oaks, CA: Sage Publications.

—— (2004) "Intimacy Expectations in Same-Sex Friendships: A Prototype Interaction-Pattern Model," *Journal of Personality and Social Psychology*, vol. 86, no. 2: 265–84.

Ferri, C.P., Prince, M., Brayne, C., Brodaty, H., Fratiglioni, L., Ganguli, M., Hall, K., Hasegawa, K., Hendrie, H., Huang, Y., Jorm, A., Mathers, C., Menezes, P.R., Rimmer, E., Scazufca, M. and Alzheimer's Disease International (2005) "Global Prevalence of Dementia: A Delphi Census Study," *Lancet*, vol. 366: 2112–17.

Fessenden, F. (2005) "Health Mystery in New York: Heart Disease," *New York Times*, 18 August. Online. Available HTTP: <http://www.nytimes.com/2005/08/18/nyregion/18heart.htm> (accessed 16 May 2008).

Fetterman, D. (2003) "Empowerment Evaluation Strikes a Responsive Chord," in S. Donaldson and M. Scriven (eds) *Evaluating Social Programs and Problems: Visions for the New Millennium*, Mahwah, NJ: Lawrence Erlbaum Associates.

Fischer, D. and Glennon, R. (1993) "Restorative Environments: A Way to Attract and Serve Museum Visitors," *The Sourcebook*, Washington, DC: American Association of Museums.

Follett, M.P. (1918) *The New State – Group Organization, the Solution for Popular Government*, New York: Longman, Green, and Company.

Forster, E. M. (1982) *Alexandria: A History and a Guide*, London: Michael Haag.

Frankl, V. (1981) *Man's Search for Meaning*, New York: Washington Square Press.

Franklin, K. (2000) "Shared Histories: Teaching and Learning at the Judaica Museum in the Bronx," *Museum News*, vol. 79, no. 2: 46–7, 74–5.

Fraser, J. (2006) "Group Identity, Protest, and Evolution Exhibits in America," *Museums & Social Issues*, vol. 1, no. 1: 87–102.

Fraser, M. (ed.) (2004) *Risk and Resilience in Childhood: An Ecological Perspective*, 2nd edn, Washington, DC: NASW Press.

Fraser, J. and Heimlich, J. (2008) "Where Are We?" *Museums & Social Issues*, vol. 3, no. 1: 5–14.

Frederick News-Post (2008) "Woman Donates Family Relics for History Museum," *The Frederick News Post*, 25 September. Online. Available HTTP: <http://www.wtopnews. com/?nid=25&sid=1484938> (accessed 2 December 2008).

Fukuyama, F. (1999) "Social Capital and Civil Society," paper prepared for delivery at the IMF Conference on Second Generation Reform. Online. Available HTTP: <http:// www.imf.org/external/pubs/ft/seminar/1999/reforms/fukuyama.htm> (accessed 7 August 2004).

—— (2002) "Social Capital and Development: The Coming Agenda," *SAIS Review*, vol. 22, no. 1: 23–37.

Furman, R. and Langer, C. (2006) "Managed Care and the Care of the Soul," *Journal of Social Work Values and Ethics*, vol. 3, no. 2: 1–9. Online. Available HTTP: <http://www. socialworker.com/jswve/content/view/39/46> (accessed 7 January 2008).

Gablik, S. (1991) *The Reenchantment of Art*, New York: Thames and Hudson.

Gaouette, N. (2003) "For Arabs, Jews, a Bit of Healing in Shared History," *Christian Science Monitor*, vol. 95, no. 87: 1.

Garvin, C. and Galinsky M. (2008) "Groups," in T. Mizrahi and L. Davis (eds) *Encyclopedia of Social Work,* 20th edn, Washington DC and New York: National Association of Social Workers and Oxford University Press.

General Assembly of the United Nations (1948) *United Nations Universal Declaration of Human Rights.* Online. Available HTTP: <http://www.un.org/en/documents/udhr/> (accessed 16 July 2007).

George, G. (2002) "Historic House Museum Malaise: A Conference Considers What's Wrong," *Forum Journal*, vol. 16, no. 3: 12–19.

Giles, L., Glonek, G., Luszcz, M., and Andrews, G. (2005) "Effect of Social Networks on 10 Year Survival in Very Old Australians: The Australian Longitudinal Study of Aging," *Journal of Epidemiology and Community Health*, vol. 59: 574–9.

Gillis, J. (1997) *A World of Their Own Making: Myth, Ritual, and the Quest for Family Values*, Cambridge, MA: Harvard University Press.

—— (2001) "Your Family in History: Anthropology at Home," *OAH Magazine of History*, vol. 15, no. 4: 31–4.

Gitterman, A. (2004) "The Mutual Aid Model," in C. Garvin, L. Gutierrez and M. Galinsky (eds) *Handbook of Social Work with Groups*, New York and London: The Guilford Press.

Goldenberg, H. and Goldenberg, I. (2002) *Counseling Today's Families*, Pacific Grove, CA: Brooks/Cole.

Gordon, P. (1998) "Community Museums: The Australian Experience," in *Community Museums in Asia: Report on a Training Workshop*, Tokyo: The Japan Foundation Asia Centre.

Gottman, J. (1999) *The Marriage Clinic: A Scientifically Based Marital Therapy*, New York: W.W. Norton and Company.

Graburn, N. (1977) "The Museum and the Visitor Experience," in S. Nichols, M. Alexander, and K. Yellis (eds) *Museum Education Anthology*, Washington, DC: Museum Education Roundtable.

Graceffo, A. (2009) "Remnants of the Khmer Rouge: Genocide as Tourism Part I: The New Cambodian Land Mine Museum," *Foreign Policy Journal*. Online. Available HTTP: <http://www.foreignpolicyjournal.com/2009/02/20/the-new-cambodian-land-mine-museum> (accessed 27 December 2008).

Granito, D. (2008) "Photography Changes the Ways Families Are Formed." Online. Available HTTP: <http://click.si.edu/Story.aspx?story=131> (accessed 6 November 2008).

Gray, M., and Fook, J. (2004) "The Quest for a Universal Social Work: Some Issues and Implications," *Social Work Education,* vol. 23, no. 5: 625–44.

Greene, R. (1994) *Human Behavior Theory: A Diversity Framework*, Hawthorne, NJ: Aldine De Gryter.

Groce, K. (1996) "Their Better Day in Court," *Museum News,* vol. 75, no. 2: 10, 12.

Group for Large Local Authority Museums (GLAMM) (2000) *Museums and Social Inclusion: The GLLAM Report,* Leicester: Research Centre for Museums and Galleries.

Guido, H.F. (1973) *Final Report of the Round Table on the Development and the Role of Museums in the Contemporary World*, Paris: UNESCO. Online. Available HTTP: <http://unesdoc.unesco.org/images/0000/000027/002784EB.pdf> (accessed 7 August 2004).

Gurian, E. (1988) "The Museum as a Socially Responsible Institution," keynote speech for Museums as Socially Responsible Institutions Conference, George Washington University, Washington, DC.

—— (1995a) "Offering Safer Public Spaces," *Journal of Museum Education*, vol. 20, no.3: 14–16.

—— (1995b) "A Blurring of the Boundaries," *Curator*, vol. 38, no.1: 31–7.

—— (2001) "Function Follows Form: How Mixed-Use Spaces in Museums Build Community," *Curator*, vol. 44, no. 1: 87–113.

—— (2006a) "The Opportunity for Social Service, 1991," in E.H. Gurian (ed.) *Civilizing the Museum: The Collected Writings of Elaine Heumann Gurian*, London and New York: Routledge.

—— (2006b) "A Savings Bank for the Soul: About Institutions of Memory and Congregant Spaces, 1996," in E.H. Gurian (ed.) *Civilizing the Museum: The Collected Writings of Elaine Heumann Gurian*, London and New York: Routledge.

Gutierrez, L., DeLois, K. and Glen, M. (1995) "Understanding Empowerment Practice: Building on Practitioner-Based Knowledge," *Families in Society: The Journal of Contemporary Human Services*, vol. 76, no. 9: 534–43.

Habitot Children's Discovery Museum (2008) "Special Campaigns." Online. Available HTTP: http://www.habitot.org/hab/programs_Parent_Education.htm (accessed 18 November 2008).

Hannah, C. (1992) "A Mural on Mental Illness and Wellness," *American Journal of Art Therapy,* vol. 31, no. 2: 34–9.

Hare, I. (2004) "Defining Social Work for the 21st Century: The International Federation of Social Workers' Revised Definition of Social Work," *International Social Work* vol. 47, no. 3: 407–24.

Harris, D. (2007) *New Solutions for House Museums: Ensuring the Long-Term Preservation of America's Historic Houses*, Lanham, MD: AltaMira Press.

Harris, T., and Molock, S. (2000) "Cultural Orientation, Family Cohesion, and Family Support in Suicide Ideation and Depression Among African American College Students," *Suicide and Life-Threatening Behavior*, vol. 30, no. 4: 341–53.

Harrison, M. (1993) "Art and Social Regeneration: The Ancoats Art Museum," *Manchester Region History Review*, vol. 4: 63–72.

Hartman, A. and Laird, J. (1983) *Family-Centered Social Work Practice*, New York: Free Press.

Harvey, A., Garcia-Moreno, C. and Butchart, A. (2007) "Primary Prevention of Intimate-Partner Violence and Sexual Violence: Background Paper for WHO Expert Meeting May 2–3, 2007," Geneva: World Health Organization. Online. Available HTTP: <http://www.who.int/violence_injury_prevention/publications/violence/IPV-SV.pdf> (accessed 9 August 2008).

Harvey, J. and Hansen, A. (2000) "Loss and Bereavement in Close Romantic Relationships," in C. Hendrick and S. Hendrick (eds) *Close Relationships: A Sourcebook*, Thousand Oaks, CA: Sage Publications, Inc.

Haynes, K. and Mickelson, J. (2003) *Affecting Change: Social Workers in the Political Arena*, 5th edn, Boston, MA: Allyn and Bacon.

Hazan, C. and Shaver, P. (1990) "Love and Work: An Attachment-Theoretical Perspective," *Journal of Personality and Social Psychology*, vol. 59, no. 2: 270–80.

Healy, L.M. (2001) *International Social Work: Professional Action in an Interdependent World*, Oxford: Oxford University Press.

—— (2004) "Standards for Social Work Education in the North American and Caribbean Region: Current Realities, Future Issues," *Social Work Education*, vol. 23, no. 5: 581–95.

Heimlich, J. and Koke, J. (2008) "Gay and Lesbian Visitors and Cultural Institutions: Do They Come? Do They Care? A Pilot Study," *Museums & Social Issues*, vol. 3, no. 1: 93–104.

Hein, G.E. (2005) "The Role of Museums in Society: Education and Social Action," *Curator*, vol. 48, no. 4: 357–63.

Helsinki Citizens' Assembly Georgian National Committee (2005) "International Day of Missing Persons." Online. Available HTTP: <http://www.yellowtulips.hcav.am/gnk_events.htm> (accessed 2 December 2008).

Hemming, S. (1992) "Chinese Homes," *Journal of Education in Museums*, vol. 13: 33–4.

Hendrix, H. (2007) *Getting the Love You Want: A Guide for Couples*, 20th anniversary edn, New York: Holt Paperbacks.

Heritage Lottery Fund (2004) *New Life: Heritage and Regeneration*, London: Heritage Lottery Fund.

Herman, A. (2007) "How the Long Arm of the Law is Reaching the Frick Collection," *Museum News*, vol. 86, no. 3: 84–90.

Hewitt, J.P. (1997) *Self and Society: A Symbolic Interactionist Social Psychology*, Needham Heights, MA: Allyn and Bacon.

Highland Council (2006) "Highland Support Group Presents Exhibition in Inverness Museum and Art Gallery," press release. Online. Available HTTP: <http://www.highland.gov.uk/yourcouncil/news/newsreleases/2008/January/2008-01-21-03.htm> (accessed 16 December 2008).

Hilke, D. (1989) "The Family as a Learning System: An Observational Study of Families in Museums," in B. Butler and M. Sussman (eds) *Museum Visits and Activities for Family Life Enrichment*, New York: Haworth Press.

Hirzy, E. (2002) "Mastering Civic Engagement: A Report from the American Association of Museums," in Museums and Communities Project, American Association of Museums, *Mastering Civic Engagement: A Challenge to Museums*, Washington, DC: American Association of Museums.

Hjorth, J. (1994) "Traveling Exhibits: The Swedish Experience," in R. Miles and L. Zavala (eds) *Towards the Museum of the Future: New European Perspectives*, London and New York: Routledge.

Holston, M. (2004) "Paintings of the Psyche," *Americas*, vol. 56, no. 2: 6–13.

Hood, M.G. (1989) "Leisure Criteria of Family Participation and Nonparticipation in Museums," *Marriage and Family Review*, vol. 13: 151–67.

Hooper-Greenhill, E. (1992) *Museums and the Shaping of Knowledge*, London and New York: Routledge.

—— (2000) *Museums and the Interpretation of Visual Culture,* London and New York: Routledge.

Hooper-Greenhill, E., Dodd, J., Moussouri, T., Jones, C., Pickford, C., Herman, C., Morrison, M., Vincent, J. and Toon, R. (2003) "Measuring the Outcomes and Impact of Learning in Museums, Archives, and Libraries: The Learning Impact Research Project End of Project Paper," Leicester: Research Centre for Museums and Galleries. Online. Available HTTP: <http://www.le.ac.uk/ms/research/rcmgpublicationsandprojects.html> (accessed 27 October 2004).

How, N. (2007) "MLA Yorkshire Family Learning Research Findings." Online. Available HTTP: <http://www.mlay-skillsforlife.org.uk/downloads/Family%20Learning%20 Report(Final).pdf> (accessed 11 November 2008).

Hubert, F. (1985) "Ecomuseums in France: Contradictions and Distortions," *Museum*, vol. 37, no. 4: 217–23.

Imber-Black, E. (2005) "Creating Meaningful Rituals for New Life Cycle Transitions," in B. Carter and M. McGoldrick (eds) *The Expanded Family Life Cycle: Individual, Family, and Social Perspective*s, 3rd edn, Boston, MA: Allyn & Bacon.

Impey, O. and MacGregor, A. (2001) "Introduction," in O. Impey and A. MacGregor, (eds) *The Origins of Museums: The Cabinets of Curiosities in Sixteenth and Seventeenth Century Europe*, London: House of Stratus.

Institute for Plastination (2006) "Visitors' Reactions to Body Worlds." Online. Available HTTP: <http://www.bodyworlds.com/en/media/press_kit.html>   (accessed   15   June 2008).

Institute of Museum and Library Services (IMLS) (2005) "Archived Project Profiles: Young at Art Children's Museum." Online. Available HTTP: <http://www.imls.gov/profiles/ sept05.shtm> (accessed 11 September 2008).

—— (2007) "Outcome Based Evaluation Overview." Online. Available HTTP: <http:// www.imls.gov/applicants/basics.shtm> (accessed 18 March 2007).

Institute of Museum Ethics (IME) (2008) "Institute of Museum Ethics." Online. Available HTTP: <http://www.museumethics.org> (accessed 16 May 2009).

International Coalition of Sites of Conscience (2009) Homepage. Online. Available HTTP: <http://www.sitesofconscience.org> (accessed 28 February 2009).

International Commission on Missing Persons (2004) "The ICMP Exhibition 'Voices of the Missing' Held in Novi Sad." Online. Available HTTP: <http://www.ic-mp.org/ press-releases/the-icmp-exhibition-voices-of-the-missing-held-in-novi-sad> (accessed 5 December 2008).

International Council of Museums (ICOM) (2001) "ICOM Statutes". Online. Available HTTP: <http://icom.museum/statutes.html> (accessed 4 August 2004).

—— (2006) "Code of Ethics for Museums." Online. Available HTTP: <http://icom. museum/ethics.html> (accessed 16 July 2007).

International Federation of Social Workers (IFSW) (2000) "Definition of Social Work." Online. Available HTTP: <http://www.ifsw.org/en/p38000208.html> (accessed 16 July 2007).

International Federation of Social Workers and International Association of Schools of Social Work (IFSW and IASSW) (2004) "Ethics in Social Work, Statement of Principles." Online. Available HTTP: <http://www.ifsw.org/en/p38000324.html> (accessed 4 July 2007).

International Museum of Women (2008) "First Money, Then Power: Microcredit Loans Make a Difference for Women." Online. Available HTTP: <http://www.imow.org/wpp/ stories/viewStory?storyId=889> (accessed 4 October 2008).

International Network of Museums for Peace (2005) Homepage. Online. Available HTTP: <http://www.museumsforpeace.org/about-the-international-network-museums-for-peace.htm> (accessed 1 March 2009).

Itkonen, S. (2008) "Abstracts 2/2008," *Museo Quarterly*. Finnish Museums Association. Online. Available HTTP: <http://www.museoliitto.fi/en.php?k=9684> (accessed 30 July 2008).

Jacobs, E., Masson, R. and Harvill, R. (2002) *Group Counseling Strategies and Skills,* 4th edn, Belmont, CA: Brooks/Cole.

James, P. (2005) "Building a Community-Based Identity at Anacostia Museum," in G. Corsane (ed.) *Heritage, Museums and Galleries: An Introductory Reader*, London and New York: Routledge.

Janes, R.R. (2007) "Museums, Corporatism and the Civil Society," *Curator*, vol. 50: 219–37.

Janes, R.R. and Conaty, G.T. (eds) (2005) *Looking Reality in the Eye: Museums and Social Responsibility*, Calgary: University of Calgary Press.

Janis, I. (1972) *Victims of Groupthink: A Psychological Study of Foreign Policy Decisions and Fiascoes,* 2nd edn, Boston, MA: Houghton Mifflin.

Johnson, R. (2007) "A Life Off the Streets in Mexico," *Los Angeles Times*, 5 April 2007: A5.

Jordan, B. (2007) *Social Work and Well-Being,* Dorset: Russell House Publishing.

Jung, C. (1946) "The Psychology of the Transference," in H. Read, M. Fordham, G. Adler and W. McGuire (eds) *The Collected Works of C.G. Jung,* vol. 16, Princeton, NJ: Princeton University Press.

Kahn, E. (2007) "Nothing Down, $0 a Month, Hammer Required," *The New York Times*, 30 August 2007: F1, F6.

Kalessopoulou, D. (2002) "Children's Museums in Hospitals," in R. Sandell (ed.) *Museums, Society, Inequality*, London and New York: Routledge.

Kamerick, M. (2008) "Festival Helps Women Artisans Gain Self-Sufficiency," *New Mexico Business Weekly*, 15 August 2008. Online. Available HTTP: <http://twincities.bizjournals.com/albuquerque/stories/2008/08/11/daily44.html> (accessed 11 September 2008).

Kamien, J. (1985) "Endings: An Exhibit on Death and Loss," *Moral Education Forum*, vol. 10, no. 3–4: 45–50.

Kaplan, R. and Kaplan, S. (1989) *The Experience of Nature: A Psychological Perspective*, New York: Cambridge University Press.

Kaplan, R. and Talbot, J. (1983) "Psychological Benefits of a Wilderness Experience," in I. Altman and J.F. Wohlwill (eds) *Behavior and the Natural Environment*, New York: Plenum.

Kaplan, R., Bardwell, L.V. and Slakter, D.B. (1993) "The Restorative Experience as a Museum Benefit," *Journal of Museum Education,* vol. 18, no. 3: 15–18.

Kaplan, S. (1983) "A Model of Person-Environment Compatibility," *Environment and Behavior,* vol. 15, no. 3: 311–22.

Karger, H. and Stoesz, D. (2002) *American Social Welfare Policy A Pluralist Approach, Fourth edition*, Boston, MA: Allyn & Bacon.

Karls, J. and Wandrei, K. (eds) (1994) *Person-In-Environment System: The PIE Classification System for Social Functioning Problems,* Washington, DC: NASW Press.

Karp, I. and Lavine, S.D. (eds) (1991) *Exhibiting Cultures: The Poetics and Politics of Museum Display*, Washington, DC: Smithsonian Institution Press.

Kaslow, F. (1987) "Marital and Family Therapy," in M. Sussman and S. Steinmetz (eds) *Handbook of Marriage and the Family*, New York: Plenum Press.

Kavanaugh, G. (2000) *Dream Spaces: Memory and the Museum*, London and New York: Leicester University Press.

Kelly, L. (2006) "Measuring the Impact of Museums on Their Communities: The Role of the 21st Century Museum." Paper presented at New Roles and Missions for Museums:

Intercom Conference 2006, Taipei, Taiwan. Online. Available HTTP: <http://www.intercom.museum/documents/1-2Kelly.pdf> (accessed 16 February 2009).

—— (2007) "Visitors and Learners: Adult Museum Visitors' Learning Identities," unpublished doctoral dissertation, University of Technology, Sydney.

Kelly, L., Savage, G., Griffin, J. and Tonkin, S. (2004) *Australian Families Visit Museums,* Sydney and Canberra: Australian Museum and National Museum of Australia.

Kelly, L., Savage, G., Landman, P. and Tonkin, S. (2002) *Energised, Engaged, Everywhere: Older Australians and Museums,* Sydney and Canberra: Australian Museum and National Museum of Australia.

Kernan, M. (1996) "Around the Mall and Beyond," *Smithsonian,* vol. 26, no.10: 26–9.

Kilpatrick, A. (2003) "Levels of Family Need," in A. Kilpatrick and T. Holland (eds) *Working with Families: An Integrative Model by Level of Need,* 3rd edn, Boston, MA: Allyn and Bacon.

Kilpatrick, A. and Holland, T. (eds) (2003) *Working with Families: An Integrative Model by Level of Need,* 3rd edn, Boston, MA: Allyn and Bacon.

Kimmelman, M. (2001) "The Solace in Sharing the Beauty of Great Art and Music; Museum Can Be a Haven From All the Anxiety of Devastating Events," *The New York Times,* 17 September: E1, E3.

Kinard, J.R. (1985) "The Neighbourhood Museum as a Catalyst for Social Change," *Museum,* vol. 37, no. 4: 217–23.

King, D. and Wynne, L. (2004) "The Emergence of 'Family Integrity' in Later Life," *Family Process,* vol. 43, no. 1: 7–21.

Kirst-Ashman, K.K. (2003) *Introduction to Social Work and Social Welfare: Critical Thinking Perspectives,* Pacific Grove, CA: Brooks/Cole.

Knudson, D., Cable, T. and Beck, L. (1995) *Interpretation of Cultural and Natural Resources,* State College, PA: Venture Publishing, Inc.

Koppel, L. (2008) "Mortals Amid the Immortals, Savoring the Romance of Art," *New York Times,* 14 February, B: 3.

Koster, E. and Baumann, S. (2005) "Liberty Science Center in the United States: A Mission Focused on External Relevance," in R. Janes and G. Conaty (eds) *Looking Reality in the Eye: Museums and Social Responsibility,* Calgary: University of Calgary Press.

Koven, S. (1994) "The Whitechapel Picture Exhibitions and the Politics of Seeing," in D. J. Sherman and I. Rogoff (eds) *Museum Culture: Histories, Discourses, Spectacles.* Minneapolis, MN: University of Minnesota Press.

Kraybill, K. and Olivet, J. (2006) *Shelter Health: Essentials of Care for People Living in Shelter,* Nashville, TN: National Healthcare for the Homeless Council.

Kregel, J. and Dean, D. (2002) "Sheltered vs. Supported Employment: A Direct Comparison of Long-Term Earnings Outcomes for Individuals with Cognitive Disabilities," in J. Kregel, D. Dean and P. Wehman (eds) *Achievements and Challenges in Employment Services for People with Disabilities: The Longitudinal Impact of Workplace Supports Monograph,* Richmond, VA: Virginia Commonwealth University.

Kropotkin, P. (1902) *Mutual Aid: A Factor of Evolution,* London: William Heinemann.

Kumashiro, M., Rusbult, C. and Finkel, E. (2008) "Navigating Personal and Relationship Concerns: The Quest for Equilibrium," *Journal of Personality and Social Psychology,* vol. 95, no. 1: 94–111.

Lagiovane, D. (2006) "Study of Dinosaurs and Other Fossils: Part of Plan by Pitt Medical School to Graduate Better Doctors Through Unique Collaboration with Carnegie Museum of Natural History," Press release. Online. Available HTTP: <http://www.upmc.com/MediaRelations/NewsReleases/2006/Pages/StudyFossils.aspx> (accessed 28 February 2008).

LaMarche, G. (2008) "Same Sex Marriage: Culture, Law, and Advocacy on Three Continents," *Atlantic Currents,* 31 July. Online. Available HTTP: <http://atlanticphilanthropies.org/

about/atlantic_currents/archive/same_sex_marriage_culture_law_and_advocacy_on_three_continents> (accessed 16 August 2008).

Lamb, P., Spacey, R. and Thomas, M. (2008) *Renaissance North West: Evaluation of the North West Museum Hub Family Learning Initiatives,* Leicester: National Institute of Adult Continuing Education.

Late, M. (2002) "New Partnership Formed in November: Nation's Museums Team Up with Public Health Community," *The Nation's Health*, vol. 32, no. 10: 3.

Layne, V. (2006) "Keynote Presentation: Empowering Communities: A Focus on South Africa's District Six Museum, New Museum Models – Transforming Communities," 2006 Seminar Series presented by Museums & Galleries NSW and the Museum of Sydney. Online. Available HTTP: <http://mgnsw.org.au/uploaded/MoS206.pdf> (accessed 28 February 2009).

LeBlanc, S. (1999) "The Slender Golden Thread, 100 Years Strong," *Museum News*, vol. 78, no. 6: 49–55, 63.

—— (2008) "Written Testimony by Suzanne LeBlanc, Long Island Children's Museum To the Subcommittee on Healthy Families and Communities Committee on Education and Labor of the U.S. House of Representatives." Submitted 4 September 2008. Online. Available HTTP: <http://edlabor.house.gov/testimony/2008-09-11-SuzanneLeBlanc.pdf> (accessed 16 October 2008).

LeCroy, C. and Stinson, E. (2004) "The Public's Perception of Social Work: Is it What We Think it Is?" *Social Work*, vol. 49, no. 2: 164–74.

Ledesma, R. (2007) "The Urban Los Angeles American Indian Experience: Perspectives from the Field," *Journal of Ethnic & Cultural Diversity in Social Work*, vol. 16, no.1–2: 27–66.

Lee, J. (2001) *The Empowerment Approach to Social Work Practice: Building the Beloved Community,* 2nd edn, New York: Columbia University Press.

Leiba, T. and Weinstein, J. (2003) "Who are the Participants in the Collaborative Process and What Makes Collaboration Succeed or Fail?" in J. Weinstein, C. Whittington and T. Leiba (eds) *Collaboration in Social Work Practice*, London and New York: Jessica Kingsley Publishers.

Leiberich, P., Loew, T., Tritt, K., Lahmann, C. and Nickel, M. (2006) "Body Worlds Exhibition – Visitor Attitudes and Emotions," *Anatomischer Anzeiger*, vol. 188, no. 6: 567–73.

Leinhardt, G. and Knutson, K. (2004) *Listening In on Museum Conversations*, Walnut Creek, CA: AltaMira Press.

L'Engle, M. (1980) *Walking on Water: Reflections on Faith and Art*, Wheaton, IL: H. Shaw.

Lester, S. and Russell, W. (2008) *Play for a Change Summary Report*, London: National Children's Bureau.

Letts, Q. (2007) "Cripes! I'm Not Sure I Wanted to Know That – My Visit to London's First Sex Museum," *Daily Mail*. Online. Available HTTP: <http://www.dailymail.co.uk/femail/article-464897/Cripe-Im-sure-I-wanted-know--visit-Londons-sex-museum.html> (accessed 11 August 2008).

LeVine, R.A. (1973) *Culture, Behavior and Personality*, Chicago, IL: Aldine.

Levinson, D. (ed.) (2004) *Encyclopedia of Homelessness*, Thousand Oaks, CA: Sage.

Lightsey, O. and Sweeney, J. (2008) "Meaning in Life, Emotion-Oriented Coping, Generalized Self-Efficacy, and Family Cohesion as Predictors of Family Satisfaction Among Mothers of Children with Disabilities," *The Family Journal*, vol. 16, no. 3: 212–21.

Linde, C. (1993) *Life Stories: The Creation of Coherence*, New York: Oxford University Press.

Linesch, D. (2004) "Art Therapy at the Museum of Tolerance: Responses to the Life and Work of Friedl Dicker-Brandeis," *The Arts in Psychotherapy*, vol. 31, no. 2: 57–66.

Logan, S., Rasheed, M. and Rasheed, J. (2008) "Family," in T. Mizrahi and L. Davis (eds) *Encyclopedia of Social Work,* 20th edn, Washington, DC and New York: National Association of Social Workers and Oxford University Press.

Lowry, G.D. (2004) "A Deontological Approach to Art Museums and the Public Trust," in J. Cuno (ed.) *Whose Muse? Art Museums and the Public Trust*, Princeton, NJ and Oxford: Princeton University Press.

Luecke, R. and Katz, R. (2003) *Managing Creativity and Innovation*, Boston, MA: Harvard Business School Press.

Maccio, E. (2008) "Marriage and Domestic Partners," in T. Mizrahi and L. Davis (eds) *Encyclopedia of Social Work*, Oxford: Oxford University Press Online. Available HTTP: <http://www.oxford-naswsocialwork.com/entry?entry=t203.e234> (accessed 28 July 2008).

Maines, R.P. and Glynn, J.J. (1993) "Numinous Objects," *The Public Historian*, vol. 15, no. 1: 9–25.

Malt, C. (2005) "Museums, Women, and Empowerment," *ISIM Review*, no. 16: 58.

Maluwa, A. (2006) "The Role of Museums in Addressing Community Needs in the 21st Century." Online. Available HTTP: <http://www.museumsnett.no/alias/HJEMMESIDE/icme/icme2006/maluwa2006.pdf> (accessed 10 January 2009).

Maritime Museum of San Diego (2006) "Team Building Events." Online. Available HTTP: <http://www.sdmaritime.com/PrivateEvents.asp?ContentID=239> (accessed 27 January 2009).

Marsh, C. (1968) "A Neighborhood Museum That Works," *Museum News,* vol. 47, no. 2: 11–16.

Maslow, A. (1943) "A Theory of Human Motivation," *Psychological Review*, vol. 50: 370–96.

McCaffrey, R. (2007) "The Effect of Healing Gardens and Art Therapy on Older Adults with Mild to Moderate Depression," *Holistic Nursing Practice*, vol. 21, no. 2: 79–84.

McCallie, E., Simonsson, E., Gammon, B., Nilsson, K., Lehr, J. and Davies, S. (2007) "Learning to Generate Dialogue: Theory, Practice, and Evaluation," *Museums & Social Issues,* vol. 2, no. 2: 165–87.

McLean, C. (2002) *Creating the Past: Report on a Youth Program at the Royal Museum of Scotland*, Edinburgh: National Museums of Scotland.

McManus, P. (1988) "Good Companions: More on the Social Determination of Learning-Related Behaviour in a Science Museum," *International Journal of Museum Management and Curatorship*, vol. 7, no. 1: 37–44.

McManus, R. (2004) "'Vital Visionaries:' Program Improves Medical Students' Attitudes Toward Elderly," *The NIH Record*, vol. 56, no. 17: 1–2.

McMichael Canadian Art Collection (1996) "Art Therapy at the McMichael." Online. Available HTTP: <http://www.mcmichael.com/art_therapyprog.htm> (accessed 27 January 2004).

Mehalick, C. (2009). Personal communication. (2 January 2009).

Mercer, C. (1998) "Inside and Out," *Reading the Museum Newsletter*, vol. 4, no. 2: 4, 8.

Mercy Corps (2008) "Action Center to End World Hunger, Design in Action, May 29, 2008." Online. Available HTTP: <http://www.actioncenter.org/design-in-action> (accessed 6 June 2008).

Mertens, D. (2003) "The Inclusive View of Evaluation: Visions for the New Millennium," in S. Donaldson and M. Scriven (eds) *Evaluating Social Programs and Problems: Visions for the New Millennium,* Mahwah, NJ: Lawrence Erlbaum Associates.

Meyerson, J. (2008) "Success with Couples Therapy – A Step-by-Step Approach," *Social Work Today*, vol. 8, no. 3: 16.

Michalchik, V., Llorente, C., Lundh, P. and Remold, J. (2008) "A Place to Be Your Best: Youth Outcomes in the Computer Clubhouse." Menlo Park, CA: Center for Technology in Learning, SRI International.

Middleman, R. and Wood, G. (1990) "From Social Group Work to Social Work with Groups," *Social Work with Groups*, vol. 14, no. 3/4: 75–86.

Midgely, J. (1981) *Professional Imperialism: Social Work in the Third World*, London: Heinemann.

Miller, J. (1991) "The Development of Women's Sense of Self," in J.V. Jordan, A.G. Kaplan, J.B. Miller, I.P. Stiver and J.L. Surrey (eds) *Women's Growth in Connection: Writings from the Stone Center*, New York: The Guilford Press.

Moore, K. (1997) *Museums and Popular Culture*, London and Washington: Cassell.

Morris, J., Orchard, K. and Davison, F. (2007) "Refugee Heritage Project: Report on the London Museum's Hub Project to Record Refugee Heritage, 2004–06." Online. Available HTTP: <http://www.mlalondon.org.uk/uploads/documents/Refugee_Heritage_Report.pdf> (accessed 16 May 2008).

Morrissey, K.A. (2002) "Pathways Among Objects and Museum Visitors," in S.G. Paris (ed.) *Perspectives on Object-Centered Learning in Museums*, Mahwah, NJ: Lawrence Erlbaum Associates.

Morry, M. (2005) "Allocentrism and Friendship Satisfaction: The Mediating Roles of Disclosure and Closeness," *Canadian Journal of Behavioural Science*, vol. 37, no. 3: 211–22.

Moussouri, T. (2007) "Implications of the Social Model of Disability," *Visitor Studies*, vol. 10, no. 1: 90–106.

Mower, J. (2008) "Celebrity Shots Help Adoption Scheme," *BBC News*, London. Online. Available HTTP: <http://news.bbc.co.uk/2/hi/uk_news/england/london/7362798.stm> (accessed 5 December 2008).

Mueller, W. (2001) "Mathematical *Wunderkammern*," *The American Mathematical Monthly*, vol. 108, no. 9: 785–96.

Mukherjee, K. (2007) "Sex Museum Makes HIV Lessons Fun," Reuters. Online. Available HTTP <http://www.reuters.com/article/oddlyEnoughNews/idUSDEL6107920070209> (accessed 22 August 2008).

Mumola, C.J. (2000) *Incarcerated Parents and their Children*, Washington, DC: Bureau of Justice Statistics.

Murray, N. (1999) "Sharing the Story of the Movement: The Project HIP-HOP Experience," *Radical Teacher*, no. 57: 8–15.

Museum of Broken Relationships (2007) Homepage. Online. Available HTTP: <http://www.brokenships.com/about.php> (accessed 9 August 2008).

Museum of Modern Art (2007) "The MoMA Alzheimer's Project: Making Art Accessible to People with Dementia: A Guide for Museums." Online. Available HTTP: <http://www.moma.org/docs/learn/GuideforMuseums.pdf> (accessed 14 September 2008).

Museums, Libraries and Archives Council (MLA) (2004) "Inspiring Learning for All: GLO." Online. Available HTTP: <http://www.mla.gov.uk> (accessed 9 November 2006).

Musser, G. (2005) "The Climax of Humanity," *Scientific American*, vol. 293, no. 3: 44–7.

National Association of Social Workers (NASW) (1973) *Standards for Social Service Manpower*, Washington, DC: National Association of Social Workers.

—— (1996) *Code of Ethics for Social Workers*, Washington, DC: NASW.

National Institute on Aging (2004) "Vital Visionary Collaboration". Online. Available HTTP: <http://www.nia.nih.gov/ResearchInformation/ConferencesAndMeetings/Vital+Visionary+Collaboration.htm> (accessed 5 July 2008).

National Museum of Australia (2008) "National Museum to Screen National Apology." Online. Available HTTP: <http://www.nma.gov.au/media/media_releases_index/national_museum_to_screen_national_apology> (accessed 11 December 2008).

National Museums Liverpool (2006) "Gay, Lesbian, Transgender and Bisexual Singles Night." Press Release, 3 August 2006. Online. Available HTTP: <http://www.liverpoolmuseums.org.uk/mediacentre/displayrelease.aspx?id=572> (accessed 4 July 2008).

—— (2008) "Living It Up: The Tower Block Story." Online. Available HTTP: <http://www.liverpoolmuseums.org.uk/mol/exhibitions/livingitup/> (accessed 16 September 2008).

National Museums Scotland (NMS) and Rural and Urban Training Scheme (RUTS) (2007) *Wheels of Time,* Edinburgh: NMS and RUTS.

National Youth Violence Prevention Resource Center (2007) "Community-Based Collaboration Fact Sheet," Rockville, MD: National Youth Violence Prevention Resource Center. Online. Available HTTP: <http://www.safeyouth.org/scripts/facts/community.asp> (accessed 4 July 2007).

Neil, S. (2007) "Putting a Face on Children Awaiting Adoption," *The Boston Globe*, 19 April. Online. Available HTTP: <http://www.boston.com/news/local/articles/2007/04/19/putting_a_face_on_children_awaiting_adoption> (accessed 9 November 2008).

Netting, F., Kettner, P. and McMurtry, S. (2004) *Social Work Macro Practice,* 3rd edn, Boston, MA: Allyn and Bacon.

New Freedom Commission on Mental Health (2003) *Achieving the Promise: Transforming Mental Health Care in America, Final Report,* Rockville, MD: Department of Health and Human Services.

Newman, A. (2005a) "Understanding the Social Impact of Museums, Galleries and Heritage Through the Concept of Capital," in G. Corsane (ed.) *Heritage, Museums and Galleries: An Introductory Reader,* London and New York: Routledge.

—— (2005b) "'Social Exclusion Zone' and 'The Feelgood Factor,'" in G. Corsane (ed.) *Heritage, Museums and Galleries: An Introductory Reader,* London and New York: Routledge.

Newman, A. and McLean, F. (2004) "Capital and the Evaluation of the Museum Experience," *International Journal of Cultural Studies,* vol. 7, no. 4: 480–98.

—— (2006) "The Impact of Museums Upon Identity," *International Journal of Heritage Studies,* vol. 12, no. 1: 49–68.

Nicholls, J. (2009) "The Cambodian Landmine Museum and Children's Refuge." Online. Available HTTP: <http://www.allappys.com/cambreport.doc> (accessed 27 January 2009).

Northen, H. and Kurland, R. (2001) *Social Work with Groups,* 3rd edn, New York: Columbia University Press.

Ogbu, J. (1995) "The Influence of Culture on Learning and Behavior," in J. Falk and L.D. Dierking (eds) *Public Institutions for Personal Learning,* Washington, DC: American Association of Museums.

Olmi, G. (2001) "Science–Honour–Metaphor: Italian Cabinets of the Sixteenth and Seventeenth Centuries," in O. Impey and A. Macgregor (eds) *The Origins of Museums: The Cabinets of Curiosities in Sixteenth and Seventeenth Century Europe,* London: House of Stratus.

Olson, D. (2000) "Complex Model of Marital and Family Systems," *Journal of Family Therapy,* vol. 22, no. 2: 144–67.

Olson, D., Sprenkle, D. and Russell, C. (1979) "Circumplex Model of Marital and Family Systems: Cohesion and Adaptability Dimensions, Family Types, and Clinical Applications," *Family Process,* vol. 18, no. 1: 3–28.

O'Neill, M. (1995) "Curating Feelings: Issues of Identity in Museums," *Canadian Art Gallery/Art Museum Educators,* January: 18–30.

—— (2006) "Essentialism, Adaptation and Justice: Towards a New Epistemology of Museums," *Museum Management and Curatorship,* vol. 21: 95–116.

Ornish, D. (1998) *Love and Survival: The Scientific Basis for the Healing Power of Intimacy,* New York: HarperCollins.

Osborn, E.C. (1953) *Manual of Travelling Exhibitions,* Paris: United Nations Educational, Scientific and Cultural Organization.

Osbourne, S. and Brown, K. (2005) *Managing Change and Innovation in Public Service Organizations,* London and New York: Routledge Press.

Packer, J. (2006) "Learning for Fun: The Unique Contribution of Educational Leisure Experiences," *Curator,* vol. 49, no. 3: 329–44.

—— (2008) "Beyond Learning: Exploring Visitors' Perceptions of the Value and Benefits of Museum Experiences," *Curator*, vol. 51, no. 1: 33–54.

Paris, S.G. and Mercer, M.J. (2002) "Finding Self in Objects: Identity Exploration in Museums," in G. Leinhardt, K. Crowley, and K. Knutson (eds) *Learning Conversations in Museums*, Mahwah, NJ: Lawrence Erlbaum Associates.

Patel, U. (2008) "Some Turn to Morikami for Healing," *South Florida Sun-Sentinel*. Online. Available HTTP: <http://www.sun-sentinel.com/features/home/sfl-bocagarden,0,6034348,print.story> (accessed 10 April 2008).

Patton, M. (1998) "Intergenerational Play: Parents and Children," in D. Fromberg and D. Bergen (eds) *Play From Birth to Twelve and Beyond: Contexts, Perspectives, and Meanings*, London and New York: Routledge.

Pearce, S.M. (1995) *On Collecting: An Investigation into Collecting in the European Tradition*, London and New York: Routledge.

Pearlin, L. and Johnson, J. (1977) "Marital Status, Life Strains and Depression," *American Sociological Review*, vol. 42, no. 5: 704–15.

Pedretti, E. (2004) "Perspectives on Learning Through Research on Critical Issues-Based Science Center Exhibitions," *Science Education*, vol. 88, no. S1: S34–47.

Pekarik, A., Doering, Z. and Karns, D. (1999) "Exploring Satisfying Experiences in Museums," *Curator*, vol. 42, no. 2: 152–73.

Perin, C. (1992) "The Communicative Circle: Museums as Communities," in I. Karp, C. Kreamer and S. Levine (eds.) *Museums and Communities: The Politics of Public Culture*, Washington, DC: Smithsonian Institution Press.

Petersilia, J. (2003) *When Prisoners Come Home: Parole and Prisoner Reentry*, New York: Oxford University Press.

Pettigrew, T. and Tropp, L. (2006) "A Meta-Analytic Test of Intergroup Contact Theory," *Journal of Personality and Social Psychology*, vol. 90, no. 5: 751–83.

Pieschel, J. (2005) "Telling It Like It Is: The Calgary Police Service Interpretive Centre," in R. Janes and G. Conaty (eds) *Looking Reality in the Eye: Museums and Social Responsibility*, Calgary: University of Calgary Press.

Plath, D. (2006) "Evidence-Based Practice: Current Issues and Future Directions," *Australian Social Work,* vol. 59, no. 1: 56–72.

Pointe, S. (2005) "Is Art Good for You?" in R. Janes and G. Conaty (eds) *Looking Reality in the Eye: Museums and Social Responsibility*, Calgary: University of Calgary Press.

Polakow, V. and Guillean, C. (eds) (2001) *International Perspectives on Homelessness*, Westport, CT: Greenwood Press.

Poulet, D. (1994) "Identity as Self-Discovery: The Ecomuseum in France," in D.J. Sherman and I. Rogoff (eds) *Museum Culture: Histories, Discourses, Spectacles*, Minneapolis, MN: University of Minnesota Press.

Prager, K. (1995) *The Psychology of Intimacy*, New York: Guilford.

—— (2000) "Intimacy in Personal Relationships," in C. Hendrick and S. Hendrick (eds) *Close Relationships: A Sourcebook*, Thousand Oaks, CA: Sage Publications, Inc.

Pratt, C., Gill, K., Barrett, N. and Roberts, M. (2002) *Psychiatric Rehabilitation*, San Diego, CA: Academic Press.

Presto, S. (2008) "Weaving Project Revives Traditions, Empowers Kurdish Women," *Voice of America News*, 17 June. Online. Available HTTP: <http://www.voanews.com/english/archive/2008-06/2008-06-17-voa68.cfm?CFID=46384252&CFTOKEN=51690278> (accessed 16 September 2008).

Providence Children's Museum (2007) "Partnering with the Child Welfare System: A Tool Kit." Online. Available HTTP: <http://www.childrensmuseums.org/programs/providencetoolkit.htm> (accessed 24 September 2008).

Putnam, R.D. (1995) "Bowling Alone: America's Declining Social Capital," *The Journal of Democracy,* vol. 6, no. 1: 65–78.

174 Bibliography

—— (2000) *Bowling Alone: The Collapse and Revival of American Community*, New York: Simon and Shuster.

Randi Korn & Associates, Inc. (1999) *United States Holocaust Memorial Museum: Evaluation of School Programs*, Washington, DC: United States Holocaust Memorial Museum.

—— (2007a) *Front-End Evaluation: Interpretative Planning of Ellis Island's Hospital and Medical Facilities*, New York: Save Ellis Island.

—— (2007b) *Summative Evaluation: Ferry Building Exhibition*, New York: Save Ellis Island.

—— (2007c) *Audience Research: Telephone Interviews with Visitors*, New York: Lower East Side Tenement Museum.

Rayner, A. (2008) "Amora London: The Art of Seduction Explored," PRWeb Press Release *Newswire*. Online. Available HTTP: <http://www.prwebdirect.com/releases/2008/prweb1049584.htm> (accessed 5 September 2008).

Reilly, J., Ring, J. and Duke, L. (2005) "Visual Thinking Strategies: A New Role for Art in Medical Education," *Family Medicine*, vol. 37 no. 4: 250–2.

Research Centre for Museums and Galleries (2001) *Small Museums & Social Inclusion*, Leicester: Research Centre for Museums and Galleries.

Richter, K. (2007) "Homeschoolers Are Always Late," *Museum News*, vol. 86, no. 2: 47–51.

Riis, J.A. (1902) *The Battle with the Slum*, New York: The Macmillan Company.

Ripley, D. (1969) *The Sacred Grove: Essays on Museums*, Washington, DC: Smithsonian Institution Press.

Robbins, S., Chatterjee, P. and Canda, E. (2006) *Contemporary Human Behavior Theory: A Critical Perspective for Social Work*, 2nd edn, Boston, MA: Pearson, Allyn & Bacon.

Roberts, L.C. (1997) *From Knowledge to Narrative: Educators and the Changing Museum*, Washington, DC: Smithsonian Institution Press.

Robertson, J. and Law, A. (2005) "Stigma, Identity, and Human Rights," *International Journal of Leprosy*, vol. 73, no. 4: 283–97.

Rodenhauser, P., Strickland, M. and Gambala, C. (2004) "Arts-Related Activities Across U.S. Medical Schools: A Follow-Up Study," *Teaching and Learning in Medicine*, vol. 16, no. 3: 233–9.

Rooney, R. (ed.) (2009) *Strategies for Work with Involuntary Clients*, 2nd edn, New York: Columbia University Press.

Rose, M.E. (1993) "The Manchester University Settlement in Ancoats, 1895–1909," *Manchester Region History Review*, vol. 7: 55–62.

Rounds, J. (2006) "Doing Identity Work in Museums," *Curator*, vol. 49, no. 2: 133–50.

Rubin, B. (2008) "Cool Your Heels in U.S. Museums This Summer." Online. Available HTTP: <http://www.frommers.com/articles/5264.html> (accessed 24 October 2008).

Ryff, C. and Singer, B. (2001) *Emotion, Social Relationships, and Health*. New York: Oxford University Press.

Saleebey, D. (ed.) (2002) *The Strengths Perspective in Social Work Practice*, 3rd edn, Boston, MA: Allyn and Bacon.

Saley, M. (1976) "Action to Help the Blind and Physically Handicapped, Niger National Museum, Niamey," *Museum*, vol. 28, no. 4: 210–11.

Sampson, C. (2008) "Civil Rights Exhibit Powered by Family Memories." Online. Available HTTP: <http://blog.uwgb.edu/inside/index.php/featured/leading-learning/10/23/learning-history-pullman-porter-story> (accessed 22 November 2008).

Sandell, R. (2002) "Museums and the Combating of Social Inequality: Roles, Responsibilities, Resistance," in R. Sandell (ed.) *Museums, Society, Inequality*. London and New York: Routledge.

—— (2007) *Museums, Prejudice and the Reframing of Difference*, London and New York: Routledge.

Santayana, G. (1905). *The Life of Reason, or the Phases of Human Progress.* New York: George Scribner's Sons.

Schriver, J. (2004) *Human Behavior and the Social Environment: Shifting Paradigms in Essential Knowledge for Social Work Practice*, 4th edn, Boston, MA: Pearson, Allyn & Bacon.

Schwartz, W. (1971) "On the Use of Groups in Social Work Practice," in W. Schwartz and S. Zalba (eds) *The Practice of Group Work*, New York: Columbia University Press.

—— (1976) "Between Client and System: The Mediating Function," in R. Roberts and H. Northen (eds) *Theories of Social Work with Groups*, New York: Columbia University Press.

Schwarzer, M. (2006) *Riches, Rivals, & Radicals: 100 Years of Museums in America*, Washington, DC: American Association of Museums.

Schwarzer, M. and Koke, J. (2007) "Talking the Talk: A Call to Action," *Museums & Social Issues*, vol. 2, no. 2: 151–6.

Scopelliti, M. and Giuliani, M.V. (2005) "Restorative Environments in Later Life: An Approach to Well-Being from the Perspective of Environmental Psychology," *Journal of Housing for the Elderly*, vol. 19, no. 3–4: 203–26.

Scott, C. (2002) "Measuring Social Value," in R. Sandell (ed.) *Museums, Society, Inequality*, London and New York: Routledge.

—— (2006) "Museums: Impact and Value," *Cultural Trends*, vol. 15, no. 57: 45–75.

Scottish Museums Council (2000) *Museums and Social Justice*, Edinburgh: Scottish Museums Council. Online. Available HTTP: <http://www.scottishmuseums.org.uk/pdfs/Publications/Museums_and_Social_Justice.pdf> (accessed 27 January 2007).

Scottish Public Health Observatory (2008) *Health, Wellbeing and Disease: Overview*. Online. Available HTTP: <http://www.scotpho.org.uk/home/Healthwell-beinganddisease/HealthWellBeingAndDisease.asp> (accessed 5 May 2008).

Sedikides, C., Gaertner, L. and Toguchi, Y. (2003) "Pancultural Self-Enhancement," *Journal of Personality and Social Psychology*, vol. 84, no. 1: 60–79.

Semmes, M. (2005) "Vital Visionaries: The Museum Cure," *Museum News*, vol. 84, no. 3: 60–2.

Sharpley, C.F. (1986) "Public Perceptions of Four Mental Health Professions: A Survey of Knowledge and Attitudes to Psychologists, Psychiatrists, Social Workers, and Counsellors," *Australian Psychologist*, vol. 21, no. 1: 57–67.

Shaw, G. (2006) "Patients at an Exhibition," *Neurology Now*, November/December: 28–30.

Sheafor, B., Horejsi, C. and Horejsi, G. (2000) *Techniques and Guidelines for Social Work Practice*, 5th edn, Boston, MA: Allyn & Bacon.

Sheldon, B. (2001) "The Validity of Evidence-Based Practice in Social Work: A Reply to Stephen Webb," *British Journal of Social Work*, vol. 31, no. 5: 801–9.

Sheldon, K., Elliot, A., Kim, Y. and Kassner, T. (2001) "What is Satisfying About Satisfying Events? Testing 10 Candidate Psychological Needs," *Journal of Personality and Social Psychology*, vol. 80, no. 2: 325–339.

Sheppard, B. (2000) "Do Museums Make a Difference? Evaluating Programs for Social Change," *Curator*, vol. 43, no. 1: 63–74.

Siebert, A. (2001) "The Resilience of Oklahoma City Bomb Survivors: An Interview with Richard Williams." Survivor Guideline.org. Online. Available HTTP: <http://www.survivorguidelines.org/articles/williams01.html> (accessed 1 March 2009).

Silverman, L.H. (1989) "Johnny Showed Us the Butterflies: The Museum as a Family Therapy Tool," *Marriage and Family Review*, vol. 13, no. 3/4: 131–50.

—— (1990) "Of Us and Other 'Things': The Content and Functions of Talk by Adult Visitor Pairs in an Art and a History Museum," unpublished doctoral dissertation, University of Pennsylvania, Philadelphia.

—— (1991) "Tearing Down Walls," *Museum News*, November/December: 61–4.

—— (1995) "Visitor Meaning Making in Museums for a New Age," *Curator*, vol. 38, no. 3: 161–70.

—— (1998) *The Therapeutic Potential of Museums: A Guide to Social Service/Museum Collaboration*, Bloomington, IN: Institute of Museum and Library Services.

—— (1999a) "Meaning Making Matters: Communication, Consequences, and Exhibit Design," *Exhibitionist*, vol. 18, no. 2: 8–14.

—— (1999b) "Meeting Human Needs: The Potential of Museums," *Museum National*, vol. 8, no. 1: 17–19.

—— (2002a) "Taking a Wider View of Museum Outcomes and Experiences: Theory, Research and Magic," *Journal of Education in Museums*, vol. 23: 3–8.

—— (2002b) "The Therapeutic Potential of Museums as Pathways to Inclusion," in R. Sandell (ed.) *Museums, Society, Inequality*, London and New York: Routledge.

—— (2007) *Expanding the Healing Arts at Columbus Regional Hospital: Towards a Care for the Caregiver Pilot Program Using Contemporary Museum Exhibit Techniques as a Healing Art. Project Summary and Final Report*, Bloomington, IN.

Silverman, L.H. and McCormick, B. (2001) *Museums as Therapeutic Agents: An Integrated Approach to Theory-Based Program Design and Evaluation*, Bloomington, Indiana: Institute of Museum and Library Services.

Silverman, L.H. and O'Neill, M. (2004) "Change and Complexity in the 21st-Century Museum," *Museum News*, November/December: 37–43.

Simon, N. (2007) "The Move on Model: Inciting Visitor Social Action," *Museum 2.0*, Online. Available HTTP: <http://museumto.blogspot.com/2007/06/move-on-model-inciting-visitor-social.html> (accessed 16 May 2008).

Simpson, Thomas K. (2000) "The Museum as Grove of the Muses," *Journal of Museum Education*, vol. 25, no. 1–2: 28–31.

Singapore Association of Social Workers (2008) "Welcome to SASW!" Online. Available HTTP: <http://www.sasw.org.sg/site> (accessed 16 May 2009).

Sivesind, J. (1981) "Sheltered Employment to Help Shoulder Responsibilities," *Museum*, vol. 33, no. 3: 145–50.

Skramstad, H. (1999) "An Agenda for American Museums in the Twenty-First Century," *Daedalus: Journal of the American Academy of Arts and Sciences*, vol. 128, no. 3: 109–28.

Social-Work.co.uk (2006) Homepage. Online. Available HTTP: <http://www.Social-Work.co.uk> (accessed 4 July 2007).

Solomon, B. (1976) *Black Empowerment: Social Work in Oppressed Communities*, New York: Columbia University Press.

Sone, Y., Harada, T., Miyamoto, M., Fukumoto, Y., Tani, N., Shintani, A., Shinoda, M., Nakanisi, A., Miki, T. and Nomura, T. (2007) "The Effect of Group Reminiscence in Nostalgic Room for Mildly Demented Elderly: Evaluation with NIRS During Dementia Assessment Test (Proceedings of the 56th Meeting of Japan Society of Physiological Anthropology)," *Journal of Physiological Anthropology*, vol. 26, no. 6: 613.

Speers, S., Montgomery, S. and Brown, D. (1994) "Toward Reconciliation: A Role for Museums in a Divided Society," *Journal of Museum Education*, vol. 19, no. 1: 10–13.

Spicer, G. (2006) "World Museum Liverpool Launches Youth Theatre Groups," *24 Hour Museum*. Online. Available HTTP: <http://www.culture24.org.uk/places+to+go/north+west/liverpool/art41042> (accessed 27 January 2009).

Spiny Babbler Museum (2007) "Ropka International." Online. Available HTTP: <http://www.spinybabbler.org/programs/education_focus/people_at_risk/rokpa.php> (accessed 16 November 2008).

Spousta, C. (2005) "Warming Up to the Museum: One Sexy Event at a Time," *WestMuse*, Summer 2005: 5–9.

Stapleton, E.R. (2006) "Yoga at Sessions Get People Exercising Inside Museums," *Hoosier Times*, April 2, F3.

Stapp, C. (1998) "Museums and Community Development," *Curator*, vol. 41, no. 4: 228–34.

Staricoff, R. L. (2004) *Arts In Health: A Review of the Medical Literature.* Arts Council England Research Report 36. Online. Available HTTP: <http://www.artscouncil.org.uk/publications/publication_detail.php?rid=0&sid=&browse=recent&id=405> (accessed 9 January 2007).

State of Queensland (2008) "Travelling for Love – a Virtual Exhibition (State Library of Queensland)." Online. Available HTTP: <http://www.slq.qld.gov.au/whats-on/exhibit/online/travelling> (accessed 9 August 2008).

Steinsaltz, A. (1989) *The Talmud: The Steinsaltz Edition*, multiple volumes, New York: Random House.

Stocking, G.W. Jr. (ed.) (1988) *Objects and Others: Essays on Museums and Material Culture.* Madison, WI: University of Wisconsin Press.

Stubbs, M. (1983) *Discourse Analysis: The Sociolinguistic Analysis of Natural Language*, Chicago, IL: University of Chicago Press.

Suchy, S. (2006) "Museum Management: Emotional Value and Community Engagement." Paper presented to the International Committee on Management 2006 Annual Meeting and Conference, 2–4 November, Taipei, Taiwan. Online. Available HTTP: <http://www.intercom.museum/documents/3-1Suchy.pdf> (accessed 1 December 2008).

Sutter, G. (2008) "Promoting Sustainability: Audience and Curatorial Perspectives on *The Human Factor*," *Curator*, vol. 51, no. 2: 187–202.

Sutter, G. and Worts, D. (2005) "Negotiating a Sustainable Path: Museums and Societal Therapy," in R.R. Janes and G.T. Conaty (eds) *Looking Reality in the Eye: Museums and Social Responsibility*, Calgary: University of Calgary Press.

Szekeres, V. (2002) "Representing Diversity and Challenging Racism: The Migration Museum," in R. Sandell (ed.) *Museums, Society, Inequality*, London and New York: Routledge.

Tanassi, L.M. (2007) "Plasti-Nation," *American Journal of Public Health*, vol. 97, no. 11: 1998–2000.

Tejero Coni, G. (2007) "Why Create a Museum on Women?" *Museum International*, vol. 59, no. 4: 63–9.

Tilinca, M. (2007) "The Creativity Workshop: The Romanian Peasant Museum," European Approaches to Inter-Generational Lifelong Learning (EAGLE) Case Study. Online. Available HTTP: <http://www.eagle-project.eu/welcome-to-eagle/practice-showcase/Romania_2_MTR_ID.pdf> (accessed 28 February 2009).

Toft, M.D. (2003) *The Geography of Ethnic Violence: Identity, Interests, and the Indivisibility of Territory*, Princeton, NJ: Princeton University Press.

Toon, R. (2000) "Solitude and Reflection in Science Centers," *Journal of Museum Education*, vol. 25, no. 1–2: 25–8.

Towle, C. (1987) *Common Human Needs*, revised edn, Washington, DC: National Association of Social Workers.

Travis, J. and Waul, M. (2004) *Prisoners Once Removed: The Impact of Incarceration and Reentry on Children, Families, and Communities*, Washington, DC: The Urban Institute.

Treadon, C.B., Rosal, M. and Wylder, V.D. (2006) "Opening the Doors of Art Museums for Therapeutic Processes," *The Arts in Psychotherapy*, vol. 33, no. 4: 288–301.

Trotter, C. (2006) *Working with Involuntary Clients: A Guide to Practice*, 2nd edn, London and Thousand Oaks, CA: Sage.

Tucker, D. (1993) "A Traditional View or a Radical Re-Think," *SHCG News*, vol. 32: 6–8.

Turner, G. l'E. (2001) "The Cabinet of Experimental Philosophy," in O. Impey and A. MacGregor (eds) *The Origins of Museums: The Cabinets of Curiosities in Sixteenth and Seventeenth Century Europe*, London: House of Stratus.

Tuyet, N. (2007) "The Vietnam Women's Museum: The Promotion of Women's Rights to Gender Equality and Gender Issues," *Museum International*, vol. 59, no. 4: 70–9.

United States Holocaust Memorial Museum (USHMM) (2001) *Teaching About the Holocaust: A Resource Book for Educators*, Washington, DC: USHMM.

United Way of America (1996) *Measuring Program Outcomes: A Practical Approach*, Alexandria, VA: United Way of America.

van Mensch, P. (1995) "Magpies on Mount Helicon," in M. Schärer (ed.) *Museum and Community*, ICOFOM Study Series 25, Paris: ICOFOM.

Vanegas, A. (2002) "Representing Lesbians and Gay Men in British Social History Museums," in R. Sandell (ed.) *Museums, Society, Inequality*. London and New York: Routledge.

Veterans Museum and Memorial Center (2003) "About Us." Online: Available HTTP: <http://www.veteranmuseum.org/aboutus.html> (accessed 1 October 2008).

Vilna Gaon Jewish State Museum (2006) "The Vilna Gaon Jewish State Museum." Online. Available HTTP: <http://www.jmuseum.lt> (accessed 1 July 2007).

Vinson, I. (2007) "Editorial," *Museum International*, vol. 59, no. 4: 4–6.

Vitez, M. (2008) "Guiding Each Other and Others; Making Friends, Finding Purpose Through 203 Museums," *Philadelphia Inquirer*, 19 February, A1.

vom Lehn, D. (2006) "Embodying Experience: A Video-Based Examination of Visitors' Conduct and Interaction in Museums," *European Journal of Marketing*, vol. 40, no. 11/12: 1340–59.

vom Lehn, D., Heath, C. and Hindmarsh, J. (2001) "Exhibiting Interaction: Conduct and Collaboration in Museums and Galleries," *Symbolic Interaction*, vol. 24, no. 2: 189–216.

Waterfield, G. and Smith, N. (1994) "Art for the People," *History Today*, vol. 44, no. 6: 55–8.

Weil, S. (1997) "The Museum and the Public," *Museum Management and Curatorship*, vol. 16, no. 3: 257–71.

—— (1999) "The Ongoing Transformation of the American Museum," *Daedalus*, vol. 128, no. 3: 229–58.

Weiss, I. (2005) "Is There a Global Common Core to Social Work? A Cross-National Comparative Study of BSW Graduate Students," *Social Work*, vol. 50, no. 2: 101–10.

Westerlund, S. and Knuthammar, T. (1981) "Handicaps Prohibited – Traveling Exhibitions in Sweden," *Museum*, vol. 33, no. 3: 176–9.

White, J. (2000) "Introduction," in J. White and A. Freeman (eds) *Cognitive-Behavioral Group Therapy for Specific Problems and Populations*, Washington DC: American Psychological Association.

Whittington, C. (2003a) "Collaboration and Partnership in Context," in J. Weinstein, C. Whittington, and T. Leiba (eds) *Collaboration in Social Work Practice*, London and New York: Jessica Kingsley Publishers.

—— (2003b) "A Model of Collaboration," in J. Weinstein, C. Whittington, and T. Leiba (eds) *Collaboration in Social Work Practice*, London and New York: Jessica Kingsley.

Wigington, H. (1995) "Intergenerational Play: Playing to Learn, Learning to Play," unpublished master's thesis, Texas Christian University, Fort Worth.

Wikoff, N. (2004) *Cultures of Care Monograph: A Study of Arts and Humanities in U.S. Hospitals*, Washington, DC: Americans for the Arts.

Williams, R. (1994) "Honoring the Museum Visitors' Personal Associations and Emotional Responses to Art: Work Towards a Model for Educators." Unpublished paper presented to the Faculty at Harvard University. Cambridge, Massachusetts.

—— (2008) Personal communication (16 June 2008).

Wilson, C. (2007) "The 5 Minute Guide To: LONDON," *Gay Community News*, September, no. 213: 29.

Wilson, E. (2002) *The Future of Life*, New York: Alfred A. Knopf.

Winch, P., Leontsini, E., Rigau-Perez, J., Ruiz-Perez, M., Clark, G. and Gubler, D. (2002) "Community-Based Dengue Prevention Programs in Puerto Rico: Impact on Knowledge,

Behavior, and Residential Mosquito Infestation," *American Journal of Tropical Medicine and Hygiene*, vol. 67, no. 4: 363–70.

Winn, P. (2000) "Arts for Health: Art Therapy at the National Gallery of Australia." Online. Available HTTP: <http://www.christchurchartgallery.org.nz/icomceca2000/papers/Philippa_Winn.pdf> (accessed 14 September 2004).

Wisker, C. (1997) "What One Museum Does for Prison Art," in D. Gussak and E. Virship (eds) *Drawing Time: Art Therapy in Prisons and Other Correctional Settings*, Chicago, IL: Magnolia Street Publishers.

Wolin, S. and Bennett, S. (1984) "Family Rituals," *Family Process*, vol. 23, no. 3: 401–21.

Women's Active Museum on War and Peace (WAM) (2006) *Newsletter*, issue 1, Fall 2006. Online. Available HTTP: <http://wam-peace.org/eng/newsletter_06_sml.pdf> (accessed 16 September 2008).

Woodson-Boulton, A. (2007) "Industry Without Art Is Brutality: Aesthetic Ideology and Social Practice in Victorian Art Museums," *Journal of British Studies*, vol. 46: 47–71.

World Health Organization (1946) Preamble to the Constitution of the World Health Organization as adopted by the International Health Conference, New York 19–22 June 1946; signed on 22 July 1946 by the representatives of sixty-one States (Official Records of the World Health Organization, no. 2, p. 100) and entered into force on 7 April 1948.

—— (2002) *World Report on Violence and Health: Summary*, Geneva: World Health Organization. Online. Available HTTP: <http://whqlibdoc.who.int/hq/2002/9241545615.pdf> (accessed 20 January 2007).

Worts, D. (1990) "In Search of Meaning: 'Reflective Practice' and Museums," *Museum Quarterly*, vol. 18, no. 4: 9–20.

—— (1995) "Extending the Frame: Forging a New Partnership with the Public," in S. Pearce (ed.) *Art in Museums*, London: Athlone Press.

—— (1997) "Assessing the Risks and Potential of The OH! Canada Project," *Muse*, vol. 15, no. 2: 19–23.

—— (2006a) "Measuring Museum Meaning: A Critical Assessment Framework," *Journal of Museum Education*, vol. 31, no. 1: 41–9.

—— (2006b) "Transformational Encounters: Reflections on Cultural Participation and Ecomuseology," *Canadian Journal of Communication*, vol. 31, no. 1: 127–45.

Wroclawski, C. (2009) Personal communication (27 April 2009).

Yalom, I. (2005) *The Theory and Practice of Group Psychotherapy*, 5th edn, New York: Basic Books.

Yarmouth County Historical Society (2007) "Family Reunions." Online. Available HTTP: <http://yarmouthcountymuseum.ednet.ns.ca/reunions.html> (accessed 17 August 2008).

Yellow Horse Brave Heart, M. (2005) "From International Trauma to Intergenerational Healing," *Wellbriety! White Bison's Online Magazine*, vol. 6, no. 6: 2–8. Online. Available HTTP: <http://www.whitebison.org/magazine/2005/volume6/wellbriety!vol6no6.pdf> (accessed 6 December 2008).

Yonzon, S. (2007) "A Year of Small Achievements. Ropka International," *Volunteer Voice*, Spiny Babbler Museums. Online. Available HTTP: <http://spinybabbler.org/programs/education_focus/articles/rokpa_volunteer_voice.php> (accessed 14 July 2008).

Index

Made in the USA
Columbia, SC
27 May 2022